NAVIGATING COMMERCE IN LATIN AMERICA

The forces of globalization, technology, and information diffusion, as well as the processes of democratic consolidation have served to improve and expand opportunities for business in Latin American markets. These changes have not occurred uniformly, and this insightful book will help future business leaders determine which economies are likely to prosper, and therefore present better business opportunities for the foreseeable future.

A chapter dedicated to the history of Latin America helps readers understand why things appear the way they do, giving them the context they need to understand the underlying business conditions. The book also addresses key challenges and issues that are unique to Latin America, and offers practical advice for tackling them. Each chapter features a focus country in order to provide a more in-depth understanding of what business opportunities exist in this region, how businesses operate and thrive there, as well as what internal and external factors affect the ability to do business in Latin America. The cases at the end of each chapter explore actual business ventures in a particular country.

A highly practical book, *Navigating Commerce in Latin America* will give international business people the tools they need to manage successful businesses in this region.

John E. Spillan is Professor of Management and Director of International Affairs in The School of Business at the University of North Carolina at Pembroke, U.S. Dr. Spillan has written four books and several articles on International Business, Global Supply Chain Management, and International Marketing in various academic journals. He has been a guest lecturer in Chile, Peru, Bolivia, Guatemala, Mexico, Spain, China, Germany, Finland, and Ghana.

Jase R. Ramsey is Associate Professor of International Business at Saint Louis University, U.S. Previously, he has worked as Professor of International Business and Coordinator of the Center for International Business at Fundação Dom Cabral (FDC) in Brazil. He has published numerous articles on doing business in Latin America and is currently a visiting professor at FDC.

NAVIGATING COMMERCE IN LATIN AMERICA

Options and Obstacles

John E. Spillan and Jase R. Ramsey

Routledge
Taylor & Francis Group

NEW YORK AND LONDON

First published 2019
by Routledge
711 Third Avenue, New York, NY 10017

and by Routledge
2 Park Square, Milton Park, Abingdon, Oxon, OX14 4RN

Routledge is an imprint of the Taylor & Francis Group, an informa business

Library of Congress Cataloging-in-Publication Data
A catalog record for this book has been requested

ISBN: 978-1-138-30469-7 (hbk)
ISBN: 978-1-138-30471-0 (pbk)
ISBN: 978-0-203-72988-5 (ebk)

Typeset in Bembo
by Wearset Ltd, Boldon, Tyne and Wear

CONTENTS

List of figures   *vii*
List of tables   *ix*
Foreword   *xii*
Acknowledgments   *xvi*

1 Contemporary Thoughts About Doing Business in
   Latin America   1

2 The Current Business Environment   18

3 Historical Business Perspective   38

4 Cultural Issues Affecting Business   58

5 The Political Climate   81

6 The Economic Climate   108

7 Global Competitiveness   132

8 Establishing a Business   162

9 The Marketing Process   191

10 Entrepreneurship and Innovation   214

11 Conclusion   233

Index   *236*

FIGURES

1.1	Map of Latin America	4
1.2	Map of Corruption for Latin America	13
2.1	Recent GDPs	22
3.1	US$/Argentine Peso Foreign Exchange Rate	54
4.1	The Cultural System	59
4.2	Central Open Market in Typical Latin American Community	64
4.3	Graphical Depiction of Social Structure in Latin America	67
4.4	Picture of Old Ruins in Petén, Guatemala	73
5.1	Corruption Perceptions Index	88
5.2	Political by Credit Risk	97
5.3	Institutional Trust	99
5.4	Rule of Law Indicator	100
6.1	Annual Inflation	109
6.2	Annual Inflation	110
6.3	Annual Inflation	111
6.4	GDP Annual Inflation Growth Rate	112
6.5	GDP by Sector, 1995	119
6.6	GDP by Sector, 2015	120
6.7	Percentage of Individuals Working by Sector, 1995	121
6.8	Percentage of Individuals Working by Sector, 2015	122
7.1	Global Competitiveness Index Components	136
8.1	Picture of Multinational Corporation in Guatemala	167
8.2	Example of an Informal Market Setting in Latin America	169

8.3   Huanza Hydroelectric Project in Peru   180
8.4   Stakeholders in Cross-Border Negotiations   183
9.1   Informal Market – They Exist across Latin America   198
9.2   Typical Retail Outlet in Guatemala   201
9.3   Customer Value and How it Relates to the other
      Components of Marketing Strategy   207

TABLES

1.1	Latin America and the Caribbean: Gradual Recovery (GDP Growth In Percentage)	9
2.1	GDP and GDP per Capita by Country (Current US$)	20
2.2	Net Inflows of FDI (Billions of US$)	23
2.3	Labor Productivity	25
2.4	Poverty Rates at 1.90 US$ a Day	27
2.5	Trading Blocs in Latin America	31
3.1	Latin American Exports, 1860–1929	41
3.2	Per Capita GDP by Region	43
3.3	Percetage Growth in GDP per Capita	48
3.4	Single-Commodity Exports as a Percentage of Total Exports, 1938	52
3.5	State Enterprise Share in the Brazilian Economy, 1973	53
4.1	Gini Coefficient – Latin American Countries	66
4.2	Summarizes the Religion Distribution Percentage among 16 Latin American Countries	68
5.1	Poverty Rates and Rural-Urban Divide	83
5.2	Intentional Homicides per 100,000 People	85
5.3	Political Stability and Absence of Violence	87
5.4	Fragile States Index	89
5.5	Freedom in the World, 2018	91
5.6	Democracy Index Ranking	93
5.7	Selected Global Competitive Index Component Ranks	96
5.8	Property Protection Ranks	101
6.1	Imports and Exports of Goods and Services (US$ billions)	113

6.2	Top Trading Partners of Latin American Countries (US$ billions)	116
6.3	Change in the KOF Index of Globalization, 2005–2015	118
6.4	Inequality in Latin America: Gini Index, 2006–2016	123
6.5	Informal Employment	125
7.1	Rankings of Selected Indicators from Doing Business Index	133
7.2	Classification by Each Stage of Development	134
7.3	Overall GCI	137
7.4	Institutions	139
7.5	Infrastructure	141
7.6	Macroeconomic Environment	142
7.7	Health and Primary Education	143
7.8	Higher Education and Training	145
7.9	Goods Market Efficiency	147
7.10	Labor Market Efficiency	148
7.11	Financial Market Development	150
7.12	Technological Readiness	151
7.13	Market Size	152
7.14	Business Sophistication	154
7.15	Innovation	155
7.16	GCI Pillar Median Ranks by Region	157
7.17	Panama	158
8.1	28 of the Top Latin American Multinationals	165
8.2	Major Export Destination for Goods Made in Respective Countries (Percentage)	166
8.3	Informal Employment Rate by Country – Non-Agricultural – Informal Jobs as a Percentage of Total Employment	169
8.4	Summarizes Capital Flows to Latin America (US$ billions)	172
8.5	Summarizes the Global Logistic Performance Rankings (LPI) for Latin American Countries	174
8.6	Ranking on Element for Starting and Doing Business in Latin America	176
8.7	Economy Ranking according to Ease of Doing Business	176
8.8	Infrastructure Investment Projections in Latin America in Year 2015 (US$ billions)	179
8.9	Latin American and the Caribbean Transportation Infrastructure Projects	179
9.1	Population Statistics, 2018	194
9.2	The Extent of Internet Connection and Potential use in Respective Countries	195
9.3	Latin America Countries Consumer Potential Based on Disposable Income and E-Commerce Potential	196

9.4	Retail e-commerce in Latin America 2014–2019 (US$ billions)	197
9.5	Latin American Countries and the Size of their Middle Class	199
9.6	Latin American Global Consumer Spending and Global Advertising (US$ millions)	203
9.7	Popular Products According to Latin America Countries	206
9.8	Summarizes the Most Popular Brands in LA	207
10.1	Global Innovation Index	220
10.2	Entrepreneurial Attitude and Perceptions (Percentage)	223
10.3	Occupational Groupings (Percentage of Working Population)	224
10.4	Entrepreneurs and Social Origin (Percentage of Social Class)	224
10.5	Entrepreneurs: By Social Origin	224

FOREWORD

We live in a globalized world. It is no longer possible to be highly successful in business by remaining in the confines of one country or region. Countless opportunities exist in the exchange of goods and services across borders and different cultures. With this new standard of the vast scope of business, it is essential to understand the risks and opportunities of each country or region as well as the cultural, political, geographic, and economic factors that compose each region's unique business environment. This book focuses on the challenges, opportunities, and realities of doing business in Latin America.

Due to its proximity to the United States, one might easily make the mistake of assuming that the business environment in Latin America is not too different or any more difficult to understand than that of the U.S. This assumption, however, would grossly underestimate the complexity of the region's history, culture, political institutions, and economic conditions. Not only is the region unique from the rest of the Western Hemisphere, but the countries within the region each have their own governments, natural resources, infrastructure, cultural heritage, social structure, etc., that differ widely from each other. To understand Latin America is to understand how these factors interact within the region and the world at large to create a complex business environment.

Latin America is composed of countries in both Central and South America with multiethnic heritage but shared cultural and historic roots. Various international organizations such as the World Bank, the International Monetary Fund (IMF), and the Organization for Economic Cooperation and Development (OECD) differ in their classification of which countries are included in Latin America; the most common debate is whether the Caribbean should be included in the region. For the purpose of this book, we will consider Latin America the collective region of 18 countries in South and Central America:

Argentina, Bolivia, Brazil, Chile, Colombia, Costa Rica, Dominican Republic, Ecuador, El Salvador, Guatemala, Honduras, Mexico, Nicaragua, Panama, Peru, Paraguay, Uruguay, and Venezuela. These countries are majority Spanish-speaking with the exception of Brazil. A general consensus of organizations or individuals studying the region is that Argentina, Brazil, Chile, and Mexico are of particular note due to their size and growth. Although Latin America has been shaped by political instability, economic hardship, and social tension, these four countries have been regional leaders in making strides to embrace modernization and development to overcome their struggles. Progress, however, has not been easy or fast. Anyone seeking to do business in Latin America must understand that even the most promising opportunities come with challenges and risks.

While this book is primarily intended for the instruction of business students at various academic levels, business professionals and interested individuals alike can benefit from the information discussed and analyzed throughout this text. The content includes the most recent data at the time of publication from international organizations such as the World Bank and the OECD, analyses and commentary from experts in the region, and information sourced from reputable publications such as *The Financial Times* and *The Economist*. A case study accompanies each chapter to provide a real-world example of both countries' and companies' successes and struggles.

Readers will first be presented with an overview of the current business climate in Latin America to establish an understanding of today's realities. Some of the trends presented will have entire sections or chapters dedicated to the topic later in the book because of their significant impact. Although Latin America is enjoying a favorable outlook currently, a worldwide economic slowdown requires further examination and careful consideration of structural reforms and strategy implementation. This section analyzes trade, investment, and the social structure (in particular the rising middle class) among other factors that are affecting the current business climate of the region.

Next, the historical perspective provides a context of how the present situation came to be. While Latin America has a long, rich history of indigenous peoples and was especially impacted by European colonization, much of the current situation as well as many struggles and crises seen today can be traced back primarily to 19th century economic policies. The trajectory of most countries' economies shifted when governments began nationalizing industries and avoiding imports to reduce dependency on foreign trade partners. Major changes to the economic structure of Latin America had and continue to have profound effects on not only the economic state but also the attitudes of people living in Latin America towards foreign investment and trade.

The current climate is further understood by delving into the cultural, political, and economic factors affecting business. Latin America experiences a unique interaction of all three factors due to their complexity and the diversity between countries. For example, the cultural makeup of each country differs from the strong indigenous populations in Bolivia, Guatemala, and Peru to a more blended cultural composition seen in the influence of Portugal in Brazil or Spain and Italy in Argentina. Understanding culture is a key component to success in a certain region, and so businesses must know how to adapt to each country's diverse populations.

Similarly, the political system and risks vary widely from country to country. In general, Latin American politics are characterized by corruption and transparency issues that increase risk. However, investors would be much safer with investments in pro-market Chile or Uruguay when compared to protectionist and crises-ridden Venezuela. Still, inequality, poverty, and crime are all political issues that influence the stability of the region, and investors must understand the degree of political risk in each country and the extent to which they can tolerate it to reap the potential reward.

The economic climate follows a similar pattern in the fact that while regional trends suggest an overall shift to freer trade and economic growth, the economic successes and shortcomings diverge on a per-country basis. In particular, there is a sharp contrast between the degree of economic liberalization in some countries and its consequential impact on human development.

The preceding three factors – especially the economic climate – contribute to the competitiveness climate in Latin America. Each country has unique opportunities and advantages to offer. At the same time, each one presents risks and obstacles. It is important for investors to understand what makes a country competitive and in which areas they can benefit from its key competencies.

Then, once the business environment is understood from a wide range of perspectives, readers will delve into the act of establishing a business in Latin America. A chapter of this book is dedicated to the considerations investors should take before diving right in and the processes that are necessary to follow.

For those who do choose to do business in the region, the penultimate chapter details marketing strategies and processes to effectively reach the diverse market segments that compose the target audience. Finally, the book presents an exploration of the emerging spirit of entrepreneurship and innovation that is shaping the development on the region before concluding.

The authors of this textbook provide a unique perspective to doing business in Latin America; they both have lived, worked, and traveled in the region for decades. They have seen the progress (or in some cases, lack of) that has resulted in the current business climate. They have formed close relationships with people living in Latin America and experienced the culture, language, and customs that are so deeply ingrained in every aspect of life. They have seen the joys and hopes of the people yearning and working for better lives, and at the same time, they have seen the struggle and frustration of being unable to shake off years of oppression, corruption, and hardship. The facts and data in this book are enriched by the personal encounters that the authors contribute. Their insights offer a distinctive combination of outside perspective and first-hand experience.

Since the first edition of this textbook, the situation of many countries in Latin America has drastically changed (e.g., Venezuela) and sometimes wildly from what was predicted. Doubtless there will once again be many radical and unpredictable changes after the publication of this text; however, the overall themes that are essential to understanding the business climate have persisted over several decades. The purpose of this book is to convey these overarching themes, provide a historical context and current overview of the business environment, and perhaps most importantly, offer insights into how to be successful while pursuing ventures in the region. It is the hope of the authors that all readers – whether students, academics, professionals, or interested individuals – are enriched with a deeper understanding of the unique challenges, opportunities, and realities of doing business in Latin America.

Kelsie Eckert
International Business and French
Chaifetz School of Business
Saint Louis University Class of 2018

ACKNOWLEDGMENTS

Dr. Ramsey would like to thank Amanda Coors and Kelsie Eckert for their diligent work editing this book. Additionally, he would like to thank the Saint Louis University 'Doing Business in Latin America' classes of 2017 and 2018 for their constructive criticism of each chapter, as well as contributing to the cases. Finally, financial support from the Boeing Institute of International Business was much appreciated.

1

CONTEMPORARY THOUGHTS ABOUT DOING BUSINESS IN LATIN AMERICA

Overview

The word "Latin America" came to be customary only in the middle of the twentieth century. Indigenous peoples inhabited the Americas for thousands of years before the European conquest. What is considered today as Latin America was fashioned by hundreds of years of European imperialist rule, battles for independence from colonial powers, civil and world wars, and both voluntary and involuntary migration (Turner-Trujillo, Del Toro & Ramos, 2017).

Latin America has a rich and very diverse history of indigenous cultures including European colonization, African slavery, and global immigration. These aspects of the region make it difficult to describe its people with one single ethnic class, and potential businesspeople to the region would be wise to pay attention to differences among the nations. External to Brazil, where the predominant language is Portuguese, Spanish is the dominant language spoken throughout Latin America. Each of these Latin-derived languages is recent import to the Americas. Latin America is the homeland to hundreds of indigenous languages; before the European conquests, it is estimated that there were as many as 1,750 of them (Turner-Trujillo, Del Toro & Ramos, 2017). Latin America is a region important to a variety of stakeholders. Academics, practitioners, tourists and curious individuals can find an enormous value, opportunities in studying, investing in and visiting this region. The region consists of some 20 countries in both Central and South America. It has a combined population of more than 600 million, and 3 main languages: Spanish, Portuguese, and English. The biggest economies in order of projected 2018 GDP growth are those of Brazil 1.9%, Mexico 2.3%, Colombia 3.0%, Argentina 2.5%, Peru 4.0%, Venezuela −15.0%, and Chile 3.0% (Werner, 2018). Unquestionably,

Latin America represents significant business potential for venturing entrepreneurs. Investment and business opportunities in Latin America are expanding, predominantly in those countries that have committed to developing efficient market systems. Over the last 50 years its population has more than tripled to almost 600 million people, yet its GDP per capita has not kept pace with its population rate of change. While this inequity is obvious, Latin America is still one of the fastest growing regions both economically and demographically. A major advantage of the large growing population is the immediate access to large potential labor pools and potential customers. This is important for future growth and development.

Latin America can be described as a land of contradictions. It has huge natural resource stocks that offer it great competitive advantages for trade, as well as, resources for its own consumption. With a predominantly young and hard-working population this resource has been recognized as a major asset in attracting businesses to the region. The region has demonstrated an ability to successfully turn new capital investments into wealth and welfare, even though the success *rate* has been up and down for some countries. Latin America is a region with a predominantly market-oriented education and culture which has the potential to grow tremendously, given the proper institutional settings. Culturally, Latin America is much closer to many industrialized nations (e.g., United States) than many people realize and thus presents a much easier path for entry into its markets than is the case in other developing areas of the world.

Even though the Latin American region has presented a steady record of economic growth over the last decade, the sustainability of this progress is not guaranteed. With its incomplete and sub-par infrastructure along with its political uncertainties, anything can happen to derail its progress. All these variables present barriers to business entry. Foreign investment and local business investment shy away from expanding their businesses when these weaknesses and uncertainties exist (Vassolo, DeCastro & Gomez-Mejia, 2011).

Exploring the international business background and activities in Latin America, specifically in the seven focal countries, is one of the main contributions of this book. Since there is a scarcity of books focused on the domestic and international business activity in Latin America, this book furnishes a foundation for a more in-depth understanding of what business opportunities exist in this region, how businesses operate and thrive there, as well as what internal and external factors affect the ability to do business in Latin America.

Introduction

This chapter introduces Latin America as an important region of the world. As aforementioned, over 600 million people live in this area of the world, and accounts for an enormous amount of purchasing, economic, and political power. At the same time, it is a region that has many similar yet very different societies. Over the years, attentive observers have witnessed turbulent times (especially in Central America in the 1980s), good times generally the major part of the 21st century and waning times, those periods in the most recent years 2014–2018. Even with all this dynamic activity the Latin American region has provoked major interest of investors from many parts of the world especially Europe and China. The last decade and a half has offered interested business developers a generally peaceful and profitable environment to place their investments and businesses. Additionally, many of the Latin American citizens have witnessed more prosperity than ever before in their lives. As such, a new middle class has emerged that has offered hope and encouragement to many of the Latin American citizens. Yet with all of these positives occurring, severe poverty and major disparities in income and wealth distribution continues to be evident throughout the Latin American region. With all the recent changes such as the forces of globalization, the exchange of ideas, information and technology, and the processes of democratic consolidation have served to improve and expand Latin American market systems. These changes are presenting potential opportunities for business investment in the region. However, these important transformations have not occurred uniformly across the Latin American region. Latin America continues to be a very important region of the world and hence it is for this reason that a comprehensive, contemporary understanding is needed to inform and educate the world about its importance. We see widespread corruption throughout Latin America. This is major issue to be discussed in this book because of its impact on economic and social development.

Geography – Where is Latin America?

Before we get into a detailed substantive discussion of the theoretical and practical concepts and issues of doing business in Latin America, it is important to understand the geography of the area being discussed. In Figure 1.1, the map presents all areas of Latin America from Mexico all the way to Tierra del Fuego in Chile. It is a vast landmass with both densely concentrated population centers (Buenos Aires, Argentina) and sparsely populated areas (Amazonas, Brazil). Mere inspection indicates that Brazil occupies the largest landmass of all the Latin American geography. Equally, Brazil is also a member of the BRIC (Brazil, Russia, India and China) quartet of the most powerful and fastest growing emerging nations in the world.

Of all the countries presented on this map, Argentina is the only country that has exhibited, over the long term, an economic and political environment that is similar to the U.S. and Western Europe. All the other LA countries are growing countries eager to become equal to the industrialized nations of the world.

Latin America is a vast and elegant geographic area. Latin American countries are all located south of the United States/Mexican border. It begins with

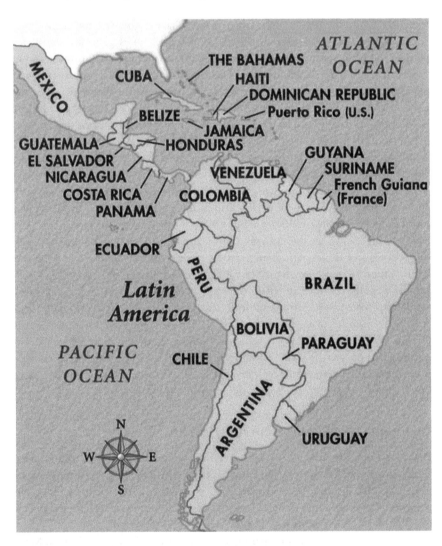

FIGURE 1.1 Map of Latin America

Mexico in North America and passes through Central America and continues to the southern-most part of South America or area called Terra del Fuego (McKeown, 2017). It is composed of the countries in the isthmus of Central America with a population of close to 45 million people and the continent of South America with over 426 million inhabitants. Each expanding their geographic perimeters as their population continues to grow (World Population, 2017).

The physical geography of Latin America is composed of six major areas. They are as follows:

1   The Andes Mountains – this mountain range is long and rugged. It extends from Venezuela, Colombia, Ecuador, Peru, Bolivia, Argentina, and Chile. It reaches the heights of 6,000 meters above sea level causing many tourists to experience temporary respiratory problems when they initially travel high in the Andes. The climate is cold and dry. Even in these rugged conditions many indigenous people live in very primitive conditions. They have been living and farming in this region for centuries. The llamas and alpaca live and roam the altiplano of this region.

2   The second major region is the Amazon basin. This area denominates the interior of the continent. Its main component is the Amazon River, which is the largest river and rainforest in the world, 1,553.76 meters. The rainforest is enormous with vast swaths of vegetation and wildlife.

3   The third significant region consists of the Pampas grasslands that cover southern part of Argentina and Chile. It is a great area for raising cattle and one of the reasons why Argentina has such great beef production and export.

4   The fourth and area is the Patagonia region located at the southern-most point of South America. It is commonly called the Tierra del Fuego region. It is a cold and windy area that attracts brave and adventurous people (McKeown, 2017).

5   The fifth area consists of Central America and Mexico. This area generally has a hot climate in the low lands and cooler climates in the mountains. The region has some significant rainforests in the eastern part and many active volcanoes. Nicaragua has the most active volcanoes in the area.

6   Finally, there is the Caribbean region consisting of a group of tropical islands. The climate is generally hot and sunny and has frequent visits from large numbers of tourists annually (McKeown, 2017).

The Organization of the Book

This book contains ten chapters, which comprehensively introduce and discuss the contemporary issues and ideas that are germane to the conduct of Doing Business in Latin America in the 21st century. The book is designed to be accessible and practical, with an emphasis on useful and applicable information. To this end, each topic is introduced with an overview, which helps to give the reader a sense of direction for what is in the chapter. Separate cases are introduced at the end of each chapter to exemplify and illustrate the concepts presented in the book. The following outline of each chapter will show the reader what to expect and how each chapter is linked to the main theme of Doing Business in Latin America.

Chapter 1 – Contemporary Thoughts About Doing Business in Latin America – This chapter introduces Latin America as an important region of the world. Over 600 million people live in this area of the world, and accounts for an enormous amount of purchasing, economic, and political power. At the same time, it is a region that has many similar yet very different societies. Over the years, attentive observers have witnessed turbulent times (especially in Central America in the 1980s), good times generally the major part of the 21st century and waning times, those periods in the most recent years 2014–2018.

Chapter 2 – The Current Business Environment – This chapter sets forth the current economic situation and trends in Latin America. Presently the outlook is less favorable than it was a few years ago. Some of the economic progress seems to be losing some of its power. This relates to a worldwide slowdown and specifically to a decrease in China commodity exchanges and the increase in interest rates in the United States that began in 2017.

Chapter 3 – Historical Business Perspective – This chapter on the history of doing business in Latin America is meant to ground the reader on various events that have helped shape Latin Americans in general and ultimately how they do business.

Chapter 4 – Cultural Issues Affecting Business – This chapter presents a discussion of how the diversity and sameness of cultures have an impact on the economic, political and social activities in Latin America. Since Latin America is ethnically mixed, describing this region from a "one shoe fits all" point of view is extremely inaccurate.

Chapter 5 – The Political Climate in LA – The political climate is one of the fastest changing elements of present day Latin America. Since the first edition of the book, the Brazilian president has been impeached, a pro-business president elected in Argentina, and signs have emerged that the Venezuelan government might finally crack.

Chapter 6 – The Economic Climate – When the first edition of this book was written, Brazil, as part of the BRICs was the star and perceived future of Latin America's economy. Since then, problems in Brazil that were discussed in the previous chapter have slid the country into the worst recession in its history.

Chapter 7 – Global Competitiveness – This chapter extends the previous one by more specifically focusing on the competitiveness of the region per the World Competitiveness Report.

Chapter 8 – Establishing a Business in Latin America – This chapter is a culmination of the previous chapters with a focus on pulling them together in order to form a strategy for entering the Latin American market.

Chapter 9 – The Marketing Process in Latin America – This chapter describes and discusses the major marketing topics that relate to assessing consumer behavior and developing marketing plans to meet the needs of the customers in Latin America.

Chapter 10 – Entrepreneurship and Innovation in Latin America – This chapter will present a discussion of "what it all means" to the curious or interested business investor.

Brief History of Business in Latin America

Globalization has had a major impact on the economic transformation of Latin America. By and large, globalization can be both good and bad for a country or region. With the intensification and pervasiveness of the digital world, borders are shrinking, and peoples' connections are becoming instantaneous. The rapidity of information exchange through the internet with its e-mail, Twitter, blogs, WhatsApp, and Facebook tools have created an environment that is more inclusive and more knowledgeable than ever before in world history. People can make consumption and business decisions more rapidly because they have more timely and accurate information. Great progress with new strategies and business models focused on different ways of promoting, selling and distributing products has provided people new ways to increase their incomes. It has offered more opportunities for careers that are assisting them in their wealth creation efforts. All of these attributes have given many people a higher quality of life. Yet on the darker side, globalization has presented many complex challenges. Globalization has raised the concern about people's movement, labor availability, terrorism, cultural conflicts and socioeconomic challenges; never before thought about among the have and have nots.

Everyone is more global today. We cannot escape it. The news broadcasts operate 24/7 with commentators and documentaries about and from all corners of the globe.

Clearly globalization has affected business and the way we do business among every type of business. The Eurozone is a clear example of these phenomena. More patently are the CAFTA, MERCOSUR, and the ANDEAN pact trade arrangements that have been strengthened and have become more active in promotion of business activity and business development among Latin American countries.

Latin America has a long history of foreign direct investment (FDI). This investment actually dates back to the 19th century (Behrman, 1974). Initially MNEs from developed countries export orientation and resources pursuits as a means of entry into Latin American markets and investments. However, post WWII, there was an alteration in Latin American country business policy thinking that began to focus more on manufacturing for local consumption (Godinez, 2016) than FDI. Although Latin American countries exhibited attractiveness for investment, it was the local governments that had an unfavorable effect on foreign business by posing significant regulations that constrained the ability to invest in the developing countries. The prohibition of most imports and restriction on FDI in the region caused many countries to create a poor business climate and thus it became unattractive to MNEs to invest in these countries (Godinez, 2016). In addition, the problems of foreign currency shortages caused significant problems around the region. The result was the closing of economies and the stoppage of FDI from MNEs from developed countries (Godinez,

2016). These regulations and restrictions hindered economic and business development. These restrictive policies continued until the 1980s.

It was at this juncture, in 1980, and beyond, the local governments began opening the region to foreign MNEs. Even though a few of the negative attributes continued to exist, over the last 30 years there have been significant market-oriented reforms, movement and activity among Latin American countries. Some of the major reforms included tax law changes, liberalization of trade, and market and procedure reform along with the removal of barriers to international capital flow. All this positive economic activity has helped the investment community and motivated them to seek business and investment opportunities in Latin America (Godinez, 2016).

While the FDI flows saw ups and downs during the 1970s and 1980s there was no real distinctive tendency to rise. However, all that changed in the 1990s. The region saw an explosion of investment in the 1990s (Godinez, 2016). Because of the major reforms associated with de-regulation and the implementation of other business investment incentives, all caused the doors to open to trade and FDI from MNEs (Godinez, 2016).

The main investor in the Latin American region has historically been the U.S., so this region depends heavily on U.S. trade relations.

Central America has also seen steady FDI flows over the last 30 years. The region's FDI investment amounts are very high when compared to other regions of the world.

The Latin American economy has profited from its continued growth. For example, it has experienced an overall 1.1% increase in the second quarter of 2017, which has produced positive feelings among most of the people who manage the countries' economies. However, in Mexico the data shows some downturn due to higher inflation. This is affecting purchasing power of the Mexican people. Argentina has had some growth while Colombia's declining inflation has caused its GDP to increase. Chile's economy has been slowly recovering while Peru's economy is making some encouraging improvements after the massive flooding in 2017. All of this positive news in the face of the 2018 elections is an interesting circumstance. This economic news should make for some major political chatter among the political hopefuls and their parties. The elections could change the political and economic landscape in Latin America. There is ambivalence about how new leadership, if it comes, could affect the economic dynamics of the Latin American economies. The unpredictable elections and the U.S. President Donald Trump's pledges could have a volatile effect on Latin America as a whole (Economic Snapshot for Latin America, 2018).

Opportunities

The following Table 1.1 summarizes the economic growth of the significant areas of Latin America. One can see over the last three years there have been good and bad stories among the member countries of this region. The year 2018 portends to be positive for everyone except Venezuela, but even that country sees positive change in GDP growth (albeit still negative for the year).

Be it as it may, Latin American countries are positioned to offer great prospects for investing and doing business in the respective regions. The numbers are good, the attitudes seem to be appropriate and the structures are improving sufficiently to accommodate investment and entrepreneurial activity.

Latin America (LA) presents an appealing location to start or invest in a business venture. In most of LA's environment, there is a desire for economic development, business creation and investment. The environment depends on where investors would like to place their business or investment. Some areas are more attractive than others. Some countries offer better economic, social and technological environments than others. A review of a cross section of LA countries will illustrate the business situations that exist in those countries.

1   Mexico – has been pursuing strong macroeconomic policies in order to strengthen its economy. It has a continuous anti-corruption effort in place to counter the constant corruption incidents that exist in Mexico. Corruption reform is a common term in the Mexican economic and social development discussions. Mexico has been experiencing a tight money policy,

TABLE 1.1 Latin America and the Caribbean: Gradual Recovery (GDP growth in Percentage)

Region and Country	2015	2016	2017	2018
Latin America and the Caribbean				
South America	−1.2	−2.6	0.4	1.6
Excluding Contracting Economies	2.9	2.5	2.2	3.1
Central America	4.4	3.7	3.8	3.9
Caribbean	4.2	3.5	3.6	4.2
Latin America				
Argentina	2.6	−2.2	2.4	2.2
Brazil	−3.8	−3.6	0.3	1.3
Chile	2.3	1.6	1.6	2.3
Colombia	3.1	2	2	3
Mexico	2.6	2.3	1.9	2
Peru	3.3	3.9	2.7	3.8
Venezuela	−6.2	−18	−12	−4.1

Source: Adapted from IMF (2017b) (Contracting economies include: Argentina, Brazil, Ecuador, Suriname, and Venezuela).

which could inhibit private consumption. Economic vigilance and constant attention to the macroeconomic and trade policies is important to keep the economy and business environment on a positive trajectory.

2   Central America and the Dominican Republic's economic activity have been strong and continue to show positive assent. The policy makers in this region can begin to advertise their economic strength and show how investment in this arena can be beneficial with these favorable conditions.

3   South America (SA) – Outlook is mixed across SA. Argentina, Brazil, Paraguay and Uruguay in the East have had great harvest seasons that have been beneficial for their economies. Argentina's recovery is showing very positive signs with positive growth expected to be between 2–3% in 2018. Its exporting activity is improving especially to Brazil.

4   Peru and Colombia have experienced some natural disaster issues but have demonstrated that because of their economic strength and public management capabilities, they are able to manage adversity and move forward with a very positive economic environment. The Peace Accord in Colombia has been a positive step forward. Domestic demand has been somewhat weak in these countries and as such needs attention with vigilance and appropriate adaptive economic policies (Werner, 2017).

5   Brazil – is beginning to turn the corner with some positive economic news and an increase in consumption. Additionally, a reduction in inflation has helped to stabilize and initiate economic growth. The concerns about domestic demand and political uncertainty continue to be issues that create uncertainty in 2018.

6   Chile – has a projected 2.3% growth rate for 2018. A tight labor market, weakening public and private consumption along with reduced public spending are issues that may have an impact on the economy as 2018 moves into the second quarter of business activity.

7   Colombia – domestic demand slowdown has emerged as a concern. The Peace Accord, infrastructure reform and friendly tax reform are all policies that ignite economic growth again (Werner, 2017).

8   Peru – had some set backs due to natural disasters (flooding), and the Odebrecht corruption scandal. However, these events have ignited increased public spending to resolve the damage from the natural disaster and to correct the impact of the scandal. Projected growth in Peru is 3.8% in 2018. This is a very respectable growth projection (Werner, 2017).

9   Venezuela – the negative political crisis that exists in Venezuela is doing significant harm to the economy and the entire society. Real GDP is expected to continue to decline and the entire political, economic and social structure is deteriorating causing major harm to the society.

As one can see there are opportunities and challenges in this great region. With its rich natural resources, its large young population with a variety of valuable skill sets in agriculture and manufacturing and generally stable governments, business opportunities abound in many areas of LA. Investors have to analyze, investigate and compare the pros and cons of each country of the LA environment. Big returns are available with smart investment decisions.

Threats – Dangerous Issues in Latin America

Public Safety and Corruption

Since the LA region is noted for large rates of inequality (social and economic) and violence (gangs and drug cartels), there are concerns regarding how long it will be before some of these issues will emerge as tension points of instability. There is a real tendency for LA to encounter boom and bust cycles. Because LA has resources that countries in other parts of the world want and need (e.g., China) it is possible that this cycle of economic activity will continue as the demand and supply of natural resources are extracted from the earth.

The other large issue relates to LA's significant under investment in education, infrastructure, public service and technology. In today's world these areas are critical to successful economic development. Many of these problems are generated by failure of LA governments to collect taxes and minimize the illicit activities that are pervasive in their economies. With the absence of financial resources, governments are weakened and unable to invest in programs and services that promote stable growth and a progressive society (i.e., public safety, and education).

Law and order is the foundation or platform for a stable society. In addition, it is imperative if countries are going to attract investment, grow markets and ignite the engines of economic development. The improvements in and strengthening of the judicial system and public safety arrangements in LA are vital to making this region suitable for investment and business activity. Hopefully this stability will come sooner rather than later such as it appears to be changing in Brazil.

Corruption is sapping an incredible amount of energy, resources and talent from LA societies and economies. The seriousness of corruption is legion and has deep roots. Much of it is caused by the huge economic inequality that exists among LA country populations. As long as corruption exists, weakness and vulnerability will exist. Countries will need to reframe their government structures and ways of doing business. This is difficult and very time consuming, but it must be done if investment and successful economic development is going to emerge.

The prospects for the future have some major obstacles in its path. As mentioned above, corruption seems to be a disease that is pulling down the positive economic possibilities. With enormous potential at hand all over LA, governments and societies must find a way to minimize or eradicate the corruption that presently exists. Moreover, the existence of the major drug trafficking routes and enterprises located in many parts of LA but especially in Central America have had a huge negative impact on the LA societies and economies. The weak, corrupted governments are having difficulties controlling the wealthy, powerful drug lords. Fear among the people de-motivates them to seek opportunities. Risk takers who would generally venture into new businesses or entrepreneurship ideas are cautious or seriously concerned about the long-term success of any venture. This pervasive drug trafficking mess has polluted the political and judicial system. Since political leaders cannot agree on solutions or are intimidated by the power of the drug lords, nothing substantial has developed to eradicate this huge nemesis in the side of the governing bodies. Fear is a giant de-motivator. It discourages FDI and local investment.

Political leaders in LA have a great deal to think about regarding a safe, stable and prosperous society. The sooner they create strong transparent mechanisms that counter acts of corruption, drug trafficking and illicit activity, the better society will be for its people. Hope is not lost. Brazil, Chile, and Colombia have all demonstrated that growing economies can strengthen public institutions and give them the chance to address the negative public issues that confront its people. Brazil's hugely successful economic programs, Argentina's lengthy devotion to democracy and free market economy and Chile's economic performance demonstrates that it can be done. One of the remarkable turnarounds is Colombia. After many years of being stigmatized as the Drug Capital of the World, Colombia is now reforming and becoming an economic power in Latin America. While it has not eradicated all of it problems, it has made substantial progress towards stability and economic prosperity. Colombia is becoming a model for other countries in the region. If Colombia can change and make the hard choices, it seems that other countries in LA can pursue the same path and provide its citizenry the stable and economically growing society that they need for their families to live free politically and economically.

Corruption has afflicted Latin America for a very long time. For centuries, ever since it emerged from the Spanish and Portuguese colonial rule, corruption has been an integral part of Latin America's way of life. The difference today is the response to this plague of corruption. Latin American societies and institutions refuse to remain complicit with the corruption, nor have resigned themselves to its inevitability. This attitude is illustrated by the proliferation of trials, investigations, demonstrations, convictions, and resignations relating to corruption. This is particularly stark in Brazil and Venezuela, and to a lesser extent Mexico and Guatemala. In all four countries, major scandals have erupted, with high-level convictions (Castaneda, 2015). Although no nation is invulnerable to corruption there is a difference between normal corruptions, which is generally for the most part controlled by various anti-corruption entities of government. Systemic corruption is corruption that is embedded in the society and has no effective anti-corruption mechanisms to eliminate its impact on society. It is in most cases just accepted.

One of the most alarming reports about corruption has evolved in Brazil. Before the reports emerged, unrest about corruption had already been brewing. First, protests against excesses and abuses regarding the preparations for the World Cup erupted in 2013. Then the alleged *petroleum* scandal hit. Large sums of money, it was revealed, had been transferred directly, or via immense construction companies, from Brazil's state-owned oil company, Petrobras, to President Dilma Rousseff's Workers' Party (Castaneda, 2015). This is just one example of a major incident of corruption that was reported by the press. Hundreds of other incidents go unreported because the people of the communities are in fear for their lives or of retribution. Since there are weak or non-existent institutions to counteract these corrupt practices, the people are held hostage and can only tolerate the actions of a few who make life problematic for the many. See Figure 1.2 for an illustration of the corruption challenge of the region.

Trends

Change and creative destruction wait for no one. Everyday events or policies emerge that have an impact on the way businesses operate or are conducted in various parts of Latin America. The corruption and scandals in Brazil have derailed the positive economic direction that the whole world was watching for so long.

FIGURE 1.2   Map of Corruption for Latin America

Nicholas Maduro, the President of Venezuela has brought his country's economy to a state of collapse causing enormous uncertainty for its people and the country itself. Trends are movements or directions that create change. In Latin America, political and economic trends are occurring all the time. One of the trends that has been occurring for a long time relates to Latin American trade.

It is interesting that 40% of all merchandise exported from Latin America and the Caribbean goes to the U.S.A. With regard to Mexico and Central America this figure is 80%. Trends that Latin America governments should continue to sustain the positive economic climate that presently exists should do the following:

1 Keep global markets open. This is critical to maintaining growth and development

2 Make regional integration a reality. This approach would expand and deepen intra-regional trade and inter-relations along with an increase in productivity, a factor critically important for economic development. This is the catalyst for expansion of millions of micro-, and SME businesses. (Layla Gonzalez, 2017).

3 Job markets in Latin America are uncertain. It offers opportunity and concern. Opportunity in that entrepreneurship, innovation and inclusion are possible yet the traditional jobs are disappearing and being replaced with digital skill sets. This trend is of concern because the majority of the population does not possess these skills.

4 Education and training are moving center stage because without an education and a trained population, companies cannot take advantage of the digital network that is driving almost all businesses in the contemporary business environment. Automated production is happening sooner rather than later. Latin American countries need to move fast to educate its population in order to survive in the business world (Botifoll, 2017).

5 Renewed thrust for industrialization. Pursuing a framework for investment using public/private collaboration approach. There is a need to create a new form of capitalism, one that has both an economic and social impact (Capote, 2017).

6 Creating livable cities by legislating policies and programs that make Latin American cities more attractive. Using clean energy i.e., gas fired plants. Additionally, introducing hybrid or electric cars to cities across Latin American cities. Tesla, GM, Toyota and Ford are bringing their technology to the region (Capote, 2017).

7 Political uncertainty that has an impact on economic policy. The elections of 2018 are deciding what direction several countries take. And the uncertainty from the North with President Trump's rhetoric places many people asking, "what is next?" All this has an impact on policy and the realization of business goals in the short run and also in the long run (Spillan, Virza & Garita, 2014).

Conclusion

Investors or business people looking to expand or invest in Latin America and benefit from the vast economic opportunities the region offers, must be sure about the risks, threats, and challenges that exist in the entire ecosystem this environment presents. The geography of LA is enormous but also extremely resourceful. The fact that the region is bordered by two of the greatest bodies of water (Pacific and Atlantic Oceans) is in itself a major asset. As a global world transport of goods via trade is the name of the game. The ability to import and export goods is a huge competitive advantage and LA over time has shown that trade is a vital part of its economic DNA. The political stability of the region also enhances the regions' capability of becoming a great place to do business. While the last decade has manifested an up and down economic cycle, with the exception of Venezuela, there have not been major economic disasters as has been the history over the years. New forecasts predict increasing growth and solid opportunities for those investors who want to venture into this region. Concrete opportunities exist, large potential returns on investment loom over the horizons.

It is without saying that there are some major issues that LA must deal with such as reduction and elimination of corruption, significant investments in education and infrastructure and implementing structural reforms and policies in the governing process among many countries of this region. While there are major risks, major opportunities also exist. However, with careful analysis, an open mind, and an entrepreneurial perspective, investments in LA can be very beneficial to potential investors.

CASE

Auteco – Colombia

Mr. Paul Vasquez founded ATECO Colombia in 1941. Its original name was Autotecnica Colombia, S.A. During the initial stages of operation, Auteco only dealt with auto parts and petrol. As it grew over the years it took on other product lines. In 1945 it began importing American Indian motorcycles as a means of satisfying a market opportunity. This product line and market focus began to become the main focus of the business. In 1954 Auteco began offering Lambrettas to the Colombian market. This scooter type product became very popular and a strong product line. Later, rather than importing them, Auteco established its own manufacturing sites and manufactured them in Colombia. Seeing the expanding opportunities for motorcycle type products, Auteco in 1972 entered into a business partnership with Kawaski to manufacture motorcycles under their license grew into electric generators and motors. The Kawasaki brand an imported Japanese product has for a long time been popular among Colombians. As technology increased and became more popular, Auteco formed another partnership with India Bajia Co. to redistribute scooters to Colombian customers. Further expansion came in 2003 when Auteco began importing Taiwanese Kymco motorcycles. Today in 2018 Auteco is in a strong position. As an importer Auteco is involved with a variety of international business transactions, customs issues and cross-border negotiations. Colombia has very active motorcycle clubs, which seem to be very united and have a high interest in the quality of the motorbikes. The customer base seems to be large and heterogeneous. This means the products that Auteco sells can satisfy their customer population.

This case is an example of how a very small parts and petro business evolved into one of the main motorbike businesses in Colombia. Even during the many years of internal strife around the country, Auteco was able to grow, expand and become international in its business dealings. Importing products has been the lifeblood of the business. Interacting with suppliers from Asia (Taiwan and Japan) from Europe (Italy and Spain) have become customary to meet the sales desires of Auteco's clients.

In 2016, Auteco celebrated its 75th anniversary of business. The company appears to be strong a prospering.

Source: www.auteco.com.co, 2017

References

Andra, Jacob (2016). "Entering Latin America." *Focus.* http://ustranslation.com/pubs/latam.pdf, accessed January, 2018.

Auteco (2017). www.auteco.com.co, accessed March, 2018.

Behrman, Jack, N. (1974). "Decision Criteria for Foreign Direct Investment in Latin America." *New York Council of Americas,* 89(8), pp.1–89.

Botifoll, Jordi (2017). "Creating (And Filling) Jobs in Latin America's New Digital Economy." www.weforum.org/agenda/2017/04/creating-and-filling-jobs-in-latin-america-s-new-digital-economy, accessed January, 2017.

Capote, Alfredo (2017). "Three Key Trends for The Future of Latin America's Economy." www.weforum.org/agenda/2017/04/three-trends-future-lat-am, accessed January, 2017.

Castaneda, Jorge (2015). "Latin America's Anti Corruption Crusade." *Project Syndicate.* www.project-syndicate.org/commentary/latin-america-corruption-scandals-by-jorge-g-casta-eda-2015-07?barrier=accessreg, accessed February, 2018.

Economic Snapshot for Latin America (2018). www.focus-economics.com/regions/latin-america, accessed April, 2018.

Godinez, Jose (2016). "Corruption in Latin America and How it Affects FDI: Causes, Consequences and Possible Solutions." In Mauricio Garita and Jose Godinez (Eds), *Business Redevelopment Opportunities and Market Entry: Challenges in Latin America* (pp.30–46). Hershey, Pennsylvania, USA: Business Science Reference.

IMF (2017a). "World Economic Outlook Database, and IMF staff calculations." www. imf.org/external/pubs/ft/weo/data/changes.htm, accessed April, 2018.

IMF (2017b). "Latin America and the Caribbean: Bouncing Back from Recession." www.imf.org/en/News/Articles/2017/05/18/NA190517Latin-America-and-the-Caribbean-Bouncing-Back-from-Recession, accessed January, 2018.

Layla Gonzales, Avancha (2017). "5 Reasons Not to Give Up on Global Trade." www. ups.com/us/en/services/knowledge-center/article.page?name=5-reasons-not-to-give-up-on-global-trade&kid=cd1adfbc, accessed January, 2018.

McKeown, Marie (2017). "What is Latin America? Geography, Language and Culture." https://owlcation.com/social-sciences/What-is-Latin-America, accessed January, 2018.

Schwab, Klaus "Latin America's Biggest Challenge and a Plan to Tackle it." *Global Competitive Report, 2016–2017,* World Economic Forum. www3.weforum.org/docs/GCR2016-2017/05FullReport/TheGlobalCompetitivenessReport2016-2017_FINAL.pdf, accessed February, 2018.

Spillan, John, E., Nicholas Virzi, & Mauricio Garita (2014). *Doing Business in Latin America: Challenges and Opportunities.* New York: Taylor & Francis.

Turner-Trujillo, Emma, Marissa Del Toro, & April Ramos (2017). "An Overview of Latino and Latin American Identity: A Primer for Pacific Standard Time: LA/LA on the Many Facets of Latin American and Latino Geography, Culture, and Heritage." http://blogs.getty.edu/iris/an-overview-of-latino-and-latin-american-identity, accessed March, 2018.

Vassolo, R. S., J. O. De Castro, & L. R. Gomez-Mejia (2011). "Managing in Latin America: Common Issues and a Research Agenda." *Academy of Management Perspectives*, 25(4), pp.22–36.

Werner, Alejandro (2017). "Latest Outlook for The Americas: Back on Cruise Control, but Stuck in Low Gear." http://blogs.imf.org/2017/latest-outlook-for-the-americas-back-on-cruise-control-but-stuck-in-low-gear/, accessed January, 2018.

Werner, Alejandro (2018). "Latin America and the Caribbean in 2018: An Economic Recovery in the Making, IMF Blog Insights and Analysis on Economic and Finance." https://blogs.imf.org/2018/01/25/latin-america-and-the-caribbean-in-2018-an-economic-recovery-in-the-making/, accessed March, 2018.

World Population (2017). "Central America – World Population Review." http://world populationreview.com/continents/central-america-population/, accessed January, 2018.

2

THE CURRENT BUSINESS ENVIRONMENT

Overview

This chapter sets forth the current business environment and trends in Latin America. Many of the items briefly discussed here will be the subjects of entire chapters later in the book (e.g., competitiveness). We mention these concepts now to build off the introductory chapter and set the stage for delving into the next chapter on historical perspectives of Latin America.

Presently the outlook is less favorable than it was a few years ago. Some of the economic progress seems to be losing momentum. This can be partially attributed to a worldwide economic slowdown, and of particular interest to Latin America, to a decrease in China's commodity demand and an increase in interest rates in the United States. These economic trends have had an impact on capital flow into the region. This slowdown has also influenced the structural reforms needed to increase productivity and competitiveness. There is a need for a focused growth strategy that makes productivity its centerpiece. This strategy needs to be implemented as soon as possible to halt the slow economic growth. It is also necessary to sustain the economic and social transformation that many Latin American countries have implemented over the last ten years. Millions of people have been pulled out of poverty and entered the middle class. This is a major transformation that occurred during a commodity boom that emanated from the global economic growth earlier in the decade. Domestic reforms were implemented which created opportunities for the poor and disadvantaged to better their lot in life. Now, governments are finding it more difficult to satisfy this new group of people. Investing in people, education, and infrastructure and eliminating obstacles to economic growth is imperative. Making labor laws flexible and financial regulations reasonable is important to drive economic growth.

Before the conclusion section and case on Colombia, a discussion on trading blocs within the region demonstrates how Latin American countries trade with each other. Contrary to protectionist policies that seem to be taking hold in other parts of the world (e.g., Great Britain and the U.S.), most Latin American countries continue to value free trade as a source of prosperity. Evidence from the Trans-Pacific Partnership illustrates how countries in Latin America are not content just trading with each other but seek to open new markets in Asia and Australia.

The case of Colombia illustrates how a recent trade agreement with the United States and a long overdue cease-fire with the FARC have improved the current business environment.

Major Trends Affecting Business Activity in Latin America

Gross Domestic Product

A good place to start to evaluate the current business environment of a region is with its overall production of goods and services by country during a particular period (see Table 2.1). Throughout this book we will provide the reader with the most recent year that accurate data is available (in this case 2016). The most current GDP data allows the reader to objectively evaluate how each country is doing in Latin America. For benchmark purposes, we have included Latin America as a whole along with the United States and China. For this section of the chapter, we have also included the world figures since we are focusing on a general global trend that is affecting Latin America.

We will progress with our analysis of Table 2.1 with GDP and GDP change over the past decade. Next, in order to get a feel for what these numbers mean per person, we'll move to GDP per capita along with the change over the past decade. The GDP column for the year 2016 indicates that Brazil and Mexico make up nearly half of the region's GDP. They are by far the biggest countries in terms of production. The two Central American nations of Nicaragua and Honduras anchor the other end of the spectrum.

In terms of GDP growth, Panama has led the way over the past decade. As we'll demonstrate in future chapters, Panama and its pro-market policies have led to a high level of foreign direct investment, which has fueled its economy over the past decade. Furthermore, the recent expansion of the Panama Canal should only boost its already robust growth rates. More revenues are generated by ships using its unique location advantage as the narrowest point in the Americas to get from the Atlantic to the Pacific Ocean. Somewhat surprising is the fact that Bolivia has the 2nd highest growth rate in the region (195%), over triple the regional average of 56%. Bolivia's economy has been growing steadily in the last few years mostly due to exports of commodities including natural gas, silver, zinc, and soy. Bolivia has the second largest natural gas reserves in South

TABLE 2.1 GDP and GDP per Capita by Country (Current US$)

Country	GDP (US$ Billions)			GDP per Capita (US$)		
	2006	2016	% Change	2006	2016	% Change
Argentina	233	545	135	5,879	12,440	53
Bolivia	11	34	195	1,234	3,105	60
Brazil	1,108	1,796	62	5,860	8,650	32
Chile	155	247	60	9,485	13,793	31
Colombia	163	282	74	3,709	5,806	36
Costa Rica	23	57	154	5,245	11,825	56
Dominican Republic	36	72	99	3,836	6,722	43
Ecuador	47	99	111	3,351	6,019	44
El Salvador	19	27	44	3,063	4,224	27
Guatemala	30	69	127	2,257	4,147	46
Honduras	11	22	98	1,438	2,361	39
Mexico	965	1,047	8	8,768	8,209	−7
Nicaragua	7	13	96	1,241	2,151	42
Panama	18	55	204	5,349	13,680	61
Peru	89	192	117	3,171	6,049	48
Paraguay	11	27	158	1,810	4,078	56
Uruguay	20	52	168	5,878	15,221	61
Venezuela, RB	183	236	29	6,736	7,620	12
Latin America	3,127	4,874	56	3,773	6,386	69
China	2,752	11,199	307	2,099	8,123	74
U.S.	13,856	18,624	34	46,437	57,638	19
World	51,364	75,847	48	7,782	10,194	24

Source: The World Bank (2017).

Notes
Venezuela is an estimate from IMF database.

America and holds the world's largest known reserves of lithium, which are yet to be explored (Trading Economics, 2018).[1] It should also be noted that Bolivia had (and still has) a lot of room to grow in terms of GDP per capita since it had the lowest value in all of Latin America in 2006 ($1,234 USD$). Even with this caveat, Bolivia's growth should not be discounted. Many people are being pulled out of poverty in that country, which has numerous political effects as illustrated in Chapter 5 of this book.

Another interesting observation from Table 2.1 is that nearly every country in Latin America grew faster in the decade leading to 2016 than the overall world figures. Many believe that this is a very positive trend that the region intends on continuing for the foreseeable future. The primary reason that the Latin American regional number is "only" at 56% is largely due to Mexico's relatively small growth of only 8% during the period. The fact that such a big economy had by far the lowest rate in the region brought down the regional average. Removing Mexico from the regional total results in an increase from 56% to 77%. An in-depth case analysis of Mexico will be covered in Chapter 9.

Next, the interested reader coming from either the United States or China can analyze the differences in GDP growth from those regions and how they might be affecting Latin America. The spectacular rise in China's GDP (>300%) has had a remarkable influence on Latin America. As one can imagine, such a significant growth rate in an already massive economy (now the world's second largest, trailing only the United States) creates a high demand for many natural resources. Latin America has been keen on providing them. From iron ore needed for steel production to crude oil, Latin America has enjoyed the strong demand coming from Chinese companies and the hefty profits associated with it. Yet the growth rate in China over the last few years has slowed along with its demand for raw materials, thus, prices have fallen. We argue that only increasing productivity levels in Latin America will result in sustainable long-term growth rates in the region. This topic will be covered in more depth later in this chapter.

Shifting to the GDP per capita information, one can see that the Uruguayans are the wealthiest in the region at over $15,000 USD$/person. Along with the Panamanians, their wealth per person has grown at 61% over the past decade. More recently, after long recessions, Brazil and Argentina still cheer when good economic news comes out. In tiny Uruguay, sandwiched between them, it is commonplace. On March 22, 2018, the central bank reported that GDP grew by 2.7% in 2017, bringing the country's growth streak to 15 years – the longest expansion in its history. Uruguay's growth since 2011, when global prices of commodities started to fall, puts its neighbors to shame (see Figure 2.1). Its success shows the value of openness, strong institutions, and investment in know (The Economist, 2018).

On the other end of the continuum, Mexico is the only country in Latin America that has reported a negative figure at a decline of −7% GDP per capita. Unfortunately, the political uncertainty with an upcoming election in 2018 coupled with the claims coming from the United States' President Trump about renegotiating NAFTA has been a further drag on the country since the release of these 2016 figures (Focus Economics, 2018). Venezuela is also pulling down the region's average GDP per capita to 38% growth in the decade up to 2016. Removing these two countries from the regional average would take the per capita growth rate up an astonishing 25% to 63%. However, these two economies are too large to dismiss, which is why we will discuss them in detail as cases.

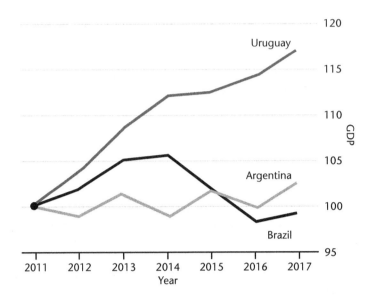

FIGURE 2.1 Recent GDPs

Foreign Direct Investment

After analyzing the growth rates by country, we next move to net inflows of investment into each country in Latin America. As before, we compared it to the influx of foreign direct investment (FDI) in China and the United States. Table 2.2 shows 2006, 2016, and the percentage change. Note that these numbers are snapshots in time and are more vulnerable to one or two outlying transactions than were the GDP numbers presented in Table 2.1. For example, Uruguay had a single investor remove US$1 billion of FDI in 2016 (IMF, 2018).

Despite Brazil's recent recession, its FDI has been steadily increasing over the last decade partially due to investments from China. In 2016, the Chinese invested over 15% of Brazil's total FDI, which is the largest share from any one country. However, investors should still be cautious because only 20–25% of the investment in 2016 was infrastructure-building greenfield investment. Much of the remaining FDI took the form of inter-company loans from foreign companies who are trying to leverage Brazil's high interest rates. These loans do not create the lasting positive impact that the greenfield investments do (Leahy & Schipani, 2017).

Comparing the net inflows of FDI in Latin America with China and the United States might make incoming investment seem relatively small. Note, however, that the economies in terms of the GDP of China and the United States are three and four times the size, respectively. It appears that the world is betting on Latin America. In general, the amount of net FDI flowing into Latin America was over twice as high in 2016 as 2006 (124%).

TABLE 2.2 Net Inflows of FDI (Billions of US$)

Country	2006	2016	% Change
Argentina	5.5	3.3	−41
Bolivia	0.3	0.3	18
Brazil	19.4	78.2	303
Chile	7.7	12.2	60
Colombia	6.8	13.7	103
Costa Rica	1.8	2.9	63
Dominican Republic	1.5	2.5	65
Ecuador	0.3	0.8	178
Guatemala	0.6	1.2	85
Honduras	0.7	1.1	57
Mexico	20.7	33.9	64
Nicaragua	0.3	0.9	210
Panama	2.9	6.0	104
Peru	3.5	6.9	98
Paraguay	0.2	0.4	119
El Salvador	0.2	0.5	102
Uruguay	1.5	−0.3	−121
Venezuela, RB	0.2	1.6	702
Latin America	74.1	166.1	124
China	124.1	170.6	37
U.S.	294.3	479.4	63

Source: IMF (2017).

That said, the Latin American region is at a difficult juncture. FDI inflows declined by 8% in 2016 to US$166 billion, representing a cumulative fall of 17% since the peak in 2011. The fall in commodity prices continues to affect investments in natural resources, sluggish economic growth in several countries has slowed the flow of market-seeking capital, and the global backdrop of technological sophistication and expansion of the digital economy has concentrated transnational investments in developed economies (Barcena, Prado, Cimoli & Perez, 2017).

According to ECLAC's report on FDI in Latin America, the perception of globalization and its economic and social effects reached a turning point in 2016. Political events, such as the referendum in the United Kingdom which resulted in the vote to leave the European Union (Brexit) and the presidential election in the United States, reflected trends that had developed over time in global production and trade. Developed economies have been more interested in repatriating production, which together with the rapid technological transition and greater competitive pressure has redirected businesses towards more technology-intensive markets. In this scenario, the Latin American region is losing ground as a recipient of FDI, with inflows decreasing for the second year in a row to levels similar to those seen in 2011. In spite of this, FDI flows stood at 3.6% of GDP while the global average was 2.5%, revealing the importance of transnational corporations in the region's economies (Barcena at al., 2017).

Structural Reforms

A key component of structural reform in Latin America is a diverse economy. For example, earlier in this chapter we discussed the impressive GDP per capita in Uruguay, but we did not discuss how it got there. After Argentina defaulted on its debt in 2002 (discussed in detail in the next chapter), Uruguay realized it needed to diversify. Thus, it entered new industries such as software and audio-visual services, which were exported to new markets (The Economist, 2018). And while the country knew that its neighbors are very important trading partners, it aimed to diversify where its products were sold. Between 2001 and 2016, the share of exports going to Brazil and Argentina fell from 37% to 21%.

In 2017, the Uruguayan government invested in raising productivity. Public spending on science and technology increased by 73% in real terms between 2007 and 2015. Even cattle farmers innovated. While Argentina initiated export tariffs on beef to hold down domestic prices, Uruguay became the first Latin American country to make all its beef exports electronically traceable in order to reassure buyers that potential contaminants or problems like foot-and-mouth disease will be caught early. Between 2005 and 2012 Argentina's beef exports fell by three-quarters (The Economist, 2018). Remarkably, Uruguay now sells more than its neighbor, which has over 15 times as much land.

A proxy for how well structural reforms are working for a nation is its labor productivity (see Table 2.3). Labor productivity is calculated by dividing each country's GDP by the average number of hours worked annually by all employed citizens. Hours worked include full-time and part-time workers, excluding holidays and vacation time. An alternative view is calculated by dividing the GDP per capita by the average number of hours worked in a year. The higher the number, the more productive a nation's workforce is.

Table 2.3 is sorted from most productive to least productive country in 2018. We did not have data for most of the Central American countries, and therefore they are not included in the table. Furthermore, data is unreliable for Venezuela and China, and thus they were also not included. Finally, the average figures reported for Latin America as a whole are not weighted, and therefore should be interpreted with caution.

As aforementioned, Uruguayans contribute the most to their GDP per hour worked (US$31.10). Structural changes that contributed to their substantial improvement include the reestablishment of collective bargaining, the increase in the minimum wage, specific regulations for domestic services, changes in unemployment insurance, advances in paternity and maternity leave, labor formalization, and the modification of the tax structure. For more detailed

TABLE 2.3 Labor Productivity

Country	2008	2018	% Change
Uruguay	22.8	31.1	36
Chile	25.2	28.1	12
Argentina	25.3	27.5	9
Mexico	20.1	20.5	2
Costa Rica	13.6	19.5	43
Brazil	17.0	18.0	6
Colombia	14.2	16.0	13
Ecuador	12.9	14.1	9
Peru	9.9	13.6	37
Latin America	17.0	19.5	15
U.S.	37.4	42.7	14

Source: The Conference Board (2018).

Note
The Latin America figure is an unweighted average.

information on the Uruguay case, the book entitled *Toward Inclusive Development: The Case of Uruguay* (Amarante & Infante, 2016 – only available in Spanish) analyzes the country's evolution from 2001 to 2014 in terms of economic growth, labor market dynamics, and social protection, which are the three fundamental pillars of inclusive development.

Mexico is fast emerging as a global industrial power, but recent growth in manufacturing has not converted into broad-based economic gains. Though factory output, employment, and exports are at new highs, Mexico's economy remains stuck. Stagnant labor productivity has kept the economy from achieving larger gains. Even though Mexico's factories are rapidly growing in sophistication, Mexican workers are barely more productive than they were a decade ago, in contrast to their South and East Asian peers (Rogers & Singh, 2017). The high degree of labor market informality and low level of educational attainment characteristic of Mexico's less developed states are all too present in the better-performing states of Mexico's industrial north and center. These structural shortcomings play a key role in undercutting productivity growth across Mexican states.

Rogers & Singh (2017) argue that Mexico's state economies are not creating enough formal-sector jobs to absorb growth in the labor force. Because of the shortage of formal-sector jobs, informal work arrangements predominate even in Mexico's fastest-growing states. The low educational attainment of Mexico's labor force, which limits opportunities for employment in the formal sector, poses an additional barrier to productivity growth (Rogers & Singh, 2017).

Almost two thirds of Mexican workers are employed informally. This is an improvement over the last decade, when nearly 70% of workers labored in the informal sector. However, informal employment in Mexico still ranks among the highest of Latin America's large economies and is well above rates reported by the U.S. and Western Europe. Indeed, in its pervasive informality, Mexico's labor market more closely resembles those in the largely underdeveloped countries of Central America (Rogers & Singh, 2017). Getting more informal workers into the formal sector of the economy should be a priority for Mexico in order to increase its productivity. That said, FDI for automotive, aerospace, and tech has recently helped Mexico in this regard.

A recent report on productivity by the OECD countries noted that differing cultural attitudes and socioeconomic factors play a key role in the number of hours employers expect from workers. In Mexico, long-standing fears about unemployment, coupled with lax labor laws, mean that the maximum 48-hour workweek is rarely enforced (Leach, 2018).[16] Since the denominator in the productivity equation is number of hours worked, the fact that Mexico has the most hours worked of OECD countries translates into poor productivity numbers.

The Rise from the Poor

While we give the subject of poverty and inequality considerable attention in Chapter 6, it is also worth noting here in the Current Business Environment chapter due to its relevance in the region. Table 2.4 demonstrates the poverty headcount ratio as the percentage of the population living on less than US$1.90 a day at 2011 international prices. As a result of revisions in purchasing power parity (PPP) exchange rates, poverty rates for individual countries are difficult to compare with poverty rates reported in earlier editions.

Comparing poverty rates is somewhat difficult, thus we used the World Bank's poverty ratio. The entity has more recently established US$3.20 a day and US$5.50 a day as poverty numbers. It might be accurate to consider US$1.90 a day as an extremely low number. The number is so low that it wasn't measured in the "rich" countries because there is an assumption that virtually no one lives below that number. Therefore, the United States is omitted in Table 2.4.

One can see that every country in Latin America has reduced the number of people living in extreme poverty. Every country except Honduras has below 10% of their population in this improved range. So, the region went from having eight countries at about 10% poverty to only one in a decade's time. We don't have reliable data from Venezuela for 2015, and thus left it blank.

The World Bank studies on Honduras have highlighted the importance of improving the quality of education and diversifying sources of rural income given that most of the country's poor live in rural areas and depend on agriculture for their livelihoods. Other studies have found that targeted social programs can potentially reduce poverty.

TABLE 2.4 Poverty Rates at 1.90 US$ a Day

Country	2005	2015	% Change
Argentina	5.4	1.7	−69
Bolivia	20.4	7.1	−65
Brazil	7.9	4.3	−46
Chile	2.3	1.3	−43
Colombia	10.4	5.5	−47
Costa Rica	4.4	1.6	−64
Dominican Republic	5.8	1.9	−67
Ecuador	13.6	4.8	−65
Guatemala	11.5	9.5	−17
Honduras	27.8	17.8	−36
Mexico	4.0	3.0	−25
Nicaragua	9.0	3.6	−60
Panama	10.3	2.2	−79
Peru	14.2	3.0	−79
Paraguay	7.0	2.5	−64
El Salvador	9.6	1.9	−80
Uruguay	0.9	0.3	−67
Venezuela, RB	17.0	n/a	−
Latin America	9.3	3.0	−68
China	18.8	1.9	−90

Source: The World Bank (2018b).

Note
The Latin America figure is an unweighted average.

On December 15, 2015, the World Bank Group Executive Board approved the new Country Partnership Framework (CPF) for 2016–2020, whose pillars are to promote inclusion, strengthen growth conditions, and reduce vulnerabilities in the country (The World Bank, 2018a).[17] The new CPF has seven specific objectives in Honduras:

1   Expand coverage of social programs
2   Strengthen the renovation of key infrastructure
3   Increase access to financing
4   Strengthen the regulatory framework and institutional capacity
5   Improve rural productivity
6   Strengthen resilience to natural disasters and climate change
7   Build capacities of local governments to prevent crime and violence.

Hopefully the country will be able to use the resources of the World Bank to dramatically reduce its numbers of extreme poor, and the next version of the book will not have any countries that have over 10% of its population in this category. We'll focus on inequality in Chapter 6. The CPF from the World Bank represents the type of structural changes needed, in particular for the especially poor countries in Central America.

The Middle Class and the Social Contract

What, if any, are the implications of a rising middle class with these characteristics – urban, better educated, largely privately employed, and with beliefs and opinions broadly in line with those of their poorer and less-educated fellow citizens – for social and economic policy? In particular, is the growth of the Latin American middle class likely to spell any changes for the region's fragmented social contract? This is the question that the World Bank set out to answer in 2013 (Ferreira, Messina, Rigolini, Lopez-Calva, Lugo & Vakis, 2013).

A "social contract" may be broadly understood as the combination of implicit and explicit arrangements that determine what each group contributes to and receives from the state. Latin America's social contract in the latter half of the 20th century was characterized by a small state to which the elite (and the small middle class associated with it) contributed through low taxes and from which they benefited largely through a truncated set of in-cash benefits such as retirement pensions, severance payments, and the like, for which only formal sector workers qualified (De Ferranti, Ferrera, Perry & Walton, 2004). Little was left for providing high-quality public services in the areas of education, health, infrastructure, and security. Public services in these areas were therefore generally of low quality. While the vast majority of the poor and vulnerable population had no choice, the rich and the small middle class opted out and chose privately provided alternatives. The essence of this implicit contract was simple: the upper and middle classes were not asked to pay much and did not expect to receive much from public services either. The poor also paid little and received correspondingly little in terms of public benefits (De Ferranti et al., 2004).

One manifestation of this social contract was a state that was typically small as well as skewed toward the provision of formal sector social security payments to the well off. To this day, with the exception of Argentina and Brazil, the region is characterized by relatively low tax revenues overall. The average total tax revenue in 2010 was 20% of GDP in Latin America, versus 34% in the OECD countries, for example.[1] In addition, the composition of these tax revenues tended to be skewed toward indirect (sales) taxes and social security contributions relative to income and property taxes, leading to a system that is not particularly progressive (Ferreira et al., 2013).

On the benefit side, the middle class and the elite participated disproportionately in the social security system (including old-age and disability pensions, unemployment protection, severance payments, and health insurance).

However, they tended to opt out of state-funded public education and health services. Rather, the upper and middle classes in Latin America often turned to private alternatives to obtain these services. This propensity to opt out extended even to services where public provision should be the uncontested norm, such as electrical power; in some Latin American countries, private ownership of generators is still found to correlate with household income. The same applies for public security, with private security in closed condominiums (the equivalent to gated communities) not uncommon in several countries in Latin America.

Over the past 10–20 years the political equilibrium has begun to shift, albeit gradually. The spread of noncontributory old-age pension and health insurance schemes and the growth of conditional cash transfers has meant that redistributive transfers from the state now reach the poor to an extent that was unheard of 20 years ago in most of the region. At the same time, in most countries in the region, the extension of cash benefits to the poor has not been matched by a return of the middle class to public health and education services. Latin America's "welfare state" may have become less "truncated," but its social contract remains fragmented (Ferreira et al., 2013).[22]

It is natural to question whether Latin America will be able to continue its recent run of "growth with equity" (or at least with declining inequality) on the basis of such a fragmented contract which inherently generates fewer opportunities for the bulk of the population. Socioeconomic progress requires a combination of economic freedom and a sound foundation of public education, health, and infrastructure. It is relatively sure that most nations in Latin America will require more changes to their social contracts to empower their states to give that foundation and sustain growth.

Whether and how the new middle class will help strengthen the region's social contract remains to be seen and will doubtless be the subject of much research in the future. Nevertheless, the World Bank report highlights three areas where reforms may help to gain the support of the middle class for a fairer and more legitimate social contract:

1   Incorporate the goal of equal opportunities more explicitly into public policy.
2   Embark on a second generation of reforms to the social protection system, encompassing both social assistance and social insurance.
3   Break the vicious cycle of low taxation and low quality of public services that leads the middle and upper classes to opt out.

Amid most of the 2000s, Latin America's enhanced policy framework allowed many countries to take advantage of a favorable external environment to begin a great change toward a middle-class society. This has created enormous expectations, which risk turning into frustration if this transition stalls. As discussed earlier in this chapter, the region cannot depend on the external environment remaining as friendly as it has been in the recent past to achieve further social and economic gains. A more prominent approach towards policy will be necessary to consolidate the process of upward mobility and to make it more resilient to potential adverse shocks. In summary, the responsibility for change will be on the political leaders and democratic institutions because they face the challenge of overhauling its social contract (Ferreira et al., 2013).

Investing in people, education, and infrastructure and eliminating obstacles to economic growth are imperative. Some countries have been able to relax rigid labor laws. For example, in July of 2017, despite his indictment on corruption charges, Brazilian president Michel Temer managed to pass a reform of labor laws that have long stalled growth. He is now trying to simplify a convoluted tax code where a typical firm has to spend 2,038 staff-hours a year on compliance. Hopes for a robust recovery ride, above all. on Mr. Temer's promise to bring public spending under control (The Economist, 2017).[24] In December 2017 he persuaded Congress to agree to a 20-year real-terms spending freeze. For it to stick, however, he will have to reform a pension system that entitles Brazilians to retire, on average, at just 58 years old. Pensions already cost 13% of GDP. Without an overhaul, government spending on pensions could reach a fifth of GDP by 2060, when the number of over-65s is projected to increase from 17 million now to 58 million.

Trading Blocs

The last topic to be covered in this chapter is trading blocs. A *free trade area* eliminates tariffs and measures having equivalent effect for goods and services traded between the member states. However, the member states don't have a common policy regarding tariffs. Each member state continues to apply different tariffs, quotas, etc., vis-à-vis non-members. Consequently, goods imported from outside countries cannot move freely inside the free trade area. Otherwise, one could evade duties and excises by importing goods into the member country having the lowest tariffs and from there into the target country. For example, Mexico will not impose import tariffs on U.S. goods and vice versa (both are part of NAFTA). However, they may impose different duties on goods from Japan. Goods from Japan imported into the U.S. cannot be freely imported to Mexico.

A *customs union* is a free trade union with a common policy regarding tariffs and measures having equivalent effect. Each member state imposes the same tariffs, quotas, etc., vis-à-vis non-members. Consequently, once goods have entered the customs union, they can move freely within the union. For example, goods from Japan imported to Argentina (which is in a customs union with Mercosur) can be freely imported into any Mercosur member state without paying any import duties. In essence, a customs union takes a free trade area one step further by not only trading freely amongst member nations but also agreeing on what tariffs to charge nonmember nations. It is a step towards a single market (e.g., EU), but a customs union doesn't include freedom of movement of people.

An advantage of a customs union over a free trade area is that the customs union eliminates the need for some regulations and customs checks at the border. This facilitates faster trade along with less administration costs. On the other hand, as part of a customs union, a country cannot negotiate separate deals because there is a common external tariff. This reduces economic and national sovereignty. Table 2.5 lists the primary customs unions and free trade agreements in Latin America.

As Table 2.5 demonstrates, every major country in Latin America except for Panama is part of either a customs union or free trade agreement. That said, Panama and the United States entered into a free trade agreement in 2012, and so the spirit of trade in the region is high. Starting with the more rigorous customs unions, MERCOSUR covers all the countries in the southern part of South America with the notable exception of Chile. Venezuela has recently been suspended in 2017 because the member nations were in doubt about whether Venezuela was complying with the union's requirements for full membership, citing human rights violations among other issues. This effectively leaves Venezuela alone in the region in terms of trading blocs.

TABLE 2.5 Trading Blocs in Latin America

	Customs Unions		Free Trade Agreements		
	MERCOSUR	Andean Community	NAFTA	TPP	DR-CAFTA
Members	Argentina Bolivia Brazil Paraguay Uruguay Venezuela★	Bolivia Colombia Ecuador Peru	Canada Mexico U.S.	Australia Brunei Canada Chile Japan Malaysia Mexico New Zealand Peru Singapore Vietnam	Dominican Republic El Salvador Guatemala Honduras Nicaragua Costa Rica U.S.
Total GDP of Bloc (trillions of US$)	2.5	0.6	21.2	10.2	18.8

Source: Global Edge (2016).

Notes
★ Venezuela's membership was suspended in 2017.

The Andean Community covers the countries in the western part of South America that contains the Andes mountain range. Once again, the notable exception is Chile (and this time Argentina). MERCOSUR has a greater GDP as a whole, principally due to the inclusion of Brazil. NAFTA and DR-CAFTA are two very large trading blocs due to Canada and Mexico alongside the U.S. in NAFTA, and the U.S.A in CAFTA. The purposes of these free trade unions were to provide access to the United States' market and vice versa, shoring up trade in all of North and Central America.

Most recently, the Transpacific partnership (TPP) has pulled together many of the fastest growing, most trade liberal countries of Latin America with parts of Asia. It took nearly seven years of negotiations. The countries that make up the free trade agreement are listed in alphabetical order in Table 2.5. In January 2017, the United States withdrew from the agreement. The other 11 TPP countries agreed in May 2017 to revive it and reached agreement in January 2018. In March 2018, the 11 countries signed the revised version of the agreement. Some have argued the trade deal would have served a geopolitical purpose, namely to reduce the signatories' dependence on Chinese trade and bring them closer to the United States. Without the United States' participation, a void exists, leaving the group potentially vulnerable to Chinese influence. Before the United States withdrawal, the signatories represented roughly 40% of global GDP and one-third of world trade. The TPP will be something to watch in the coming years since it includes the main trading countries bordering the Pacific Ocean in the Americas. In the authors' opinion, this is a missed opportunity for the United States to maintain its dominant position in the hemisphere that could have shaped trade in the region for many years to come. That said, leaving the TPP was due to the current president of the United States. It's wholly possible that the next president could pick up where President Obama left off.

Conclusions

The purpose of this chapter is to prepare the reader to delve into the components of this book in detail. Based on the introductory chapter, we have discussed recent history along with cultural, political, and economics topics. Now that you have seen the size of each country's GDP and allocation of each country's outside investment, we can begin to understand which countries have the brightest future in the short and medium term.

Part of ascertaining a country's potential is its degree of labor productivity. In every country that was measured in Latin America, the productivity rates have improved over the past decade. We then argued that by continuing to make the difficult structural changes needed (such as those currently being done in Argentina and Brazil), the region will continue to pull more people out of extreme poverty. It is possible that in the next few years, no country in the region will have greater than 10% of its population in extreme poverty.

As will be discussed in more detail in Chapter 6 and 9, having a growing middle class is important to those wanting to do business in Latin America. Demand for many of the products designed and manufactured in countries like the United States and China is surging. This was much less common even a decade ago as the price points were simply out of reach for all but the very wealthy in Latin America.

Next, we discussed the various trade blocs operating in Latin America. It is important to note that as of the writing of this book, Latin America is on track to ratify the TPP. This may be considered a pivotal move of embracing free trade even when the United States appears to be moving towards a more protectionist model.

Finally, the case of how Colombia is taking advantage of its peace deal with the FARC and its free trade agreement with the United States illustrates the opportunities in that country. Marriott seems to have taken notice that there will likely be an increase in tourism to the country, and it is poised to capture some of the likely profits.

Case of Colombia

We chose the case of Colombia for this chapter on Current Business Environment for two reasons. First, the country recently finalized peace talks to end the longest standing civil war on the planet. Second, they recently signed a free trade agreement with the United States. Marriott Hotels seems to understand what this means for its business in the country.

The peace talks with the FARC started in 2012 in Havana, Cuba, and lasted four years until 2016. A cease-fire was officially declared in August 2016. An initial peace treaty was signed in Cartagena a month later; the pen used by President Juan Manuel Santos and FARC leader Rodrigo Londoño "Timochenko" was made of a bullet casing to symbolize the end of the conflict. Everyone attending, including presidents from other countries and former UN Secretary-General Ban Ki-moon, wore white. On the October 2, 2016, a plebiscite was held in order to ratify the government's decision and the NO camp won, meaning the citizens would not accept the deal as it stood. Only 38% of the population voted, and the vote was very close: 50.2% against 49.8%, showing a very polarized country (Cobb & Casey, 2016).[25]

The outcome of the plebiscite might seem hard to understand from a foreigner's perspective since it is hard to understand why someone would say "no" to peace. However, if seen from a Colombian's point of view, the situation becomes much more complex and very heated with very strong feelings from both sides. For this case, we interviewed Colombians who voted YES and NO. NO voters' main reasons for their decision included:

1   Support for ex-president Álvaro Uribe's politics,
2   The belief that FARC is still a terrorist organization and could not come to the talks and present itself as an equal and on the same level as the Colombian government,
3   The treaty gave the FARC guaranteed seats in congress,
4   Due to the violence from the killings, rape, and displacement of thousands of civilians, there is a belief that the treaty was too lenient.

YES voters' reasoning included:

1   Colombians were tired of having the longest running civil war in history,
2   The need to move on and create a better country for future generations,
3   To prevent violent deaths due to the internal conflict, decreasing the number of firearms, and for FARC combatants to reintegrate with Colombian society and lead normal lives.

After the results of the plebiscite, changes were made to the initial treaty. One of the main changes was the option of adding jail time depending on the level of accusations. The final agreement was made and signed in November 2016. Even though the conflict is over on paper, it is still very much an ongoing process. It will take some years for the population to get fully accustomed to new realities and for former guerrillas to formally rehabilitate back to civilian life. Pope Francis visited Colombia in September of 2017, and his visit echoed themes of hope and forgiveness throughout. The visit was certainly planned on purpose to help steer the mood within the country.

The peace process with the FARC has promoted and given the country a huge boost in positive publicity and PR, More and more people are going to Colombia for both business and tourism. Publications such as the *New York Times* and *Condé Nast Traveller* have put Colombia on their watch-list and top travel destinations in recent years. Cities have had incredible transformations as well, Medellín, a city once run by drug cartels, was named the world's most innovative city in 2013. All of this has improved the pro-business climate and increased confidence, encouraging foreign direct investment and forging stronger ties with other countries around the world.

The increased safety has also proved to have a major role. From the end of the 1990s, homicide rates have halved to around 26 per 100,000 deaths in 2016. Furthermore, the reintegration of thousands of ex-FARC combatants back into the working force will mean countless contributions to the Colombian economy; future projections predict economic growth for the years to come. An example of how all these implications tie together is Caño Cristales, located in southern Colombia. It has been referred to as the most beautiful river in the world and the "liquid rainbow" because of its several tones and colors given the plants and algae that grow in the riverbed. Until the mid-2000s, it was too dangerous to visit because of the internal conflict, but today it is a major attraction and a huge contributor to the Colombian tourism industry, generating important revenue.

The growing opportunities in the tourism market have not been lost on Marriott Hotels. For them, Latin America is one of their fastest growing regions; in 2016 they had over 215 hotels and resorts in the area, with 105+ under development (Marriott, 2017). In 2015, they announced an expected 75% increase in the region until 2018 (Marriott, 2016b). The company currently has six hotels in Colombia, with plans to triple their properties in the country by the end of 2018, totaling around an extra 1,600 rooms. Marriott released a report on its hotel plans for Cartagena, a city that they state is the most important resort location in the country. In the report they highlighted that 11% of foreign visitors to Colombia, as well as millions of domestic visitors, traveled to the city in 2014. As rationale for their investment in the city, they state:

> The blend of its economic and corporate activity generated by the Port, the leisure appeal of its magical historic walled colonial city, annual festivals and nearby Caribbean beaches; combined with the group demand with its solid convention facilities and improved international connectivity, provides all the necessary ingredients for a thriving destination.
>
> *(Marriott, 2016b)*

One of the new hotels that is being constructed in Cartagena (which will be located halfway between the airport and the historic walled city, with beach and lake access) will include every possible amenity: offices, a shopping mall, a movie theatre, a casino, two restaurants, a pool bar and grill, two coffee shops, a lobby bar, a fitness center with a swimming pool and meeting and event space (Marriott, 2016a). When considering the culture of Colombia, Marriott seems to be doing an excellent job of catering to the Colombians' high orientation on Hofstede's Dimensions of both Indulgence and Collectivism (discussed more in Chapter 4). If a Colombian company had a business conference at the new hotel, its employees would not only be able to work together but also build their valuable relationships (as per Colombia's incredibly low scores on Individualism) on-site in the various leisure spaces. Marriott is likely well-aware that Colombians like to indulge and would be visiting bars, movie theaters, pools, and casinos. Creating a space in Colombia that includes all amenities in an ingenious plan.

Marriott's success in creating hotels that cater to the Colombian population is no accident; the company has a special development team to focus on its Latin American sector. Located in Miami, the team is comprised of multilingual/multicultural experts in all areas of business (development, feasibility, advertising and commercial, and legal) that provides customized support to owners and franchisees in Latin America (Marriott, 2017). The team and franchises, ensures that Marriott abides by and takes advantage of the culture in their entered Latin American countries. When considering Colombia in particular, this is a very smart method for trying to respect the country's traditions, a key outcome of the country's low score on Long Term Orientation. Having people from the area working on the development team also shows that Marriott is putting effort into establishing and maintaining relationships, which are particularly relevant in Latin America.

Note

1 In 2010, Brazil's total tax revenue was 34% of GDP, and Argentina's was 33%.

Reference

Amarante, V. & Infante, R. (2016). *Toward Inclusive Development: The Case of Uruguay.* Santiago, Chile: CEPAL, pp.1–174.

Barcena, A., Prado, A., Cimoli, M., & Perez, R. (2017). "Foreign Direct Investment in Latin America and the Caribbean." In *Economic Commission for Latin America and the Caribbean.* Santiago, Chile: United Nations.

CEPAL (2016). "Labor Income Inequality Shrank in Uruguay between 2007 and 2014 Despite an Increase in Productive Heterogeneity." www.cepal.org/en/noticias/la-desigualdad-ingresos-laborales-disminuyo-uruguay-2007-2014-pesar-incremento-la, accessed August, 2018.

Cobb, Julia & Casey, Nicholas (2016). "Colombia Peace Deal Is Defeated, Leaving a Nation in Shock." *New York Times.* www.nytimes.com/2016/10/03/world/colombia-peace-deal-defeat.html, accessed December, 2016.

De Ferranti, D., Ferrera, F., Perry, G. and Walton, M. (2004). *Inequality in Latin America: Breaking with History?* Washington, DC: The World Bank.

Ferreira, F., Messina, J., Rigolini, J., Lopez-Calva, L., Lugo, M., & Vakis, R. (2013). *Economic mobility and the rise of the Latin American middle class.* Washington, DC: The World Bank.

Focus Economics (2018). "GDP per Capital in Mexico." www.focus-economics.com/country-indicator/mexico/gdp-per-capita-USD, accessed August, 2018.

Global Edge (2016). "Trading Blocs." https://globaledge.msu.edu/global-insights/by/trade-bloc, accessed January, 2018.

International Monetary Fund (IMF) (2017). "Balance of Payments Database." www.imf.org/en/Data, accessed January, 2018.

International Monetary Fund (IMF) (2018). "Uruguay: 2017 Article IV Consultation-Press Release; Staff Report; and Statement by the Executive Director for Uruguay." www.imf.org/en/Publications/CR/Issues/2018/01/31/Uruguay-2017-Article-IV-Consultation-Press-Release-Staff-Report-and-Statement-by-the-45598, accessed February, 2018.

Johnson, David (2017). "These Are the Most Productive Countries in the World." *Time.* http://time.com/4621185/worker-productivity-countries/, accessed January, 2018.

Leach, Whitney (2018). "This is Where People Work the Longest Hours." *World Economic Forum.* www.weforum.org/agenda/2018/01/the-countries-where-people-work-the-longest-hours/, accessed February 2018.

Leahy, J. & Schipani, A. (2017) "Foreign Investors Sustain Brazil through Recession." *Financial Times*. www.ft.com/content/457b5638-6cf6-11e7-bfeb-33fe0c5b7eaa, accessed January, 2018.

Marriott (2016a). "Marriott International Sets Its Focus on Cartagena, Colombia." https://hotel-development.marriott.com/2016/02/marriott-international-sets-its-focus-on-cartagena-colombia/, accessed December, 2016.

Marriott (2016b). "Marriott 2015 Annual Report." http://investor.shareholder.com/mar/releasedetail.cfm?releaseid=935441, accessed January, 2018.

Marriott (2017). "Caribbean and Latin America." https://hotel-development.marriott.com/regions/latin-america-the-caribbean/, accessed January, 2018.

Rogers, J. & Singh, A. (2017). "Mexico's Productivity Puzzle: What the State Economies Can Tell Us." *Moody's Analytics*. www.economy.com/home/products/samples/2017-06-15-mexicos-productivity-puzzle.pdf, accessed July, 2017.

The Conference Board (2018). "Total Economy Database." www.conference-board.org/data/economydatabase, accessed April, 2018.

The Economist. (2017). "Investors seem confident that an economic recovery is under way." www.economist.com/news/americas/21726689-there-still-plenty-could-go-wrong-investors-seem-confident-economic-recovery, accessed August, 2017.

The Economist (2018). "Uruguay's Record-Setting Economic Growth Streak." www.economist.com/news/americas/21739793-how-small-country-outperforms-its-neighbours-uruguays-record-setting-economic-growth-streak, accessed March, 2018.

The World Bank (2017). "GDP per Capita." https://data.worldbank.org/ and www.imf.org/external/pubs/ft/weo/2017/02/weodata/index.aspx, accessed January, 2018.

The World Bank (2018a). "The World Bank In Honduras." www.worldbank.org/en/country/honduras/overview#2, accessed April, 2018.

The World Bank (2018b). "Poverty Rates." https://data.worldbank.org/topic/poverty, accessed April, 2018.

Trading Economics (2018). "Bolivia GDP Growth." https://tradingeconomics.com/bolivia/gdp-growth, accessed August, 2018.

3

HISTORICAL BUSINESS PERSPECTIVE

Introduction

This chapter on the economic history of doing business in Latin America is meant to ground the reader on various events that have helped shape Latin Americans in general and ultimately how they do business. While we could start with the colonization of the region by primarily the Spanish and Portuguese, we prefer to begin with the economic structure of the 19th century, which led to import substitution industrialization (ISI) encouraged by the International Monetary Fund. For better or worse, the policies set the stage for a sense of mistrust that permeates much of Latin America even to the present day. After a thorough understanding of ISI's effects on Latin America, we shift to various banking crises, debt crises, and the Washington Consensus. We conclude by looking at how various industries have emerged or struggled. Finally, a case elaborating the historical conditions of Argentina will highlight the spillover effects of past ISI policies from the 1980s on today's borrowing appetite.

The Economic Structure of Latin America in the 19th Century

Latin America during the 19th century identified an abundance of resources, particularly, natural resources. The region, however, suffered scarcity in labor. Labor mobility was restricted in the internal economies of most Latin American countries due to the pervasive influence of retrograde institutions overly influenced by Iberian traditions that were non-conducive to economic growth and development.

Latin America would not have been able to respond to the opportunities offered by the world economy had it not been for the easy access it had to the

European immigrant market. This was particularly true for the southern-most part of Latin America. Strong immigration flows from Europe to southern Latin America brought an influx of highly valuable entrepreneurial and technical talent. The influx of ideas challenged homegrown Latin American political and social institutions. The Europeans were not as docile as native Latin Americans on matters of political affairs (Spillan, Virzi & Garita, 2014).

Liberal ideas were exported from North America and Europe to Latin America to profound political, social, and economic effects. Where indigenous populations remained important, coercive measures were politically implemented to spawn labor mobility. However, indentured service and slavery would gradually be forced out. The conservative influence of the Catholic Church waned to the benefit of political, social, and economic progress.

Foreign financing was important to the development of large-scale economic activities, such as the exploitation of natural resources – primarily oil and minerals. It was also important to the spawning of the great plantation structures of the banana and sugar industries. Foreign participation in forms other than financial was important to the development of the coffee industry in countries such as Guatemala, where the local German population was instrumental in developing the industry. The purpose of this industry, like many others in Latin America, was to export to external markets abroad.

1870–World War I (1914–1918): The Export Boom

Between 1870 and 1930, the Latin American economies failed to achieve macroeconomic stability on what could be regarded as a regular basis, due to the inability of the governments to handle their exchange rates under a proper stable system. However, the introduction of railroad and modern transport systems provided substantial learning opportunities and positive externalities that enabled Latin American economies to modernize by imitation, at least in comparison to where they were before, without world trade. In countries like Brazil and Mexico, the railroads were an important impetus for economic modernization, although true modernization would not begin until after World War II. The immersion of Latin America into export markets brought about important productivity improvements in export sectors, although these improvements to other sectors were always slow.

The advent of the export age brought about not only national investment but international investment as well. However, as profits from trade grew, so did the thinking that economic dependency was a peril to be dealt with. Trade boomed among Latin American countries in the years between 1870 and 1914: the beginning of World War I. In Mexico, Argentina, Brazil, Colombia, and Cuba, trade increased significantly. Even though it may not have been a very significant part of the total economy of the developed countries, the dramatic increase in the importance of trade was certainly a factor to notice in Latin America.

The initial gains from trade naturally benefitted the economic agents that invested in land, since it was agricultural products that were typically being exported from Latin America. This aspect was further deepened where railroads were built to favor export enclaves, i.e., railroads that went directly from the farms or mines to the ports for export. However, the general story is that the trade benefitted Latin America tremendously. The boom in exports created a small but important middle class of merchants and clerical workers that deviated strongly from the previous categorization of Latin American society, which was basically rich and educated or ignorant and poor. As the export sector grew, so did Latin American modernization, since the creation of a new middle class of educated, not rich, yet aspirational people set the basis for the creation of the foundation of modern Latin American democracies (Spillan et al., 2014).

Though trade benefitted Latin America in the aggregate, there were important microeconomic effects which, ended up having macro ramifications. Since farm or mine products were the primarily exported, international trade favored the landed classes relatively more than the poorer classes, although the latter also benefitted from employment. Along with the growth in trade came a relative boom in middle-class occupations like merchants and civil professionals dedicated to the transactions of trade. Suffice to say, these beneficiaries of trade constituted the minority of the population in the bulk of Latin American countries.

Though the turn towards exports surely created an economic boom, the reality was that this boom also created an economic dependency on the continued willingness of foreign investors to choose Latin America instead of other regions of the world to send their capital. In the context of the prevailing sociopolitical culture, the safe havens required by foreign investors tended to be roughly translated to order and peace maxims, typically prejudicial to the legitimate political interest of the non-elites.

Since Latin American economies became more acceptant of the realities of the benefits of free trade, they became more dependent on the economic prospects of their trading partners. This postcolonial economic dependence would eventually become a focal point of Latin American political contention, as if there was ever a choice between competing in the world economy or not.

Nationalist rhetoric aside, there has always been a significant degree in Latin America of what Mexicans would call *malinchismo*, roughly translated as a preference for what is foreign. This surely drove the imports of European and, to a lesser extent, American manufactured and luxury goods in the 19th and 20th centuries. It is very common still today for Latin Americans to criticize everything American, while yearning to display American branded goods, such as Coca-Cola and Hilfiger, and listen to American music. In this context, Latin American economic nationalism must be taken with a grain of salt, especially when expressed at a popular level. It is when it becomes official government policy that it becomes a problem (e.g., in Venezuela).

Latin American economic expansion up to the Great Depression was primarily fueled by the growth of exports. However, export-led growth produced uneven effects in Latin American countries. Importantly, the "curse of the riches" worked against the development of entrepreneurial cultures, such as those that developed in countries less endowed in natural resources such as England, Holland, and more recently, South Korea and Japan.

Exports not only increased as a share of GDP for many Latin American countries but also Latin America's structural participation inworld trade also increased. As trade ties with the developed world progressed, precious metals declined in overall importance as produce, meat, and natural resources like oil and minerals grew in importance. Coffee, sugar, and spices also were important sources of export revenues (See Table 3.1).

Argentina in the late 19th and early 20th centuries provides the best example of export-led growth. However, virtually all Latin American economies improved with their insertion into the international economy. At first, Latin American economic dependence was focused on Europe, but as the North American economy began to catch up with and surpass Europe, the Latin American economies made the transition. As the European economies slowed down in the inter-war years, Latin American economies turned towards the U.S. economy as an increasingly important export market.

Many factors combined to create a favorable export climate for Latin America in the decades following 1870. For example, technological innovations reduced transport costs in the 19th century. This improved the terms of trade for Latin American economies focused on exporting commodity products. However, after World War I, prices for commodity goods grew increasingly volatile.

Export-led growth in Latin America engendered capital and labor movements. London was the main source of external financing for Latin America for the 19th century and the early part of the 20th. However, over time, other European powers increased their capital financing to the Latin American region, as did the United States.

TABLE 3.1 Latin American Exports, 1860–1929

	1859–1861	*1899–1901*	*1911–1913*	*1927–1929*
Value of exports (US$ million)				
Latin America	292	664	1,493	2,954
Argentina	13	163	437	964
Excluding Argentina	279	501	1,056	1,990
Share of world trade (%)	–	7	9	9
Share of their world exports (%)	42	37	38	36

Source: Jomo (2006).

Immigration flows between the developed world and Latin America were basically the inverse of what they have been until recently. People from the first world immigrated to Latin America, not vice versa. Countries like Argentina absorbed a huge quantity of Southern European immigrants, particularly Italians. Brazil and Chile absorbed massive numbers of immigrants from Europe who brought with them entrepreneurial attitudes and competencies and technical skills largely unknown to the Latin American region which can still be felt today. Chinese immigrated to countries like Peru. Or course, large contingents of slave labor were brought also, forming significant parts of the population in the Caribbean and to a lesser extent Central America.

Demonstration effects came into play as well. Latin American development was undoubtedly inspired and determined by its political and economic relations with the developed countries. The overall influence of the developed world on the developing world of Latin America was positive. It was not confined only to the realm of consumer goods and capital inputs but also to the importation of ideas of markets, democracy, and progress. There were concrete results that benefited mankind. A case in point is the Panama Canal. Had it not been for France and later the United States, Panama – and the Panama Canal – would likely not have come into existence.

By the middle of the 19th century, Latin America was in the midrange of the income hierarchy of world regions. In this period, it was claiming an increasing share of the total world per capita gross domestic product (see Table 3.2).

While Latin America was increasing its export prowess, Latin American countries failed in developing their internal economies. As a result, their governments were particularly dependent on tariff duties as sources of revenues. Investment patterns suffered with the booms and busts of international trade, further disrupting the supply of investment for important domestic economic development projects. Some of the largest countries of Latin America – Argentina, Brazil, Chile, and Colombia – suffered these types of volatile revenue swings.

The export era of Latin America has been incorrectly labeled the *laissez-faire* age. This is not true. Latin American countries typically have turned to inflationary measures and currency depreciations to recover their competitiveness in world export markets. Governments forced labor in counties like Guatemala, while at the same time intervened to ensure that the revenues from exports of agricultural and mining products did not go to the working classes.

The Impact of Export-Led Growth on the Diversification of the Socioeconomic Structure

As mentioned, Latin America's early model of export-oriented growth was largely confined to the export of primary products or commodities for industrial use in the developed world. Export-led growth in Latin America typically

TABLE 3.2 Per Capita GDP by Region

Region	1820	1870	1913	1929	1950	1965	1973	1980	1990	2000
Western Europe	1,232	1,974	3,473	4,111	4,579	8,441	11,416	13,197	13,197	19,002
U.S., Australia, Canada	1,202	2,419	5,233	6,673	9,268	12,967	16,179	18,060	22,345	27,065
Japan	669	737	1,387	2,026	1,921	5,934	11,434	13,428	18,789	21,069
Asia (w/o Japan)	577	550	658	–	634	936	1,226	1,494	2,117	3,189
Latin America	692	681	1,481	2,034	2,506	3,439	4,504	5,412	5,053	5,838
Eastern Europe and ex–USSR	686	941	1,558	1,570	2,602	4,333	5,731	6,231	6,455	4,778
Africa	420	500	637	–	894	1,164	1,410	1,536	1,444	1,464
World	667	875	1,525	–	2,111	3,233	4,091	4,520	5,157	6,012

Source: Jomo (2006).

spawned debates centered around the issues of the distribution of the benefits generated by exports, particularly of natural resources, as well as the backward and forward linkages associated with export-oriented sectors. On the distributive debate, the issue typically centered on the division of the profits between national and foreign players but also on the distribution among national economic agents. These issues have never been fully resolved in Latin America. For instance, landowners typically resist governmental attempts to tax exports and land (Spillan et al., 2014).

Latin American tariff policies were oriented to stimulate import-substitution industrialization (more on this in the next section), an assumed prerequisite by the elites to the imperative of modernization. Countries such as Chile, Mexico, Colombia, and Brazil were actively protectionist. Despite Latin America's reliance on trade, governments in the region never hesitated to practice economic protectionism to shield local economic actors from the rigors of international markets. Protectionist policies resulted in Latin America having the highest tariffs in the world in the 19th century (Coatsworth & Williamson, 2004). For example, in 1885 the poor but independent parts of Latin America (Brazil, Colombia, Mexico, and Peru) had tariffs 4.6 times higher than those in the poor and dependent parts of Asia (Burma, China, India, Indonesia, and the Philippines). Taxes were one thing; government spending was another. Where governments chose to invest in physical and human capital in the 19th century and the early part of the 20th, the economies of the region improved. Unfortunately, Latin American governments, then as now, did not always prove to be wise spenders of public revenues.

Export activities had important backward linkages that introduced new innovations into the rest of the economy. For example, mineral exportation activities introduced processing plants. Sugar processing plants also arose in response to the needs of the sugar export sector. Technological innovations like refrigeration made the transportation of meat possible. This led to the birth of meat-processing plants. The surge in new employment opportunities spread benefits throughout society. As incomes grew, a consumer class arose, and domestic demand grew. Local consumers demanded not only foreign products but also domestically grown produce, further fueling Latin American development.

Latin America did not only benefit from its exports but imports as well. While it is true that national demand for foreign manufactures benefitted foreign exports to Latin America, the importation of these manufactured goods facilitated local industrialization. The exportation of goods involved forward linkages such as processing requirements. The cement and beer industries tended to be characterized by backward linkages, through which materials, money, and information flowed between firms and suppliers, creating a network of economic inter-dependence. The high costs of transportation worked to the favor of national industries as well.

An important benefit of the export-led growth era was the transmission of technological know-how and entrepreneurial attitudes lacking in traditional Latin American cultures. Trade promoted greater specialization, innovation, and the diffusion of ideas and institutions – especially in the banking, insurance, and shipping industries. To participate in world trade, Latin America had to adopt the rules of the game of the international economy. As Latin American trade with other regions became more congruent with world rules than local shenanigans, the prospects for the general enrichment of the population through free trade reforms increased. For instance, Latin America had to create new financial institutions to facilitate trade, which over time would have positive external effects on economic growth and development in the region (Cárdenas, Ocampo & Thorp, 2000).

Finally, industrialization began during the export-led boom (Gómez-Galvarriato & Williamson, 2009).[6] The countries that experienced the most success during the export age were Argentina, Chile, Cuba, and Uruguay. Colombia, Peru, and Venezuela also benefitted tremendously. Brazil stagnated in the 19th century but rebounded in the 20th.

The Import-Substitution-Industrialization Era

The Great Depression (1929–1939) dealt a deathblow to the Latin American export model. As demand conditions in the U.S. and Europe deteriorated, the export markets for Latin American economies collapsed as commodity prices plummeted. The global financial system fell into chaos and uncertainty as countries, even the UK, abandoned the gold standard, causing FDI flows to dry up, leaving Latin America dearly short of capital. As markets for Latin American exports fell off, the Latin American countries experienced negative pressures in their external finance sectors, as well as in their fiscal situations and balance of payments accounts.

Beginning with the Smoot-Hawley Tariff Act in the U.S. in 1930, a run of protectionist policies characterized the disintegration of free trade commercial regimes all over the world. As the developed economies fell into the illiberal practices of trade restrictions, Latin American countries were prone to follow. Ill-advised multiple exchange rates were experimented with, particularly in countries that didn't use the dollar as a medium of exchange. Fiscal pressures meant that nearly all Latin American countries were pressured to abandon their foreign debt obligations (the subject of the next section).

As foreign sources of financing dried up, balance of payments accounts were stressed. Multiple policy responses failed to rebalance matters. As protectionism, exchange controls, devaluation, import controls, and the employment of multiple exchange rates failed, the measure of last recourse was all too often the decision to default on foreign debt.

The Great Depression brought great shocks to the Latin American region. Intellectual opinion in Latin America turned against the great dependency that was perceived in the economic relationships between the rich "North" and poor "South." Declining terms of trade between the North and South were commonly signaled as causal factors of poverty between the two regions (Spillan et al., 2014).[7]

In 1938, the Cárdenas administration in Mexico in a bold move nationalized U.S. oil companies operating in Mexico. The U.S. let it stand. Despite the negative implications for the commercial interests of the U.S., the Roosevelt administration gave way, understanding it could not wholly impede the nationalist aspirations of its Latin American neighbors. Thus, the Good Neighbor Policy was born, repealing the Platt Amendment, which had given the U.S. the "right" to interfere in Cuban politics. Upon the arrival of World War II and the struggle against global fascism, the U.S. was brought closer together with some of its Latin American neighbors.

Having adopted as a nationalist imperative the need to modernize politically, socially, and economically, but lacking capital to pay for industrial inputs, Latin American countries turned towards import-substitution-industrialization (ISI) as the means to achieve their developmentalist aims. ISI policies were promoted based on the idea of commercial protectionism, transfer of riches, and the creation of burgeoning local middle classes, whereby local protected industries would tend to local demand. ISI was, essentially, an infant-industries argument. Latin American countries were to adopt ISI policies in order to produce self-sufficient development based on the expansion of the internal market. ISI was essentially a state-led regime, whereby the state not only implemented protectionist trade policies but also nationalized key industries such as power generation, which were determined to be of critical importance for the purposes of national economic development.

This time, the industrialization emphasis was not to be tied to the needs of the export sectors. Instead, the development of an internal domestic market was to be the focus. The ISI trend was led by the big countries of Latin America, such as Mexico, Brazil, and Argentina, but was also followed by the smaller countries of Central America.

In the 1930s a paradigmatic change in economic thinking was under way. The classical economics underpinnings of the free trade regimes were apparently discredited, and pro-interventionist policies, later known as Keynesian economics, became the new normal. Under the new economic philosophy, domestic demand could and should be stimulated by activist fiscal and monetary policies. These ideas took hold in Latin America, where the suspension of foreign debt obligations and the creation of national banks restored (in the short term) domestic credit and financial markets.

Latin America embraced the Keynesian notions of activist monetary and fiscal policies, controls on free trade, as well as the ISI notions aimed at substituting the importation of manufactured and agricultural goods. ISI policies needed to complement Keynesian demand management policies so that Latin

American countries did not unduly stimulate the demand for imports and thus exacerbate their balance of payments problems. Domestic demand did recuperate partly and with varying degrees of success throughout the Latin American region. This led to increasingly greater levels of state intervention in subsequent decades, even when decreasing marginal returns on public investment set in.

Only time would reveal the long-term costs of unmitigated state interventionism. After adopting the Keynesian fiscal and monetary policies and ISI commercial policies, Latin American governments no longer were inclined to adopt the view that industrialization was for developed countries and exports of primary commodities for developing countries. The imperative was to pursue both industrialization and growth in the export sectors. Latin American countries all hoped to regain their former access to the developed world markets, which they had enjoyed prior to the Great Depression and World War II.

The onset of World War II provided a strong external push for Latin American industrialization because Western industrialized nations directed their industrial outputs to the existential war against fascism. Keynesian monetary policies were apparently validated as domestic inflation lowered the pressures of foreign debt holdings. As Latin American countries imported less, while continuing to export to the U.S., the financial and economic engine of the war effort resulted in improved trade balances, as did the holdings of international reserves. Domestic financing of new types of ISI investment was greatly facilitated under these unique historical conditions for Latin America. It is important to note that Latin America had the tremendous good fortune of avoiding the destructive consequences of World War II but was able to participate as the supplier of raw materials for the Allied cause.

Table 3.3 demonstrates how the performance of ISI policies varied by country, with Brazil, Mexico, and Ecuador exhibiting the strongest growth rates between 1950–1980. The production of basic consumption goods was widespread throughout the region, and some countries successfully initiated heavy-machine goods industries as well.

As a result of the apparent success of the ISI policies, Latin American governments became more activist and interventionalist in their national economies than they had been in the past. Latin American governments assumed the tasks of implementing trade restrictions, tariff controls, capital contrails, and FDI controls. In addition, the state assumed such important tasks as infrastructure developments, in terms not just of highways and railroads but also banking systems. Social infrastructure also improved with public investments in health, education, and a modicum of social safety net legislation.

As demand conditions stabilized in the developed countries during the postwar period, the international reserves that Latin America had accumulated diminished in short order. Volatile price swings made export models predicated on the selling of primary commodities abroad an unviable proposition. This was especially so given that the protectionist measures adopted in the inter-war years

TABLE 3.3 Percentage Growth in GDP per Capita

Country	1941–1949	1950–1959	1960–1969	1970–1979	1980–1989
Brazil	1.6	3.6	2.8	6.1	0.8
Ecuador	4.1	2.4	1.8	7.0	−0.1
Mexico	3.7	3.1	3.5	3.2	−0.3
Dom Republic	3.0	3.4	1.4	4.6	0.7
Panama	−2.2	1.8	4.8	1.9	−0.6
Costa Rica	4.7	2.8	2.2	3.3	−0.8
Colombia	1.6	1.8	2.1	3.2	1.6
Peru	2.5	3.0	2.5	1.2	−2.1
El Salvador	9.3	1.8	2.2	1.8	−2.6
Guatemala	0.3	0.5	1.9	3.1	−2.1
Paraguay	0.6	−0.7	1.1	5.0	0.9
Argentina	2.3	0.8	2.8	1.3	−2.3
Honduras	1.5	−0.1	1.8	2.4	−1.0
Chile	1.5	1.3	1.9	0.6	1.9
Uruguay	2.5	1.0	0.3	2.5	0.1
Nicaragua	4.2	2.4	3.6	−2.5	−3.8
Bolivia	0.6	−1.7	3.2	1.9	−3.0
Venezuela	6.7	2.9	0.0	−0.1	−3.4
Latin America	–	–	2.7	3.7	−0.1
U.S.	–	–	3.3	2.5	2.2
China	–	–	1.2	5.3	8.2

Source: Corbo (1994).

still applied. The creation of a liberal world order after World War II was to rely tremendously on the Bretton Woods scheme and the General Agreement on Tariffs and Trade. These two systems were set up to manage commercial and financial relations. This could have been advantageous for Latin America, less they both made strong exceptions for the agricultural and textile sectors – sectors in which Latin America had a strong comparative advantage. Latin America not being able to participate as much in the global expansion following World War II augmented a future debt crisis.

The Debt Crisis

As far as Latin America is concerned, the debt crisis refers to the phenomenon whereby countries of the region reached the point of being unable to service and/or repay their foreign debt. In the two decades prior to the 1980s, Latin American countries had accumulated massive debts from international creditors in order to finance their so-called infrastructure and industrialization projects. This was easy to do during periods of high economic growth. The international creditors included organizations such as the World Bank but also private banks looking for safe investment outlets for their petrodollars. Latin America quad-rupled its foreign debt in the 1975–1983 period, an alarming increase surpassed only by the rising rate of its schedule of debt service, which increased more than five-fold in the same period.

The global economy entered a worldwide recession at the end of the 1970s and the onset of the 1980s. After the successful organization of the OPEC oil cartel, oil prices increased significantly, which caused problems for Latin Amer-ican oil-importing countries. The rise in oil prices induced Latin American countries to incur greater, unsustainable levels of foreign debt. Ironically, oil-producing nations in Latin America, such as Mexico, believed oil prices would continue to rise, so they too incurred greater amounts of debt.

Interest rate increases in the developed world at the end of the 1970s caused an increase in debt payments. This made it much more difficult for the debtor countries in Latin America to even service their foreign debts, much less pay them back. Declining terms of trade in dollar terms translated into declining purchasing power coupled with more onerous debt servicing schedules for the countries of Latin America, which were suffering through a general decline of the prices of the goods they sold. Eventually, the debt levels would become unsustainable.

Mexico was the first country to effectively declare itself in default. As a result of Mexico's announcement, private banks halted lending to Latin America, which naturally aggravated the process. Adding insult to injury was the fact that good portions of the loans to Latin America were short term. Upon refusal of the international creditors to refinance these loans, the crisis was compounded significantly as the debts became almost immediately due.

The pressing concern became how to avoid a global financial panic. New loans were issued but this time under strict conditions, which often included the intervention of the International Monetary Fund (IMF). The IMF pushed the structural adjustment conditions that it felt were necessary to guarantee future loans. For instance, debt restructuring was contingent on the reduction of public-sector spending and liberalization of the economies by making them more open to trade. Additionally, rational exchange rate systems were to be implemented. If Latin American countries did these things, they would receive debt relief on the huge sums they had borrowed and irresponsibly spent.

The Latin American debt crisis of the early 1980s was grave in its immediate consequences. Economic growth in real terms stalled and real incomes plummeted. Inflation soared as Latin American governments sought to monetize their debts by printing worthless money. Progress on mitigating poverty and other social issues stalled as public spending because increasingly oriented to pay public debt.

Latin America had little choice but to abandon the failed ISI policies. As interest rates soared, capital flowed out of Latin America, depreciating national exchange rates. This only made foreign debt more expensive, bringing even the largest countries in Latin America to the breaking point.

The Washington Consensus: The Painful Restoration of Competitiveness

Confronted with the realities of market economics, Latin American countries were "forced" to abandon their ill-advised ISI policies wholesale. Most nations adopted an export-led growth and industrialization strategy. This came to be known as the neo-liberal structural adjustments advocated by the IMF. It was John Williamson who coined the term "Washington Consensus" due to the fact that the IMF, the World Bank, and the U.S. Treasury Department were all Washington, D.C. based. They were responsible for the reform package promoted for crisis-wracked developing countries such as those in Latin America in the 1980s.

The Washington Consensus centered on the policy recommendations of respect for property rights, fiscal and monetary discipline, liberalization of exchange rates and interest rates, modernization of the bloated and inefficient public sector through privatization and de-regulation schemes, and the reorientation of public spending towards education, health care, and infrastructure investments. Needless to say, it was painful for Latin Americans, and many haven't forgotten the nation that "inflicted" that pain.

Instead of the discredited ISI policies, Latin American countries found themselves with few realistic options but to adopt the unpopular neoliberal strategies associated with the IMF's structural adjustment policies. Latin America struggled to regain its competitiveness while it implemented policies that sacrificed short-term growth for long-term economic competitiveness. (Chapter 7 deals with the consequences of this in terms of competitiveness today.) Yet, as a byproduct of these strategy changes, Latin America got the cash and authority backing it would need to reimburse its obligations. However, the IMF structural adjustment reforms were so painful to implement that the 1980s has been called the "lost decade" for Latin America. Growth was close to zero and resulted in the short-term deterioration of living standards (refer back to Table 3.3) (Franko, 2007). It's therefore understandable that Latin Americans felt a perceived loss of national sovereignty to the U.S., which grew at over 2% annually on average that decade. Note that China was growing at an astonishing 8%. Although politically unpopular, the IMF reforms went a long way towards advancing free market principles in the Latin American region.

The term Washington Consensus has been used more broadly to describe the general shift towards free market policies that followed the displacement of Keynesianism in the 1970s. More commonly, commentators have suggested that the Consensus in its broader sense survived until the time of the 2008–2009 global financial crisis as market fundamentalism lost favor. The consensus as originally stated by Williamson included ten broad sets of relatively specific policy recommendations:

1 Fiscal policy discipline, with avoidance of large fiscal deficits relative to GDP;

2 Redirection of public spending from subsidies ("especially indiscriminate subsidies") toward broad-based provision of key pro-growth, pro-poor services like primary education, primary health care and infrastructure investment;

3 Tax reform, broadening the tax base and adopting moderate marginal tax rates;

4 Interest rates that are market determined and positive (but moderate) in real terms;

5 Competitive exchange rates;

6 Trade liberalization: liberalization of imports, with particular emphasis on elimination of quantitative restrictions (licensing, etc.); any trade protection to be provided by low and relatively uniform tariffs;

7 Liberalization of inward foreign direct investment;

8 Privatization of state enterprises;

9 De-regulation: abolition of regulations that impede market entry or restrict competition, except for those justified on safety, environmental and consumer protection grounds, and prudential oversight of financial institutions;

10 Legal security for property rights.

The achievement or disappointment of the much-censured Washington Consensus relies upon one's point of view. As a development program, the results leave much to be desired. However, that was not its intended purpose. The intended purpose was to restore the fiscal and monetary sectors of the Latin American economies as well as introduce economic stability. For better or worse, the world seems to believe that the Consensus is a set of neoliberal policies that have been imposed on the hapless countries by the Washington-based international financial institutions and have led them to crisis and misery. This sentiment is important to remember for those who come from the U.S. and other "market-based" economies because touting the success of such policies will likely be received with skepticism at best and distrust at worst.

The neoliberal reforms of the Washington Consensus were designed to rid Latin America of its unsustainable debt dependency. In this, the neoliberal reforms are to be considered an unqualified success. Today, Latin America is substantially readier to stand negative exogenous financial stuns, both when contrasted with its own particular past and different areas.

While the verdict on the Washington Consensus is clearly not a consensus at all, economists and policy makers have urged countries in Latin America to move beyond "first generation" reforms. Subsequent reforms should focus on productivity-boosting efforts as well as, programs directed to support the poor. This includes improving the investment climate and eliminating red tape (especially for smaller firms), strengthening institutions (in areas like justice systems), fighting poverty directly via the types of Conditional Cash Transfer programs adopted by countries like Mexico and Brazil, improving the quality of primary and secondary education, boosting countries' effectiveness at developing and absorbing technology, and addressing the special needs of historically disadvantaged groups including indigenous peoples and Afro-descendant populations across Latin America.

Specific Industries that Thrived or Failed

During each of the time frames discussed in this chapter, there were "winners" and "losers" in Latin American business. It is relevant for business people to look at what industries did well as well as those that struggled during the various epochs. In particular, one should look for patterns that evolved over time in order to extract possible opportunities and threats in future business endeavors in the region.

Table 3.4 demonstrates how countries tended to be dependent on one dominant export commodity. These commodities were either winners or losers depending on the price of that commodity in any given year. Most of the countries selected their dominant commodity based on natural endowment and agricultural advantage. Before WWI, political stability, expansion of transportation systems, and improvements in capital markets all contributed to a booming export market for Latin America.

Yet, single-commodity exports can be dangerous for an economy due to the instability in global demand for a product and the correlated prices that go with

TABLE 3.4 Single-Commodity Exports as a Percentage of Total Exports, 1938

Country	Commodity	% Total Exports
El Salvador	Coffee	92
Venezuela	Petroleum	92
Cuba	Sugar	78
Panama	Bananas	77
Bolivia	Tin	68
Guatemala	Coffee	66
Honduras	Bananas	64
Colombia	Coffee	61
Dominican	Sugar	60
Chile	Copper	52
Haiti	Coffee	51
Costa Rica	Coffee	49
Nicaragua	Coffee	47
Brazil	Coffee	45

Source: Hanson (1951).

the rise and fall of demand. Development policy was preoccupied with the needs of the export sector with little attention to the links with domestic production and demand (Franko, 2007). For example, the U.S. multinational United Fruit Company dominated the banana industry in Costa Rica and didn't pay any taxes to that government.

One of the primary components of the ISI era was that the state would either acquire or start large enterprises, which they would manage in order to compete with large foreign multinationals. Despite a number of operational problems fairly characteristic of state-owned-enterprises (SOEs), they proliferated rapidly from the 1950s to 1970s. Particularly in Brazil, it was believed that state intervention was the pragmatic response to the failure of the free market. Table 3.5 shows what types of industries were most subject to state ownership in the case of Brazil. High rates of state ownership existed especially in industries that required significant investment, such as public goods enjoyed by all citizens and critical industries, including national security enterprises.

TABLE 3.5 State Enterprise Share in the Brazilian Economy, 1973

	Proportion of Assets in SOEs
High Degree of State Participation (>50%)	
Railways	100
Port Services	100
Water, Gas, and Sewers	99
Telegraph and Telephone	97
Electricity	79
Mining	63
Developmental Services	51
Chemicals	50
Medium Degree of State Participation (20–49%)	
Water Transport	45
Banking and Finance	38
Metal Fabrication	37
Services	36
Air Transport	22
Low Degree of State Participation (<20%)	
Construction and Engineering	8
Rubber	6
Road Transport and Passengers	6
Agriculture and Forestry	4
Non-Metallic Minerals	2
Transport Equipment	2
Food and Beverages	1

Source: Adopted from Evans (1979).

The Case of Argentina

The election of Mauricio Macri in December of 2015 was a turning point in Argentine economic history after the populist Kirchners. Macri's new pro-market policies put Argentina on a trend to economic prosperity and becoming an ideal investment location. Macri has enacted a multitude of economic and fiscal reforms to make Argentina a competitive place to do business. Macri also allowed the Argentina peso to float instead of being pegged to the dollar like is has been for decades. This led to a sharp drop in the value of the peso against the dollar as seen in Figure 3.1.

This sharp devaluation allowed for any export-oriented firm to export goods cheaply compared to before and allows for any firm making an investment in Argentina to do so cheaper than before. Floating the peso also enabled disinflation to occur, which is relevant for Argentina as it trends into becoming a viable market. Historically, inflation has been extremely volatile. Macri's fiscal policies have allowed for inflation to start its descent. This allows for investors to require a smaller rate of return to beat inflation and make an investment viable. Along with currency devaluation, Macri is working to close the budget shortfall by one percentage point annually.

This responsible fiscal policy will enable Argentina to avoid future defaults. Recently, Macri has worked strenuously to de-regulate the Argentine finance and labor sector. Under the Kirchners, overseas investment by Argentines was strictly prohibited and punishable by prison sentences. Along with legitimatizing international investments, Macri will have Global Investment Advisors licensed to work for clients. With this, international financial institutions will be able to legally take on Argentine clients and help foreign clients invest in Argentina more efficiently, permitting firms to create offices and branches in the country.

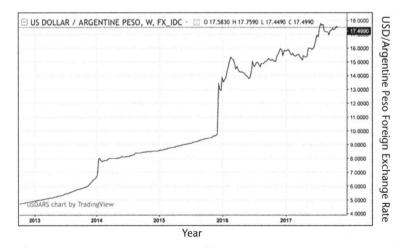

FIGURE 3.1 US$/Argentine Peso Foreign Exchange Rate

Macri has also begun dismantling the country's powerful labor unions that were stifling growth in the agricultural sector. Macri is going sector by sector, renegotiating the power of labor unions in hopes to make labor markets more competitive than they were in the Peronist era.

In conclusion, Argentina is trending towards pro-market policies with President Macri working to rein in inflation to much more competitive levels than before, significantly reducing the deficit to display fiscal responsibility not recently seen in the country.

How ISI Policies from the 1980s Impact Borrowing in Argentina Today

ISI policies in the 1980s led to soaring inflation and debt accumulation for Argentina. This cumulated in economic crashes in both the 1980s and 1990s, causing Argentina to plunge into a catastrophic default in 2001 and 2014 and withstand serious scars on the countries' ability to procure funds from foreign investors.

Firstly, ISI forced Argentina into a trend of huge inflation. Under ISI, countries work to internalize their markets and avoid imports. To do this, Argentina nationalized companies and industries. To do so, however, Argentina needed lots of money. Therefore, Argentina issued bonds that were bought by foreign governments and foreign private sector groups. The Argentine military junta did not think of the long-term implications of the debt, as the focus was on helping working class Argentines escape poverty and therefore boost the politicians' popularity.

For a time, Argentina's economy accommodated the massive amounts of debt accrued, with the populace preoccupied with the Falklands War of 1982. During this time, inflation reached 100% annually and stores were forced to change prices daily. The humiliating defeat in the Falklands War served to plunge Argentina further into debt, and inflation began to pick-up more so. The Military Junta was replaced with a civilian government that the IMF made loans to prevent a collapse. The new government chose to combat inflation through price controls, which were negotiated with top Argentine companies.

Along with price controls, the president at the time, Carlos Menem, opted to peg Argentina's currency to the dollar. This fixed the exchange rate to a 1:1 ratio. For a time, this was successful in stabilizing inflation. However, the Argentine government did not consider the full ramifications of their actions, and when the U.S. Dollar appreciated against the Brazilian Real in 1999, so did the Argentine Peso. This caused Argentine exports to drop and was the catalyst for the collapse of the Argentine economy and subsequent default.

The default was catastrophic for Argentina. Before the crash, in 1998, Argentina issued floating rate accrual notes, or FRAN bonds, onto the international markets. The idea of these types of bonds was that their yield would be inversely correlated to the credit rating of the Argentine economy, meaning that if the credit rating was good, the yield would be small and the inverse. As noted, the Argentine economy crashed and the interest rate on the FRAN bonds reached 101% annually. One of the leading creditors, Elliott Capital Partners, eventually saw a whopping return of 730 cents on the dollar for their bond holdings. U.S. Hedge Funds were the primary holders of the FRANs and were making a fortune on paper. In reality, Argentina stopped tracking the FRAN interest rate and was unable to pay the hedge funds.

Since the 2001 default, the Republic has been in court battles with U.S. "vulture" hedge funds that bought billions in Argentine bonds and have been demanding repayment. One of the most famous cases involved Paul Singer's Elliott Capital Management, who in 2012 seized an Argentine Navy Ship in Ghana in attempts to recoup its investment. The company tracked The Libertad, an Argentinian Navy Ship, to a dock in Ghana and had a court in Ghana issue injunction for the ship until the debt was repaid to ECM by Argentina. The ship was detained for 10 weeks until the International Tribunal for the Law of the Sea forced Ghana to release the ship, citing a UN convention that grants warships in foreign ports immunity from civil claims. According to the tribunal, holding the ship was "a source of conflict that may endanger friendly relations among state" (Smith, 2012). Although the ship was released, a court in New York stated that Argentina must pay ECM US$1.3 billion, the entire principal plus accumulated interest on the bonds.

Negotiations with the vulture fund holdouts have continued well into the second default in 2014, which was due to a U.S. court order that blocked Argentina from making payments to new creditors before paying the holdouts. This past year, Argentina was able to reach a deal with the vulture funds and paid out almost US$5 billion to settle. This caused the U.S. ExIm Bank to reopen financing operations in Argentina for the first time in 15 years. While this serves as wonderful news for investors looking to build a business in Argentina, it should also serve as a warning that the U.S. will punish Argentina for poor financial policies that would drastically affect any investor.

With the re-entry of Argentina into international markets, Macri's government issued US$16.5 billion in new bonds in 2016, which would be paid out in U.S. dollars. With the bonds being denominated in USD$, this made the bonds immune to Argentine inflation and created investor confidence. Fueled by U.S. pension and other fixed income funds that were seeking high yielding bonds, the issuing was oversubscribed by US$53.5 billion for a total of US$70 billion in orders. The oversubscription allowed for Argentina to not only to expand its debt offering but also negotiate more aggressive interest rates with investors. Although Argentina is rated B3, B-, and B by Moody's, S&P, and Fitch respectively, it was able to keep its later bonds' yields lower than El Salvador and other comparable borrowers. The oversubscription also enabled Argentina to also issue high yielding 100 Year Bonds, putting the country in a small group of countries to issue such debt. S&P gave Argentina's credit rating a B+ on October 30, 2017 in a show of confidence from Wall Street following Macri's mid-term election victories.

In conclusion, Argentina's history of irresponsible ISI policies in the 1980s led to soaring amounts of debt and inflation, which cumulated in a default in 2001. The default caused FRAN bonds to achieve extreme interest rates, which Argentina refused to pay, which resulted in legal battles with creditors and being frozen out of international markets until it resolved its disputes. This in turn led to Argentina having one of the most successful bond issuing of any emerging market and securing its financial future and ending an era of defaults.

References

Cárdenas, E., Ocampo, J., & Thorp, R. (2000). *An Economic History of Twentieth-Century Latin America: Volume I: The Export Age.* London: Palgrave Macmillan.

Coatsworth, J. H. & Williamson, J. G. (2004). "Always Protectionist? Latin American Tariffs from Independence to Great Depression." *Journal of Latin American Studies*, 36(2), pp.205–232.

Corbo, Vittoria (1994). "Economic Policies and Performance in Latin America." In *Economic Development: Handbook of Comparative Economic Policies*, Enzo Grilli & Dominick Salvatore (eds.). Westport, Conn.: Greenwood, p.308.

Evans, Peter (1979). *Dependent Development.* Princeton, N.J.: Princeton University Press.

Franko, P. M. (2007). *The Puzzle of Latin American Economic Development.* Lanham, Maryland: Rowman & Littlefield.

Gómez-Galvarriato, A. & Williamson, J. G. (2009). "Was it Prices, Productivity or Policy? Latin American Industrialization after 1870." *Journal of Latin American Studies*, 41(4), pp.663–694.

Hanson, Simon (1951). *Economic Development in Latin America.* Washington, C.C.: Inter-American Affairs Press, p.107.

Jomo, Sundaram (Ed.) (2006). The Great Divergence: Hegemony, Uneven Development, and Global Inequality. New York, USA: Oxford University Press.

Smith, David (2012). "Seized Argentinian Sailing Ship Leaves Ghana." *Guardian*. www.theguardian.com/world/2012/dec/20/argentina-sailing-ship-ghana-release, accessed January, 2018.

Spillan, J. E., Virzi, N. & Garita, M. (2014). *Doing Business in Latin America: Challenges and Opportunities.* New York: Routledge.

4

CULTURAL ISSUES AFFECTING BUSINESS

Introduction

This chapter presents a discussion of how the diversity and sameness of cultures have an impact on the economic, political and social activities in Latin America. Since Latin America is ethnically mixed, describing this region from a "one shoe fits all" point of view is extremely inaccurate. Many times, one can hear or observe people talking about Latin American as if everyone speaks Spanish and that if you go to one Latin American country you have seen them all. Take for example Brazil. This country is composed of people from African, Japan, Italy, Germany, and obviously Portugal. Chile has a great many citizens who are of German heritage. This composition readily indicates that these two countries are different than Peru, Bolivia and Guatemala, which have significant indigenous populations who live high in the mountains and have cultures that are far different than modern day cultures of many other Latin American countries. Issues of high and low context cultures can be seen in some Latin American countries. Religion, machismo and family centered ness are attributes that dominate the Latin American culture. Clearly Latin American societies are much more complex than they look.

Businesses exploring the opportunities of doing business in Latin America must think about how culture will affect its business negotiations and operations in a country or region. People's traditions affect human behavior and ultimately have an impact on how they think, feel and act (Spillan, Virzi & Garita, 2014).

Figure 4.1 summarizes the complex interactions that exist in any culture. They have an enormous impact on business operations both individually and collectively. The globalization process that has been occurring over the past 25 years has slowly forced Latin Americans to think differently. The business practices and processes that have historically been part of the daily lives are now changing to accommodate western business practices. This is happening because success in business requires a management process that operates congruently with contemporary global business practices. Culture remains the main variable that consistently and continuously affects just about every transaction. Language is one element of the culture system that is instrumental in making the business transactions workable. An example of this is using English as a means of negotiating business transactions. While English is necessary for many business dealings, the international business manager needs to know and understand the local cultural differences. Different parts of a country or region where business is conducted have different traditions and practices. It is very common that cultural routines and customs in rural areas are substantially different than those in large cities. As such, it is important that the international manager recognizes the differences and respects their impact on the business activities that are being conducted (Becker, 2010). So, culture is a huge concern for business managers.

Cultural Analysis

The foregoing Figure 4.1 illustrates the major components or factors that have to be dealt with as one begins thinking about developing and implementation a business in LA. These components are real and not just abstractions. For example, language and religion are real factors in doing business. They must be taken into consideration when doing business. They influence decision making, recruiting of staff and daily operation of a business.

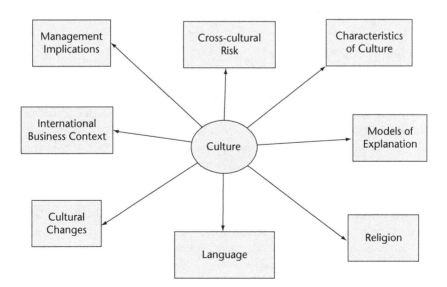

FIGURE 4.1 The Cultural System

National Values and Attitudes

Culture is a learned system of knowledge, behaviors, attitudes, beliefs, values, and norms that is shared by a group of people (Smith, 1966). In the broadest sense, culture includes how people think, what they do, and how they use things to sustain their lives (Smith, 1966). Culture is complex. What one sees on the surface is an expression of what is much more profound among the fundamental influences that reside in one's norms and values, beliefs, history and geography. Throughout LA the family is still the most important social unit. The eldest male is usually the predominate head of the household. While this is the traditional style of family, there have been alternative life styles that have emerged over the past decades. Economic and social changes in LA have led to changes to birthrate and life expectancy. Additionally, changes in technology and communication are also promoting social, political and economic change in LA.

1 The LA baby boomers were exposed to authoritarian, political, regimes, the cold war and other societal scenarios by worldwide transformations.
2 Generation Xers were exposed to democracy, narcoterrorism, and civil wars and loosing of moral and ethical standards.
3 Millennials grew up with protests against narcosis. They have been active players and promoters of the digital age instruments and tools. They are active users of the internet, Facebook, cell phones and understand democracy.

The world and LA is a different place than it was 60 years ago. Change is certain, and it does have an impact on culture.

Machismo and *Marianismo*

Gender roles and societal expectations of men and women in this area of the world have been shaped largely by cultural-specific values and beliefs. The expressions *machismo* (men) and *marianismo* (women) describe the set of attributes that has developed in the region. Machismo relates to male virility, where the man is bold, intransigent, and sexually aggressive. Conversely, *marianismo* implies feminine moral superiority. This means the ideal woman to be selfless, submissive, and possessing great spiritual strength (Chavin, 2017).

The concepts of *machismo* and *marianismo* establish the expectations of men and women in Latin America. These ideas underpin the sexual division of labor. Since women are expected to be nurturing and morally superior to men, their primary responsibilities are with the family. Primarily they are in charge rearing and education of children (Chauvin, 2017).

The traditional Latin American religious and cultural values profile of a woman defines her the as passive, selfless, and pure. Popular culture and the mass media have defined her in terms of physical appearance (Zimmerman, 2017).

Women of indigenous populations endure from 'double marginalization,' because they are both minorities and females (Zimmerman, 2017). The lives of indigenous women are generally different from that of non-indigenous women in the same countries. Because the indigenous communities of Latin America have held on to a great deal of their traditions shared by women of Hispanic heritage. Traditions die-hard and as such can make contributions to the values and norms of succeeding generations. Appreciation of the art and literature that has come from the ancestors is important. The work ethic and appreciation of family life and contribution of each member of the family to the sustainability of the ethnic group is an important dimension even in the digital 21st century. It is important for a society to know, understand and appreciate the contributions of the previous generations. These elements of society form a foundation for business and economic development.

The digital world of the 21st century in which consumers and corporations are no longer separated by geographical borders and ever more brands are being introduced into emerging markets. This means introduction into a totally different culture. As such, the marketers need to become "cross-culturally" attentive and sensitive to the manners, customers and norms of the different culture where products and services are being offered.

There is a difference between cultural awareness and cultural ignorance. Knowing one and not knowing the other has both positive and negative consequences. The reputation of the marketer and the company are on the line.

Failure to understand cultural and the relationships, norms, mannerisms and customs that exist in a foreign culture can be catastrophic for a businessperson. This ignorance can be long standing and deny a company the opportunity of doing any business in the respective country. Advanced preparation, which thoroughly readies the marketer for the new cultures, is imperative and unavoidable. This activity is not a choice it is a demand for all those marketing professionals destined to work and market products and services in international markets (Costa, 2010).

One tool for understanding culture is the use of Geert Hofstede' cultural workplace relationship framework that has become so popular and frequently used in understanding different cultures. Hofstede set apart four features that summarized cultural relationships. These features include power distance, uncertainty avoidance, individualism versus collectivism, and masculinity versus femininity. These items are briefly described below:

1 Power distance – relates to the inequality in physical and intellectual abilities. In this respect high power distance cultures were discovered in countries that let inequalities over time become inequalities of power and wealth. Low power distance was discovered in countries that paid limited attention to these differences.

2 Uncertainty avoidance – assesses how different cultures make its members behave regarding the acceptance of uncertainty. Followers of high uncertainty avoidance cultures really are concerned about job security, and career advancement issues. These members require rules and regulations to guide them in their work. On the other hand, followers of the low uncertainty avoidance cultures are able to take risks and are less resistance to change.

3 Individual vs. collectivisms – this feature deals with the relationship between individuals and their fellow citizen or workplace co-workers. Cultures that have individualistic characteristics promote individual freedom. This element is highly respected. In collectivistic cultures the relationship between individuals is close. Extended families are important and become a priority among the citizens.

4 Masculinity vs. femininity – this element of the framework relates to the relationship between gender and work roles. With regard to the masculine cultures, sex roles are dramatically different. The exercise of power in society for example is determined by tradition and cultural ideals. In feminine cultures, sex roles are not so obviously defined. As such, there are slight differences between men and women's role in society (Hill, 2011).

Hofstede's framework provides a working tool for assessing where Latin American cultures are when trying to understand the relationships to societal norms. One can see very easily where the uncertainty avoidance issue could be very easily analyzed among Latin American workers. In most cases throughout the region the workers will most likely defer almost all decisions to his or her patron (boss) rather than take responsibility for the decision-making. Additionally, it evident that Latin American worker generally like rules in the work place so the uncertainty can be minimized or eliminated. Similarly, one can see how the masculinity vs. femininity dimension is a major feature of the Latin American society. The family is a major sociological feature of just about all of Latin America. It is a priority in most countries. Additionally, the extended family is a major concern and center of attention in most Latin American countries.

With an understanding of these cultural dimensions, an investor or business developer can begin to develop his/her business plan and model understanding that these dimensions, from a cultural point of view, will have an impact on employee recruitment considerations.

Regional Subcultures

Latin America is composed of four major regions. They consist of Mexico, Central America, The Caribbean and South America. South America alone is a continent with 12 sovereign states (WorldAtlas, 2018). Mexico is a country with over 130 million residents (Worldmeter, 2018). It is a powerful economic force in Latin American with a very rich culture composed of Spanish descent and a large Aztec indigenous population continuing their culture from ancient times. Central America comprised of seven countries with a population of over 42 million inhabitants. Its cultures are similar but distinct. For instance, Guatemala has a very large Mayan indigenous population (Worldmeter, 2018). After this comes the Caribbean region with five countries and a population of about 44 million people. The cultural influences are varied from Spanish, French, British, Dutch and African. Many of these countries are very touristic because of their beautiful climate and beaches. Finally, the continent of South America has a population of 427 million residents in 14 countries (Worldmeter, 2018). The cultural influences are substantial but predominately of Spanish and Portuguese influence. Alternatively, one can see that Argentina has a large German population and distinctly Eurocentric aura in the cities of Buenos Aires and Mendoza.

To successfully achieve cultural competency in this area of the world is critical. Because Latin America has both similarities and differences in national cultures, we have divided the area into six regions based on theme names according to their economic, political and social situations and will discuss the cultural aspects from this structural perspective So essentially the Latin American region can be divided into the following geographic regions:

Region 1 – Modern and Progressive
Brazil
Argentina
Paraguay
Uruguay
Chile

Region 2 – Indigenous Influences
Bolivia
Guatemala
Ecuador
Mexico
Peru

Region 3 – Peace and Tranquility
Costa Rica
Chile

Region 4 – Political Instability
El Salvador
Honduras
Nicaragua
Venezuela

Region 5 – Fledging Economically
El Salvador
Honduras
Nicaragua
Guatemala

(IMF, 2017)

The foregoing regional descriptions provide a prospective investor/manager insight into the regional profile for countries in these regions. With this information in mind investors and managers can make decisions as to whether they will or will not enter these regions and if they do what issues they need to be prepared to address as they make their entry and investment in the region(s). As presented, each region has its pros and cons and as such preparation for these profiles is very important.

While much of LA is quite diverse, three countries have major indigenous subcultures. Guatemala, Peru and Bolivia have large distinct indigenous populations, which are thriving (although often in poverty) and retain most of the cultural attributes that were common among their ancestors of the 14th and 15th century.

One of those is the central market as depicted in Figure 4.2.

The informal market has been around for a very long time and it is the traditional center for commercial activity in many Latin American countries. Almost all Latin American countries have one large central informal market and then many informal markets scattered throughout the country.

Social Structures

Over time, many historical factors have evolved that have fundamentally affected the Latin American cultures. Essentially the class structure is based on the social relationships of the basic economic activities in the society. These relationships consist of property ownership, labor arrangements, sources of income, and supervisory/subordinate interactions. In some cases, people are relegated to certain jobs because of their gender, race or ethnicity (Gabrenya, 2003). Examples of this arrangement exist all over Latin America. For example, the indigenous housekeeper or maid seems to be ubiquitous especially in countries where the indigenous population is large.

Class structure also differs by country. For example, the fact that Argentina is more fully developed economically than many other LA nations results in a different development of class structure. The poverty level in Argentina is far

FIGURE 4.2 Central Open Market in Typical Latin American Community

less intense than that of Bolivia, Peru or Guatemala. Poverty and illiteracy rele-gates many people in Latin America to subservient status. Since they do not have the economic power or ability to articulate their positions on class issues, they remain unfortunately consigned to the lower-class status in Latin American society. There are three major social classes in Latin America. They are com-posed of the following:

1 High class – consists of the wealthy landowners, business owners and suc-cessful entrepreneurs. This class is in control of many of the economic forces and various infrastructure entities in many of the Latin American countries.

2 Middle class – this is a class of people that has grown substantially from 2000 to 2009 by nearly 30%. The people in this class are generally edu-cated, and work in the formal job sector of society. Women in this cat-egory tend to have fewer children and are a large component of the rise of the middle class. This class primarily lives in an urban setting with limited affiliation with the rural population. This movement from the lower class has reduced inequality from 44% to 30%, a substantial and welcomed reduction (The World Bank, 2012).

3 Lower class – is composed of people who are essentially in a survival mode every day. They work in the informal labor force and live on a day-to-day basis. Their wages are extremely low. Many of the members of this class are illiterate with a limited skill set that relegates them to primarily menial labor jobs. Their living conditions and quality of life can be somewhat primitive. Many do not own the land they live on but rather occupy the space because the owner of the plantation for which they work employs them. Many of the members of this class are also members of indigenous groups. Their living conditions and ways of life have not changed much for centu-ries. One could hypothetically argue that this group is poor and living in this social class because of discrimination by the dominant class of society. They have not been given the chance to move forward economically or socially.

Over the past decade, income inequality has dropped substantially as evidenced by a decline in the average Gini index by 13% from 2000–2012. Table 4.1 sum-marizes the Gini coefficients.

Table 4.1 gives a pretty good picture of the level of income inequality that exists among a majority of Latin American countries. While the Gini coefficient has fallen among some of the countries, in most of the countries the index is a long way from the 1.0 mark.

This goes against the historical trend of growing income inequality. Inequality in income in Latin America declined to some degree because of labor market shifts. Additionally, poor people's wages increased because of the commodities boom, which required more unskilled labor. Also, wages for the poor have improved due to active labor market policies such as enforcing labor laws and paying minimum wages (Ibarra, 2016). Besides these labor market changes there was a redistribution of wealth through public spending on health care, education and social protections for citizens. Even after all of these positive changes, Latin America continues to be one of the most unequal regions in the world. In 2014, the richest 10% of people in Latin America had amassed 71% of the region's wealth. If this trend continues, according to Oxfam's calculations, in just six years' time the richest 1% in the region will have accumulated more wealth than the remaining 99% (Ibarra, 2016). It remains to be seen whether the region can implement policy reforms within the employment, tax and social security sectors to decrease inequality (The World Bank, 2012). Table 4.1 gives a pretty good picture of the level of income inequality that exists among a majority of Latin American countries. While the Gini coefficient has fallen among some of the countries, in most of the countries the index is a long way from the 1.0 mark.

From another perspective, one can view social structures according to how a society is organized. It refers to the relationships of the society and its people and how they organize themselves. Most societies have two major parts – one is that of the individual (Western culture) or as a collective (Eastern culture) (Hill, 2011). The social structure also focuses on how societies are created in terms of classes or casts. How mobile a person is in a society will determine its social structure. For example: the U.S. society allows for just about unlimited mobility. Being part of a social structure can have a serious impact on one's ability to

TABLE 4.1 Gini Coefficient – Latin American Countries

Country	Date of Measurement	Gini Index
Argentina	2014	42.7
Bolivia	2016	47.0
Brazil	2014	49.7
Chile	2015	50.5
Colombia	2015	53.5
Costa Rica	2015	50.5
El Salvador	2015	37.0
Ecuador	2013	48.5
Guatemala	2014	53.0
Honduras	2014	48.2
Mexico	2014	48.2
Nicaragua	2014	47.1
Peru	2012	45.3
Venezuela	2011	39.0

Source: Central Intelligence Agency (2018).

achieve economic independence and innovative capabilities. Those individuals who seem involved in a social class that does not permit mobility are clearly constrained. As such their ability to develop businesses and achieve economic rewards and be an active consumer of goods is constrained or limited (Hill, 2011).

Figure 4.3 is a graphical depiction of the way social entities are structured in Latin America. The social structure in Latin American culture begins with the family. The family is the major social entity that everything else revolves around. Family comes first before anything else in the life of most Latin American's.

As mentioned previously in the Hofstede cultural discussions, the family is at the core of Latin American society and its presence drives all other activities among Latin American people.

Further, Figure 4.3 depicts how the social relationships operate in the Latin American culture. The concentric circle demonstrates that the family is the center of all business and cultural activities. As we move out from the most center of the circle, the loyalty and obligations are significantly affected. Groups are important in Latin America business and social situations, but they work well only when the members of the group are known to one another. Foreigners, while greeted politely and engaged, are not the primary concern of Latin Americans. Clearly this has major implications for business relationships and transactions (Becker, 2010).

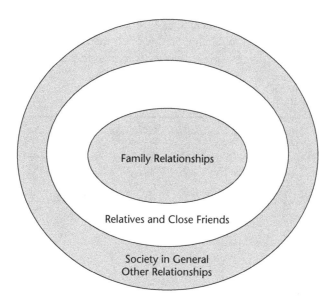

FIGURE 4.3 Graphical Depiction of Social Structure in Latin America

Religion

Religion is a set of shared beliefs, attitudes and rituals relating to a supernatural or higher being as sacred. These beliefs affect the attitudes, perceptions and thought processes of an individual. Throughout the world, cultures have religion as their underpinning and fundamental approach to living. Religion is part of culture and culture has an impact on peoples' way of thinking. Therefore, it follows that religious beliefs affect managerial and customer behavior in various ways.

Religion can also have a positive influence on GDP by reducing corruption and broadening the respect for law and order (Cavusgil, Knight & Riesenberger, 2014). Christianity has an impact on business because among many Christians consider Sunday as a day of rest and generally not a day to engage in substantive business transactions.

Latin American culture has been profoundly configured by religion (see Table 4.2). In Latin America, religion is at the core of the cultural forces that influence Latinos in their everyday lives. Latin America has had a predominately Catholic population. It is the home of close to 40% of the world's total Catholic population. From 1900 through the 1960s, 90% of Latin American population was Catholic. Since then, the number has dropped to 69%, which is a major decline (Pew Research, 2014). The religious affiliation memberships among Latin Americans have been changing for a variety of reasons. Some of those explanations are outlined below:

1   Change in religious affiliation – The reason for the falling off in Catholic membership is religion switching. Large numbers of Catholics have changed to the Pentecostal churches. It offers them the spirituality orientation that they desire. Members say they want a more personal experience.

TABLE 4.2 Summarizes the Religion Distribution Percentage among 16 Latin American Countries

Country	Christianity %	Catholics %	Other Christians %	Other, No Religion (Atheists and Agnostics %)
Argentina	84	77	7	16
Bolivia	93	76	17	7
Brazil	84	63	21	16
Chile	70	57	13	30
Colombia	78	75	3	22
Ecuador	93	81	8	4
Paraguay	96	88	8.3	1.7
Peru	87	77	10	13
Uruguay	49	41	8	51
Venezuela	91	79	12	9

Source: Corporación Latinobarómetro (2014)

2   Protestants are more committed than Catholics. Protestants support same sex marriage and abortion, and oppose the notion that wives must obey their husbands.

The Central American nations of Honduras, Nicaragua, Guatemala and El Salvador are very committed to Catholicism, while Argentina, Chile and Uruguay are more secular and have relatively low levels of religious commitment. Brazil falls in between these two groups (Lipka, 2014).

Communication

Communication is a critical factor in cross-cultural management. Culture and communication are intricately intertwined. Communication is the mechanism through which relationships are made, conflicts are resolved, and innovative ideas are developed (Deresky, 2014). The ability to communicate across borders both personally and professionally will determine the success of the business transactions. Effective communication and collaboration depends on informal understandings among the parties and the trust that has been developed between and among the parties. Language is a huge part of communication. If the communicators are not well versed in the language then the communication process can be difficult, cause misinterpretations, conflict and ultimately loss of business opportunities.

Hidden cultural differences are elements of cross-cultural communication that can cause serious problems in the communication of personal and business messages. Context and content are the critical components in any communication. In Latin America, there is a broader focus, which includes contextual factors like relationships, situations, timing and social appropriateness. Moreover, the meaning of words, gestures or messages may depend on the hierarchical status of the parties included in the transaction. It also can be contingent on the degree of trust they share and if the communication is private or public. The ability to interpret subtle hints is important in communications in Latin American transactions. To some, Latin Americans may appear to be ambiguous or evasive in the communication process (Wederspahn, 2005). Since Latin America is a high-context culture, physical distance between people, softer handshakes, more touching (e.g., hugs) and greater use of hand and arm gestures remains major attributes of how Latin Americans communicate.

Additionally, business attire is more fashionable and colorful that in some other business environments. Finally, nonverbal language is critical to face-to-face communication because it expresses feelings, intentions and reactions. Many times, non-Latin Americans see them as emotional or excitable. This is a part of their unique communication process. It distinguishes them from other people in the global business world (Wederspahn, 2005). Communication is also a silent language in Latin America that entails embraces between men, standing close together, pats on back, tugs and squeezes of the arm, energetically expressive motions and non-verbals (Becker, 2010).

Because of the unique communication process in Latin American cultures, business deals take longer to conclude. In such a high context culture, business cannot be conducted successfully until trust levels are established and parties build personal bonds by getting to know each other (Becker, 2010). This can only be achieved when an acceptable communication process is established between the individuals involved.

Education

Over the last two decades great progress has been made in providing access to education in Latin America. Yet, a great many children are not receiving high-quality education that is needed to prepare them for the contemporary work force. Depending on the country and the jurisdiction i.e., urban or rural the delivery and quality of education vary. For example, in Guatemala, private education in primary, secondary and University levels is pretty good in the major urban areas. Outside of the major urban areas the delivery and quality of education is questionable. Latin American universities, which serve approximately less than 10% of the population, get disproportionately more resources than the elementary education (Education Gap in Latin America, 2017). The consequence of this is that many students are entering the work world without the proper skills to be successful in the global economy. The information rich economy is clamoring for skilled workers who are prepared to address the complex technical, financial and socioeconomic issues that confront the societies in LA. The lack of proper skill development in the educational system is impeding economic growth and perpetuating a system of have and have nots (Education Gap in Latin America, 2017).

Latin America is lagging among the regions of the world as it relates to years of school and quality of education. Latin America was in 2015, on average, 2.5 years of schooling behind the Organization for Cooperation and Development or OECD average. Fifty years ago, Asian countries such as South Korea had similar, if not worse, educational levels than many Latin American countries. Today, South Korea boasts more years of schooling and significantly better educational outcomes than every Latin American country (Education Gap in Latin America, 2017). In recent assessments, it was found that less than 1% of Latin American students scored in the top levels in international exams. Surprisingly, at the same time it was also found that high-income students also scored below their international peers.

There is an obvious reason for the lag in quality education in Latin America. First is the issue of budget allocation for education. The actual investment in education is inadequate even with the increases over the last few years. The amounts of spending on education across the LA region are comparatively low when compared to OECD spending in Europe and elsewhere. The example of Mexico is illustrative. Mexico spends a large percentage of GDP per student age 6–15 years annually, which is 31% of the OECD average. The second issue relates to teacher development and pay. Since the quality education is connected to the quality of the teacher, it is important to get them to the level they need to deliver a quality education. With this in mind, two actions have to be taken: (a) pay increases for all the teachers and (b) program development for professional teacher development (Education Gap in Latin America, 2017).

Manners and Customs

The way Latin Americans interact with each other, foreigners and business people is based on centuries of embedded manners and customs. In many places in Latin America, the 12:00 noon to 3:00 p.m. becomes a time of meal and siesta. For example, in Guatemala the noon meal is the most important family get-together of the day. It is a gathering of the family for a large lunch. This constitutes the main meal of the day because the evening meal generally consists of some type of bread and coffee. After the noon meal, participants can take a siesta and then return to work. This is particularly customary in countries such as Guatemala, Chile and Bolivia.

From a business point of view some of the manners and customs can be outlined as presented below:

1 Dress is important for making a good impression. Latin Americans are very fashion conscious. Business suits for men and conservative suits or dresses for women.
2 Greetings are similar to that in other Western countries – a handshake. Sometimes women will lean forward for a slight kiss on the cheek. Who kisses who, and how many kisses depends on the country.
3 Personal space is important. Generally, the conversational partner will stand close to the other person and look them in the eyes.
4 Men tend to pull out a chair, help with a coat and give up a seat for women.
5 It is customary to refer to business people by their surname (e.g., Mr. Ricardo).
6 Hats and sunglasses are not to be worn inside.
7 Business appointments are required and arranged at least two weeks in advance.
8 Agendas are not common and when they are present, they are not generally followed.

9 Negotiations in Latin America take a long time. Lots of haggling is part of the process.
10 Business cards are important. They should be in English and Spanish.
11 Avoid talking about political problems, as it can create problems in establishing trust and confidence

(Business Etiquette in Latin America, 2017)

These common issues of manners and customs are important to know and understand. While they may seem simple and common sense, one would be surprised to see how they could negatively impact the interactions of business and conversation partners. Being aware of their influence in transactions can go a long way in being successful in conducting business transactions in Latin America.

Cultural Context and Content

Building and maintaining relationships is critically important. There is a real need to manage complex dimensions of relationships. In LA it simply takes more time than some businesses in other cultures. Latinos have a tendency to be more interested in you the person than you the company representative. Therefore, to understand a culture one must understand that there are really two important concepts: context and culture. There are high and low categories of culture. The high context culture is a situation where there is a need for a lot of background information and discussion. Individuals need to "get to know" each other. It may be called a "warm-up" phase where good inter-personal relationship is established. There is a lack of sense of urgency that many business people are familiar with. Low context cultures are just the opposite of the high context. Low context means that the message is explicit and direct. There is no need to establish an inter-personal relationship before the communications are transacted. Data and information are set forth directly with out any background being developed (Hooker, 2008).

Latin Americans are high context communication types. They need time to get to know their visitors, partners or collaborators. A relationship or trust must be established before transactions are processed. As such, company norms in this type of culture must be communicated personally and close supervision is essential. Rules are not strictly enforced and, in many cases, can be seen to be non-binding. Awareness of the circumstances, timing and social appropriateness are critical elements that need to be observed when doing business in LA. That is why many times Latinos may appear to be evasive to those unfamiliar with the LA cultures.

Contracts

With regard to contracts, in LA or a high context communication culture there are some dimensions that are necessary to observe and understand:

1   Not necessary to write everything down – since a good inter-personal relationship has been established, there is a trust that the items agreed to will be completed.
2   Terms of the agreements are generally vague so that adjustments are possible in the future.
3   Business plans are developed along with the relationship rather than a written plan preceding the agreements.

Cultural Artifacts

Guatemala is one example of a Latin American country that is rich in culture and an archeologist dream. Since the Mayan empire was pervasive in this country centuries ago, many of their ruins and artifacts have been and continue to be discovered. Tourists, academics and interested parties come to Guatemala annually just to visit the ancient cities and ruins that are scattered all over Guatemala. In Figure 4.4 is pictured one of the major Mayan ruins that attracts a great many tourists. This tourist activity generates large amounts of business and economic development activity across Guatemala. Each year new business ventures emerge that cater to the growing population associated with these archeological treasures.

The same is true in other Latin American countries. Colombia, Peru, Ecuador, Bolivia and Chile have numerous historic sites that attract millions of visitors every year. Such activity contributes significantly to the business and economic development in the respective countries.

FIGURE 4.4   Picture of Old Ruins in Petén, Guatemala

Bureaucracy

Many times, the procedures, transactions and practices seem to be enormously redundant and burdensome. The repetitiveness of some activities and multiplicity of documents are many times a major constraint from a low context culture person's point of view. One example can give a glimpse of this redundancy. A worker in Mexico submits a variety of travel reimbursement documents to his immediate supervisor for approval. Once that is completed, the same person has to submit another set of documents to the main office in Mexico City for their approval. The documents are generally identical but must be not only approved by the immediate supervisor but also the main office in Mexico City. It takes months to process these documents and thus for reimbursement is months into the future. The issue of timeliness or consideration of other people's time, in this case, is not a consideration. In a relationship society, the bureaucracy serves a purpose other than processing paper. It represents the power of important people. Polychromic cultures have bureaucracies that revolve around personal power rather than logical organizations (Hooker, 2008).

Culture and Business Leadership

Globalization and cross-border business transactions require businesses to understand not just basic business principles but also global business principles that are essential to successful conduct of business in various parts of the world. Latin American leaders possess many important capabilities such as integrator, goal oriented and collaborative. All these attributes focus on relationships. According to Ramsey, Rutti, Lorenz & Barakat (2017, p.462) the Latin American leader of Multilatinas is a "paternalistic figure that engenders care and loyalty as well as protects working relationships using a humanistic approach. This relationship respects power and authority." While all these relationship traits are widely held among Latin American managers, are good and have great value in managing people in the workplace, being a transformational leader is one talent that international businesses need to be competitive. In Latin America the global leaders' attributes take on more than just transformational elements. Global leader development has been recognized as a critical aspect of human resource management in multinational enterprises. Global leaders with the capability of understanding, functioning, and managing in a global setting are invaluable to achieve a competitive advantage. Besides these skills and competencies, global leaders in Latin America need the cultural intelligence proficiencies in order to be successful. These abilities give the leader the capacity to adapt to new cultural contents and function in cross-cultural settings. Having these attributes is critical to effectively interacting and negotiating in cross-border business transactions and relationships.

Conclusions

Latin America is described as a group of nations in the Americas and the Caribbean whose residents predominantly speak Spanish or Portuguese. These languages are two of the many languages descended from Latin. The geographic area that is now physically Latin America has been formed by hundreds of years of European imperialist rule. Forces from Europe through force and conquered and structured the societies based on their values and norms (Getty, 2017) Because of the different conquers; there are very important variations of culture and lifestyles across Latin America culture. Spanish is the predominant language in Latin America, except for Brazil a country of 210 million people who speak Portuguese (Worldmeter, 2018). Even though these similarities in language is generally pervasive, there are countries that have large indigenous population who speak their own native tongue and have a distinct culture that is different from modern day lifestyles. Because of poverty, traditions and political suppression they have retained cultural patterns that are not congruent with the postmodern ideas of living in the rest of LA. This circumstance has caused concern, conflict and separation in some Latin American cultures (Spillan et al., 2014).

While there are great similarities, most Latin American countries display distinct differences in employee behavior according to their cultural socialization. For example, people from Chile and Argentina have a closer association with tradition, as well as, a cultural inclination towards hierarchical institutions and more blatant gender prejudices. Brazil and Colombia are different from other Latin American countries in that from an employee point of view they prefer a flattening of both hierarchical and gender lines. Interestingly, Mexicans are constantly changing form one view to another (Vassolo, De Castro & Gomez-Mejia, 2011).

Contextual factors such, as relationships, circumstances, timing and social appropriateness are important factors that affect the cultural dynamics of doing business in LA. Business is a unique and important place to study culture in action. Business practices are heavily influenced by intensely kept cultural points of view towards work, power, trust, wealth and communication. As such, many things that occur in business are affected by a worker's cultural norms and values (Hooker, 2008).

Finally, communication is one of the main business areas that are affected by cultural inclinations. Since communication is the lifeblood of any organization and because it is a shared activity among all members of the organization, it is important to understand the whys and how it is used among the employees in a business. If not, the result may be miscommunication, costing both a deterioration of a relationship, and ultimately money.

CASE

MASISA, Chile

Chile has been one of Latin America's fastest growing economies in recent years. It is a solid trading partner with a vibrant export market, has robust market-oriented policies, maintains a stable government, has good business practices and has very low corruption. These attributes make Chile a good place to do business. During the last 25–30 years its economic growth has averaged around 5%. Lately it has slowed a bit but still has a strong economic being with a very high rating among world economic indices. Chile is an example of a country that has exploited entrepreneurship and innovation to establish and promote a rapidly expanding economy. Companies competing in this region are responding not only to new trends in technology but the dynamic fluctuations in world economic activity. Their challenges require firms to find a value proposition that meets the needs of the Chilean people. Chile has been at the forefront of this business activity and has been very successful. Chile is one country in Latin America that has been an active participant in the globalization process. Similar to consumers throughout the world, the Chilean people are required to make purchase decisions almost every day. As globalization of markets continues to be the focus of business strategy among business firms, managers need to understand the components and dynamics of buying decisions among different cultures. Entering international markets has been not only the focus of Multinational Corporations (MNCs) but also an approach of small and medium size businesses as well. One example of a company that has been part of Chile's successful business model is a company called MASISA. MASISA, S.A. Chile. It was founded in 1920 and is headquarter in Santiago Chile. MASISA is a company that is involved in the production and sale of wood boards for furniture and interior architecture. It operates from two sectors: a. Industrial and b. Forestry.

MASISA's main products consist of panels, doors, and window boards. These wood products can be classified as products listed below:

1   Medium density fiber board
2   Medium density particle board
3   Melamine or laminated boards
4   Sawn lumber
5   MDF moldings
6   Layer boards.

The company focuses on bringing design quality and sustainability to every item of furniture or interior space and improving people's lives through this process. MASISA wants to be the number "one" company in Latin America by bringing value added to peoples' environment by increasing the quality of furniture and interior space.

Within this framework MASISA wants to meet the requirements of the triple bottom-line (social, economic and environmentally sound) or continue its corporate social responsibility.

As a business MASISA's Mission and Vision are as follows:

Mission: Promote and sell high-quality and sustainable wood and furniture products that will increase the quality of life among its customers.

Vision: To be number "one" in value and facilitator in finding solutions for the interiors of Latin American homes and businesses. Being the most attractive for clients, investors and collaborators.

As such, MASISA operates within six major business principles:

1 Always look for economic value.
2 Maintain an ethical business with a high level of transparency.
3 Conduct a personal, honest relationship with its stakeholders and customers with integrity and transparency.
4 Promote excellent relations with it clients by offering high-quality products and excellent service.
5 Developing good healthy relationships with collaborators.
6 Provide mutual respect and cooperation with community.

MASISA'S business model focuses on sustainable value with a commitment to ethical and transparent conduct among ALL employees of the organization. The customer is at the center of the company's operation. They advocate long-term trust-based relationships with customers and promote high-quality service to all their clients.

Company size:

1 The company owns 302,906 hectares of land and 188,588 hectares of forest. It is essentially independent of needing wood supplies because of this huge inventory of virgin wood that is available to them. This ready availability of wood from its own land gives it a competitive advantage in the market place.
2 It has 10 industrial plants scattered around the Latin American Region – 2 in Chile, 1 in Argentina, 2 in Brazil, 4 in Mexico, and 1 in Venezuela.
3 It has 317 distribution points around the region for sale of products with 77 in Mexico, 32 in Colombia, 29 in Ecuador, 21 in Peru, 6 in Bolivia, 49 in Chile, 55 in Argentina, 1 in Uruguay, and 47 in Venezuela.

The company encourages high performance work teams that function in a healthy and safe work environment. The company has a respect for human rights. Finally, the company is committed to joining with the community and its other stakeholders in the work place and society to respect and cooperate in promoting their core values among all the people they do business with.

The revenues generated from sales as of 2011 were US$1.2 billion with a net profit of US$69.9 million.

Source: Masisa Tu Mundo, Tu Estilo (2018)

References

Becker, Thomas, H. (2010). *"Doing Business in the New Latin America" Keys to Profit in America's Next-Door Markets*, 2nd Edition. New York: Praeger.

Business Etiquette in Latin America (2017). www.kcba.org/streaming/Documents/COLLABORATIVE-Handout_1.pdf, accessed January, 2018.

Cavallos, Diego (2005). *Indigenous Peoples Divided by Faith*. Mexico City: IPS.

Cavusgil, Tamer, Gary Knight, & John R. Riesenberger (2014*). International Business: The New Realities*, 3rd edition. Boston-New York: Pearson.

Central Intelligence Agency (2018). "Gini Coefficient Index." www.cia.gov/library/publications/the-world-factbook/rankorder/2172rank.html, accessed March, 2018.

Central Intelligence Agency (2018). *The World Factbook*. www.cia.gov/library/publications/the-world-factbook/rankorder/2172rank.html, accessed January, 2018.

Chauvin, Emilie (2017). "Insertion, Integration and Inclusion of South American Women: Relation and Coordination between Socio-cultural Parameters, Economic Growth and Gender Issues in the Andean Region, Fostering Women's Empowerment." Bachelor's Thesis – Degree Program in International Business Option of Management Consulting, Tampere University of Applied Sciences, Tampere University of Technology, University of Vaasa and VVT Research, Finland. www.theseus.fi/bitstream/handle/10024/134263/Chauvin_Emilie.pdf?sequence=2, accessed July, 2018.

Corporación Latinobarómetro (2014). "Banco De Datos en Linea, Santiago de Chile." www.liportal.de/fileadmin/user_upload/oeffentlich/Honduras/40_gesellschaft/LAS_RELIGIONES_EN_TIEMPOS_DEL_PAPA_FRANCISCO.pdf, p.7, accessed January, 2018.

Costa, MaryLou, (2010). "Beware of the Cultural Gaps on the Global Growth Trail." www.marketingweek.co.uk/in-depth-analysis/cover-stories/beware-the-culture-gap-on-global-growth-trail/3018963.article, accessed January, 2018.

Deresky, Helen (2014). *International Management: Managing Across Borders and Cultures*, 8th edition. Boston-New York: Pearson.

Education Gap in Latin America (2017). https://worldfund.org/site/why-worldfund/, accessed January, 2018.

ElanBiz (2018). www.koda.ee/sites/default/files/content-type/content/2017-09/Javier%20Sanchez.pdf ElanBiz, accessed January, 2018.

Encyclopedia.com (2008). "Class Structure in Modern Latin America." www.encyclopedia.com/humanities/encyclopedias-almanacs-transcripts-and-maps/class-structure-modern-latin-america, accessed February, 2018.

Gabrenya, W.K. (2003). *Culture and Social Class: Research Skills for Psychology Majors: Everything You Need to Know to Get Started*, Version 1.0. Public Broadcasting Systems,

University of Washington, Seattle, Washington, U.S.A, available at www.pbs.org/digitaldivide.

Getty (2017). http://blogs.getty.edu/iris/an-overview-of-latino-and-latin-american-identity, accessed January, 2018.

Gini Coefficient (2018). *CIA Intelligence, 2018 – Gini Coefficient for Respective Countries in LA*. Washington D.C. USA: The World Bank.

Hill, Charles, W.L. (2011). *International Business: Competing in the Global Market Place*. New York: McGraw-Hill.

Hooker, John (2008). "Cultural Differences in Business Communication." Tepper School of Business, Carnegie Mellon University.http://public.tepper.cmu.edu/jnh/businessCommunication.pdf, accessed January, 2018.

Ibarra, Alicia Barcena (2016). "Latin America is the World's Most Unequal Region. Here's How to Fix It." www.weforum.org/agenda/2016/01/inequality-is-getting-worse-in-latin-america-here-s-how-to-fix-it, accessed January, 2018.

IMF (2017). *Economic Outlook, Latin America*. www.imf.org/en/Publications/REO/WH/Issues/2017/10/11/wreo1017, accessed March, 2018.

Informal Market (2017). www.jica.go.jp/english/countries/america, accessed February, 2018.

Lipka, Michael (2014). "7 Key Takeaway's about religion in Latin America." www.pewresearch.org/fact-tank/2014/11/13/7-key-takeaways-about-religion-in-latin-america, accessed January, 2018.

Masisa Tu Mundo, Tu Estilo (2018). "Nosotros/Estructura Organizacional Estructura Organizational", www.masisa.com/nosotros/nuestra-empresa/estructura-organizacional, accessed April, 2018.

Pew Research (2014). "Religion in Latin America: Widespread Changes in a Historically Catholic Region." www.pewforum.org/2014/11/13/religion-in-latin-america, accessed January, 2018.

Ramsey, Jase, Raina M. Rutti, Melanie P. Lorenz & Livia L Barakat (2017). "Developing Global Transformational Leaders." *Journal of World Business*, 52, pp.461–473.

Ruins in Guatemala (2018). www.jica.go.jp/english/countries/america/-Myan Ruins in Guatemala, accessed February, 2018.

Smith, G. (1966). *Communication and culture* (Ed.). New York: Holt, Rinehart and Winston. http://stonecenter.tulane.edu/uploads/Women_in_Latin_America_updated-1352754376.pdf, accessed February, 2018.

Spillan, John, E., Nicholas Virzi & Mauricio Garita (2014). *Doing Business in Latin America: Challenges and Opportunities*. New York: Taylor and Francis.

The World Bank (2012). "Latin America: Middle Class Hits Historic High." www.worldbank.org/en/news/feature/2012/11/13/crecimiento-clase-media-america-latina, accessed February, 2018.

UNESCO (2010). *Global Education Digest*. Tables 1, 3, 5 & 8, p.98, p.118, p.138 & p.162.

UNESCO (2011). *Education for all Global Monitoring Report*. Table 9, p.337.

Vassolo, Robert S., Julis O. DeCastro, and Luis R. Gomez-Mejia (2011). Managers in Latin America: Common Issues and Research Agenda. *Academy of Management Perspectives*, 25(4), pp.22–36.

Wederspahn, Gary M. (2005). *Cross-Cultural Communication Between Latin American and U.S. Managers*. Grovewell: Global Leadership Solutions.

WorldAtlas (2018). www.worldatlas.com/articles/how-many-countries-are-in-south-america.html, accessed February, 2018.

Worldmeter (2017). www.worldometers.info/world-population/brazil-population, accessed January, 2018.

Worldmeter (2018). www.worldometers.info/world-population/mexico-population, accessed January, 2018.

Zimmerman, Lisa (2017). *Latin American Resource Center Resources Focusing on Women in Latin America.* RoberThayer: Stone Center for Latin American Studies.

5

THE POLITICAL CLIMATE

Overview

The political climate is one of the fastest changing elements of present day Latin America. Since the first edition of the book, the Brazilian and Peruvian presidents have been impeached on corruption charges, a pro-business president was elected in Argentina, and signs have emerged that the Venezuelan government might finally return to democracy. It appears that Latin Americans are finally getting fed up with the corruption that has been bleeding their countries since their inception. As the rising middle class begins to pay taxes, demands for services are becoming pertinent. Whether governments will actually become transparent will likely be one of the biggest accomplishments (or failures) of the current regimes. While a number of countries could be the case focus of this chapter, we will present the current political climate of Venezuela in order to illustrate a case of possible dramatic political change in the region.

Poverty and Inequality

Poverty still afflicts some 30% of the population in Latin America. Poverty has been falling in the past two decades, but the rate of reduction has slowed. It has only been able to be reduced on account of the positive economic growth and contained inflation, according to the report "Social Panorama of Latin America 2012," published by CEPAL. According to this report, in 2011, 168 million Latin Americans (30% of the region) lived below the poverty line. Thanks to economic growth, wages have been rising for the poor, and this, not social programs, was the main reason for the reduction in poverty rates.

The executive secretary of CEPAL, Alicia Barcena, states:

> Current poverty and indigence rates are the lowest for three decades, and this is good news, but we are still facing unacceptable levels in many countries. The challenge is to generate quality jobs as part of a development model based on equality and environmental sustainability.
>
> *(CEPAL, 2012)*

Nonetheless, taking into account the entire period since the global financial crisis of 2008/2009, the income distribution gap narrowed between then and 2015 in most of the region's countries. During this period, the income of the lowest income quintile increased more than that of the highest. This occurred generally across the various sources of household income but mainly in labor income (both for wage jobs and self-employment), retirement, and transfers (CEPAL, 2017).

As shown in Table 5.1, most countries of Latin America still have relatively high poverty rates (especially in rural areas). This urban/rural divide is based on the region's initial endowments and governmental focus on agricultural competitiveness. Certainly, Latin America is a region primed to supply the world with key inputs in the areas of foodstuffs and minerals. This competitive advantage needed no governmental protection, which only introduced rigidities into the political economic systems. Nevertheless, the poverty rates can be as much as 20–30% higher in the rural areas than in the urban areas (see Table 5.1 for a by country comparison). In this respect, the national poverty rates, already relatively bad, do not tell the entire story. Higher poverty rates in the rural areas translate into exceedingly high rates of political vulnerability and risk. This is partially due to the notion that rural voters are less educated and thus more susceptible to populist false promises that introduce uncertainty into the local investment and business climates (Spillan, Virzi & Garita, 2014).

So, although progress has been made, poverty rates are still high. This is important when considering the political system because it makes it vulnerable to the populist socialist bent on deforming the market economies to their political needs. When this happens, the business climate suffers both for locals and for those would-be investors from the outside. A vulnerable political system increases policy uncertainty as well as a concern for property rights.

Urban Poverty

Urban poverty and destitution is a multidimensional issue within the overall poverty umbrella concept. The urban poor live with numerous hardships. Their day by day difficulties may include: restricted access to work openings and pay, lacking and shaky lodging and benefits, rough and undesirable conditions, almost no social security systems, and constrained access to sufficient wellbeing and education options.

TABLE 5.1 Poverty Rates and Rural–Urban Divide

Country	Urban			Rural			Rural Urban Divide		
	2000	2014	% Change	2000	2014	% Change	2000	2014	% Change
Argentina	26	4	22	n/a	n/a	—	—	—	—
Nicaragua	64	53	11	77	65	12	13	13	1
Peru	42	15	27	78	46	32	36	31	6
Brazil	34	14	20	55	29	27	21	14	7
Guatemala	45	58	-13	68	77	-9	23	19	4
Ecuador	59	31	28	66	27	38	6	-4	10
Panama	26	12	14	55	41	14	30	29	1
Bolivia	52	22	30	83	54	29	31	32	-1
Venezuela	n/a	n/a	—	n/a	n/a	—	—	—	—
Paraguay	50	37	14	71	51	20	21	14	6
Colombia	51	25	26	62	42	20	11	17	-6
Mexico	32	39	-7	55	45	10	22	6	17
Dominican	42	34	8	56	44	12	14	10	4
Honduras	66	66	0	84	82	2	18	16	2
El Salvador	38	37	1	62	49	13	25	12	12
Costa Rica	18	17	0	24	22	2	7	5	2
Chile	20	8	12	24	7	17	4	-1	5
Uruguay	11	5	6	n/a	2	—	—	-2	—
Latin America	37	24	13	64	46	18	27	22	5

Source: CEPAL, U.N. (2015).

But urban poverty is not just a collection of characteristics, it is also a dynamic condition of vulnerability or susceptibility to risks. "In order to provide a richer understanding of urban poverty, the World Bank presents these two analytical frameworks: (i) a dynamic framework of poverty (vulnerability and asset ownership) and (ii) the multiple characteristics of poverty and its cumulative impacts" (The World Bank, 2018a).

For the first time in history, more than half the world's people live in cities. Over 90% of urban growth is occurring in the developing world, adding an estimated 70 million new residents to urban areas each year. During the next two decades, the urban population of the world's two poorest regions – South Asia and Sub-Saharan Africa – is expected to double.[6] The pattern in Latin America isn't quite as extreme, but the pattern of rural to urban shift exists nonetheless.

Urban development is credited to both an increase in population growth and rural to urban shift. Urbanization helps manage financial development, which is basic to poverty alleviation. The economies of scale and agglomeration in urban communities draw in entrepreneurs and business visionaries, which are useful for general financial development. Urban communities additionally give chances to many, especially poor people who are pulled in by more prominent occupational prospects, the accessibility of services, and for many, an escape from restrictive cultural conventions in provincial towns. However, city life can also result in crowded living, blockage of transportation systems, joblessness, absence of social and group systems, stark imbalances, and devastating social issues, not least of which include crime and homicides.

Many individuals who move from rural areas will profit by the open doors in urban territories, while others, frequently those with lower ability levels, might be deserted and end up battling with the everyday difficulties of city life. A significant number of the issues of urban neediness are established in an intricacy of asset and limit constraints, insufficient government strategies at both the general and neighborhood level, and an absence of anticipating urban development and change. Given the high development projections for most urban areas in Latin America, the difficulties of urban destitution and, in general, city administration will be exacerbated in numerous locations if not tended to more forcefully.

Regional Political Issues that Affect Business

Crime

Crime is a major area of concern for not only Latin Americans but also potential investors and people considering moving there to work. In particular, Central America and Venezuela have cause to be worried. For example, Central America is the world's most violent region, and Honduras, Guatemala, and El

Salvador are perennials on the list of most violent countries. Violence is not pervasive in the entire region, as seen in the reduction of violence in Argentina, Chile, Peru, and Paraguay. As a whole, the region posts around 22 murders per 100,000 inhabitants, ranging from the lows of four and seven in Chile and Argentina/Peru, to 57, 64, and 109 by Venezuela, Honduras, and El Salvador (see Table 5.2). The statistics of those last three countries make them the most violent in all of the world, not just Latin America. Needless to say, doing business in these countries is both dangerous and costly due to the need for security forces. And the cost isn't just in terms of money. Imagine trying to convince a manager to expatriate with her or his family to one of these dangerous countries. While Brazil, Colombia, and Mexico have considerably fewer homicides, they still rank seventh, eighth, and tenth in the world as the deadliest place to be.

Taking the matter of security seriously is particularly pertinent in order to protect not only employees but also their families. Failure to understand a company's responsibility to protect the families of its employees would go against the implied trust inherent in the employer/employee relationship in Latin

TABLE 5.2 Intentional Homicides per 100,000 People

Country	2005	2015	% Δ
El Salvador	64	109	45
Honduras	47	64	17
Venezuela	45	57	12
Guatemala	44	31	−13
Brazil	23	27	4
Colombia	40	27	−13
Dominican Republic	26	17	−9
Mexico	9	16	7
Bolivia	7	12	5
Costa Rica	8	12	4
Panama	11	11	0
Paraguay	19	9	−10
Ecuador	15	8	−7
Uruguay	6	8	2
Argentina	–	7	–
Peru	11	7	−4
Chile	4	4	0
Nicaragua	14	–	–
U.S.	6	5	−1
China	2	1	−1

Source: The World Bank (2018b).

Note
Sorted by highest in 2015.

America. This is different than in the United States where the employer/employee relationship ends once the employee leaves the office.

For Latin America as a whole, it has been estimated by the Inter-American Development Bank that the economic cost of crime and violence is more than 3% of regional GDP. The figures vary from over 6% in El Salvador and Colombia to 2% in Uruguay (Jaitman, 2017). In a more recent study focused on Central America, the World Bank estimated lower numbers.

Crime and violence do not just increase the delinquency in Latin America. They take political overtones which directly impact the climate for doing business in the region. The direct intent of the efforts during the peace processes that engulfed the Latin American region upon the end of the Cold War and the transition toward democratic governments was to weaken the state apparatus on the premise that state power for law and order purposes was evil in and of itself. In the first place, this was not true. Civil war violence started with communist terrorism throughout the region. More importantly, the weakening of the state proceeded too far, enabling not only criminal groups to displace state power but also anti-establishment associations to engage in ever more violent protests to make their political point (Spillan et al., 2014). Table 5.3 shows how Latin American nations fare in the realm of political violence and instability, both areas that greatly denigrate the climate for doing business in the region.

The reader can see that Uruguay has the highest rating (in a range from −2.5 to 2.5). It's even higher than that of the United States. Uruguay has been a beacon for political stability in the region which has added to its allure as a place to do business. It could be argued that Uruguay might be one of the better countries to base an expansion into Latin America due to its safety and lack of problems with the government. The 10-year trend also bodes well for Peru, Paraguay, Ecuador, and Colombia. As mentioned earlier in this section of the chapter, one might not consider Colombia "safe," but due to recent peace deals with the FARC rebel group, the country has improved on this index, and rightfully so. Since the writing of this book, we suspect that more recent data would send Venezuela much lower than it currently is. The interested reader can follow the hyperlink under Table 5.3 for the most recent data. The recent moves by President Maduro have mired the country in political risk, especially for investors from the United States.

Latin America certainly suffers from criminal and political violence. Criminals and political dissenters alike feel empowered to take violent measures into their own hands to protest against the inequities of the system and do so with impunity. Latin American governments, particularly in countries where the military handily beat the communist revolutionaries, such as Guatemala, feel restricted to apply the self-same law and order techniques that would be applied in the United States at the first instance of violet public protests against business interests, private property, or the public order in general. Adding insult to

TABLE 5.3 Political Stability and Absence of Violence

Country	2006	2016	Δ
Uruguay	0.6	1.1	0.5
Costa Rica	0.8	0.7	0.0
Chile	0.7	0.5	−0.2
Panama	0.1	0.4	0.3
Dominican Republic	−0.1	0.3	0.4
Argentina	0.1	0.2	0.1
Paraguay	−0.5	0.2	0.7
El Salvador	−0.2	−0.1	0.2
Ecuador	−0.8	−0.1	0.7
Peru	−1.1	−0.2	0.9
Nicaragua	−0.5	−0.2	0.3
Bolivia	−0.1	−0.2	−0.1
Honduras	−0.5	−0.4	0.1
Brazil	−0.2	−0.4	−0.2
Guatemala	−1.0	−0.5	0.5
Mexico	−0.9	−0.8	0.2
Colombia	−1.6	−1.0	0.7
Venezuela	−0.6	−1.0	−0.4
U.S.	0.9	0.4	−0.6
China	−0.1	−0.5	−0.4

Source: The World Bank (2018c).

Note
Sorted by highest (best) in 2016. Range is −2.5 to 2.5, with higher being better.

injury, corruption in the public institutions is another factor that weakens the state's ability to act for the common good in Latin America. That said, countries such as Brazil and Peru seem to be attempting to change this pattern by holding politicians and business people alike to account for their corruption. The next section deals with this topic.

Corruption & Transparency Issues

The Corruption Perceptions Index by the organization Transparency International is one instrument that helps understand corruption around the world. Figure 5.1 shows the ranking each country obtained in the 2017 report. Specifically, Transparency International attempts to measure the public's perceptions of the situation of corruption in each country. Venezuela is, not surprisingly, at the bottom of the list in Latin America with a ranking of 169 out of 180 countries. Nicaragua and Guatemala don't fare much better. (Note that lower ranks are better.) Nearly all the countries in Latin America are worse off than China, which has had its own challenges recently with corruption.

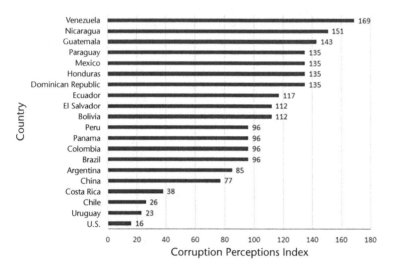

FIGURE 5.1   Corruption Perceptions Index

Pro-market Chile ranks well, indicating the application of lessons learned and an understanding of the importance of public institutions for the national achievement of global competitiveness (an important issue discussed in detail in a later chapter). Uruguay and Costa Rica would also be wise choices for the investor seeking to do business in a transparent environment.

In the 2017 Corruptions Perception Index, El Salvador and Brazil fell the furthest in Latin America from the prior year. The prominence of the FMLN party could be to blame for El Salvador's decline due to its attempts to undermine the Supreme Court. It also has rejected offers from the UN to create an anti-corruption task force, similar to the group created for Guatemala (Runde, 2017). Brazil's drop was most likely related to the corruption scandals that have been plaguing the nation in recent years. Former president Dilma Rousseff was removed in 2016 due to charges of manipulating the budget. Another scandal was "Operation Car Wash," where oil giant Petrobras, Brazil's state-owned oil company, paid exorbitant fees to construction companies in return for kickbacks. One of the accused perpetrators was former president Lula de Silva, who interestingly is the current (as of 2018) favorite in the next presidential election. As mentioned before, Odebrecht, one of Latin America's largest construction companies, has been accused of bribing politicians all over South America. Lula's replacement, Michel Temer, also has been accused of corruption for his connection to a meatpacking scandal with the firm JBS (BBC News, 2018). It remains to be seen whether these convictions stick in Brazil and whether the country is able to "turn a corner" away from corruption.

Political Systems

The Fragile States Index by the Fund for Peace relates a telling story. The reader should bear in mind that on this indicator a low score is better than a high one. The countries can be broadly categorized into three buckets: stable, warning, and alert. Referring to Table 5.4, one can see the countries are ranked from worst to best in this index. Fortunately, none of the countries fall into the "alert" category, which is the range of 90–114. Yet the majority of the countries do fall into the "warning" category, which includes a range of 60–90. Finally, five countries are considered "stable": Panama, Argentina, Costa Rica, Chile, and Uruguay. Note that Uruguay is only one spot behind the United States in this index.

From 2016 Mexico's score increased, which is negative, the most in 2017 out of all the 178 countries included in the index (not just Latin America). The country's score in 10 out of the 12 indicators reported worsened. A few of the notable increases include the Security Apparatus indicator and the Economic Decline indicator. To calculate the Security Apparatus indicator, several factors

TABLE 5.4 Fragile States Index

Country	2007	2017	Δ
Guatemala	81	83	−2
Venezuela	80	83	−3
Honduras	75	79	−4
Colombia	90	79	11
Nicaragua	80	77	3
Ecuador	80	77	3
Bolivia	82	77	5
Mexico	73	74	−1
El Salvador	75	73	2
Paraguay	73	72	1
Peru	76	70	6
Dominican Republic	81	69	12
Brazil	67	68	−1
Panama	59	51	8
Argentina	41	48	−7
Costa Rica	51	44	7
Chile	34	41	−7
Uruguay	41	37	4
Latin America	75	72	3
China	81	75	6
U.S.	34	36	−2

Source: Fund for Peace (2017).

Note
Scores are out of 120 with high scores representing unstable states. Sorted by 2017 rank.

including the use of force by the military, political violence, organized crime, arms proliferation, etc., are considered. In Mexico's 2015 mid-term elections, seven candidates were murdered and several more dropped out due to threats of violence. This continuing violence can be attributed to the increasing presence of cartels and privately-funded security forces that act without consequence. With a presidential election slated for summer of 2018, these problems are not expected to improve. Therefore, foreign investors may want to wait to see the results of the election before investing. This is a general recommendation in Latin America, not just for Mexico in 2018.

The Economic Decline indicator is determined by quantitative factors such as GDP per capita, inflation, and unemployment, as well as more qualitative measurements such as attractiveness to FDI, consumer confidence, and experts' opinions. Over the past few years Mexico's economic position has been improving, and the indicator has been decreasing, which is good. However, due to the uncertainty in the petroleum industry and the results of the recent presidential election in the United States (i.e., Trump), the economic forecast for Mexico has deteriorated. The peso has significantly weakened against the dollar which might make it attractive for investment. On the other hand, NAFTA's precarious position and a popular leftist presidential candidate should also be considered before investing in the country (Messner, 2017).

Finally, looking past the one-year change trend, we compared the 10-year trend in Table 5.4. Note that the change (delta) column represents a positive change if the number is positive and vice versa if it is negative. The Dominican Republic and Colombia are at the top of the list for positive change over the past decade. We have already discussed why Colombia's peace deal to end the longest lasting current standoff in the world would help its position (not to mention earn a Nobel Peace prize for the president). Growth in the Dominican Republic is one of the fastest in the region, and the IMF praised the country's economic and financial progress that combines economic and political stability. This stability is an important part of the country's appeal to international companies and investors (Dwyer, 2016). While it might seem counterintuitive that Argentina and Chile have the worst change over the 10-year period, it stems from the fact that they were in such good positions 10 years ago. It could be argued that they are now on their way back to their former positions as the least fragile of states on the list.

A complementing measure of the political systems described above is the Freedom in the World political rights measure. As shown in Table 5.5, about half of the countries in Latin America are considered "free," and the other half "partially free." The outlier is Venezuela which is the only country in Latin America that is not considered free. Note that Cuba falls in this column as well, but we largely aren't covering Cuba in this book.

Since 2012, there have been two changes of status in Freedom House's "Freedom in the World." Venezuela dropped from Partly Free to Not Free in

TABLE 5.5 Freedom in the World, 2018

Status		
Free	*Partly Free*	*Not Free*
Argentina	Bolivia	Venezuela
Brazil	Colombia	
Chile	Dominican Republic	
Costa Rica	Ecuador	
El Salvador	Guatemala	
Panama	Honduras	
Peru	Mexico	
Uruguay	Nicaragua	
	Paraguay	
Count: 8	9	1

Source: Freedom House (2018).

Note

Status is based on Freedom Rating which is the combination of the political rights score and civil liberties score of a given country. The following statuses are given to associated ranges: Free (1.0 to 2.5), Partly Free (3.0 to 5.0), and Not Free (5.5 to 7.0).

the 2017 report. Several factors contributed to this demotion. First, in 2016, the National Election Council refused to allow a recall of the Presidential election. Many in the opposition viewed President Maduro's election as illegitimate. Another reason for the downgrade was the refusal to pass legislation allowing for the acceptance of foreign aid, despite the worsening food and medicine shortage in the country. Furthermore, the Supreme Tribunal of Justice refused to seat three members of the opposition party that would have given the opposition party a supermajority, reversed their legislation, and stripped the body of many protections. In 2017, President Maduro and the Supreme Tribunal of Justice completely replaced the National Assembly with the National Constituent Assembly, which he controls (Freedom House, 2018).

The other change in the status involved the Dominican Republic who declined from Free to Partly Free in the 2016 report mainly due to a 2013 Constitutional Court ruling that revoked citizenships of many Dominicans of Haitian decent. There was a process put in place for them to regain their citizenship; however, many reported difficultly in trying to use it. Journalists who have reported on the Haitian citizenship issue have received threats, and a lawyer who accepted a Haitian discrimination case was murdered. Other factors that may have also played a part in the downgrade include fewer political candidates and lack of protection for media. In 2016, laws were passed to protect journalists from political defamation charges; however, it did not address the criminal penalty that remains for "defaming" private people, the president, and foreign politicians (Freedom House, 2018).

Political Risk

The Economist Intelligence Unit's Democracy Index provides a snapshot of the state of democracy worldwide for 165 independent states and 2 territories. This covers almost the entire population of the world and the vast majority of the world's states. (Microstates are excluded.) The Democracy Index is based on five categories: *electoral process and pluralism*; *civil liberties*; *functioning of government*; *political participation*; and *political culture*. Based on its scores on a range of indicators within these categories, each country is then itself classified as one of four types of regime: "full democracy"; "flawed democracy"; "hybrid regime"; and "authoritarian regime" (The Economist, 2018) (see Table 5.6).

Latin America's average score declined from 5.33 in 2016 to 5.26 in 2017 (The Economist, 2018). Nevertheless, the region remains the most democratic in the developing world. Latin America scores well above the global average for electoral process and pluralism (many parties), but its performance is less impressive in other categories. For example, Latin America's average score is only slightly ahead of the global average for functioning of government, as well as for political participation, reflecting the region's issues with corruption, organized crime (with the already high murder rate related to drug trafficking rising throughout the region in 2017), and low levels of political engagement. The region falls below the global average for political culture, reflecting relatively low levels of popular confidence in democracy. According to Latinobarómetro, a Chilean pollster which publishes annual assessments of public perceptions of democracy in eight Latin American countries, public support for democracy has steadily declined since polling began in 1995, falling to 53% in 2017. (Paradoxically, support for authoritarian rule has also declined over time) (The Economist, 2018).

Most countries had only minor changes in their overall scores in 2017 over last year. However, two countries in the region shifted categories. Ecuador improved from a "hybrid regime" to a "flawed democracy," reflecting efforts by the newly inaugurated president, Lenín Moreno, to combat some of the more controversial excesses of his predecessor, Rafael Correa, particularly with respect to press freedom and efforts to fight corruption. Venezuela, by contrast, moved from a "hybrid regime" to an "authoritarian regime," joining Cuba in that category. This reflects Venezuela's continued slide towards dictatorship as the government has side-lined the opposition-dominated National Assembly, jailed or disenfranchised leading opposition politicians, and suppressed opposition protests. The region now counts just 1 "full democracy" (Uruguay), 16 "flawed democracies," 5 "hybrid regimes," and 2 "authoritarian regimes" (The Economist, 2018).

Brazil's president, Michel Temer, narrowly avoided a trial over corruption charges after his allies in Congress voted to block two separate requests by the prosecutor-general to open a trial at the Supreme Court. The entire region felt the fallout from the corrupt practices of Brazilian construction and engineering

TABLE 5.6 Democracy Index Ranking

	Rank			Overall Score			2017 Category
	2007	2017	Δ in Rank	2007	2017	% Δ in Overall Score	
Uruguay	27	18	9	8.0	8.1	1	Full Democracy
Costa Rica	25	23	2	8.0	7.9	−1	Flawed democracy
Chile	30	26	4	7.9	7.8	−1	Flawed democracy
Panama	44	45	−1	7.4	7.1	−4	Flawed democracy
Argentina	54	48	6	6.6	7.0	6	Flawed democracy
Brazil	42	49	−7	7.4	7.0	−5	Flawed democracy
Colombia	67	53	14	6.4	6.7	5	Flawed democracy
Dominican Republic	74	55	19	6.1	6.7	10	Flawed democracy
Peru	75	61	14	6.1	6.5	7	Flawed democracy
El Salvador	70	65	5	6.2	6.4	3	Flawed democracy
Mexico	53	66	−13	6.7	6.4	−4	Flawed democracy
Paraguay	71	71	0	6.2	6.3	2	Flawed democracy
Ecuador	92	76	16	5.6	6.0	7	Flawed democracy
Guatemala	77	80	−3	6.1	5.9	−3	Hybrid regime
Honduras	69	82	−13	6.3	5.7	−10	Hybrid regime
Bolivia	81	89	−8	5.6	5.5	−2	Hybrid regime
Nicaragua	89	105	−16	5.7	4.7	−18	Hybrid regime
Venezuela	93	117	−24	5.4	3.9	−28	Authoritarian
U.S.	17	21	−4	8.2	8.0	−2	Flawed democracy
China	138	139	−1	3.0	3.1	3	Authoritarian

Source: The Economist (2018).

Note
Ranks are out of 165 independent states, and overall scores are out of 10. Sorted by 2017 rank.

firm Odebrecht who was at the center of the scandal due to its operations in several countries over the years. These allegations cost the Peruvian president, Pedro Pablo Kuczynski, his job, and led to the forced removal from office of the Ecuadorean vice-president, Jorge Glas. Investigations of possible bribes from Odebrecht received by politicians continue in Peru, Colombia, Panama, the Dominican Republic, and elsewhere.

In several countries, lower overall scores reflected departures from democratic norms. In Guatemala, President Jimmy Morales sparked a political crisis after he tried to expel Iván Velázquez, the head of the UN-backed International Commission against Impunity in Guatemala, as the body moved to investigate allegations that a drug-trafficking cartel had funded Mr. Morales's presidential campaign. The Supreme Court vetoed Mr. Velázquez's expulsion, but Congress upheld Mr. Morales's presidential immunity.

At the presidential election in Honduras in November of 2017, there were serious irregularities in the country's voting process. In Nicaragua, the ruling Frente Sandinista de la Liberación Nacional won a sweeping victory at the November municipal elections that the Organization of American States criticized as unfair. In Bolivia, President Evo Morales overrode the result of a 2016 referendum which rejected an extension of presidential term limits and had the Supreme Court (dominated by loyalists) declare him eligible for a fourth presidential run in 2019 (The Economist, 2018).

Finally, as shown in Table 5.6, we have compared a 10-year change by country in both rank and overall score. The table is sorted by 2017 rank from best to worst. For reference, the United States and China are included. A repeated message here is that not only has Uruguay done well in 2017, but it has also been relatively stable over the past decade, only moving 1% in its overall score. Costa Rica and Chile have also remained relatively steady. Nicaragua and Venezuela are not only at the bottom of the overall list, but they are also the biggest decreases per the percentage change. This is a bad signal for both of those countries as it appears that Nicaragua is on a trajectory to becoming an Authoritarian regime along with Venezuela. With that in mind, we will now shift to the Leftist threat in Latin America.

Leftist Threat in Latin America

The data from various organizations show that Latin America has not completely learned the lessons of the past. Due to poor institutions and the political culture of the strongman – which still reins in much of the region – countries in Latin America seem perennially susceptible to falling into the grip of socialist, populist governments. This is due to the continued presence of poverty in the region (discussed earlier in this chapter). Combined with very low scores on matters of human development, it leaves the region in a difficult situation, and ultimately, with a vulnerable political system.

Latin American populist political movements are all too eager to exploit the poverty and inequality that still characterizes great parts of the region. They do this in order to push for an anti-democratic and anti-capitalist agenda that is hostile to both the internal and external business interest in the region.

The leftist turn has not only afflicted small countries in Latin America, like Nicaragua, but rather large economies like Venezuela, Ecuador, and Bolivia. It should be noted that Argentina was on this list of leftist countries in the prior version of this book and has fortunately been lifted from this list with the removal of the Kirchner regime. Before the demise of the Venezuelan strong-man Hugo Chavez, Venezuela led the ALBA countries, including Ecuador, Bolivia, and Nicaragua, in a political movement he referred to as "21st-century Socialism." It is characterized mainly by attacks on private interests and the degradation from within of democratic institutions so that regularly held elections are skewed to those in power. The end result was evident to all in the aftermath of Hugo Chavez's death in Venezuela in 2013, wherein his self-appointed successor won a rigged election that has thrown the country into political and economic uncertainty. While the Leftist threat might leave the potential investor in doubt as to the public institutions in Latin America, the private institutions offer some hope.

Public vs. Private Institutions

The good news for Latin America is that its private sector is in much better shape than its public, political sector. This is relevant for both the political climate and the investment climate in Latin America. As free trade with advanced nations like the United States and the European Union progresses, and they invest in the Latin American region, there occurs a transfer of ideas and ways of organizing business and political life. This should eventually impact Latin America's political life in positive ways. A key example of this is NAFTA, which has benefited Mexico tremendously since its inception. It should be noted that it has also benefitted the United States and Canada.

Upon partnering with the U.S. and other Western nations, the Latin American countries often commit to adopt modern, more agile, and less burdensome rules and regulations. Ultimately, they need to implement them accordingly. For example, the United States fined Odebrecht US$3.5 billion for a corruption scandal that covered much of Latin America and two Portuguese speaking African countries – Angola and Mozambique. That figure is nearly double the largest record settlement ever under America's Foreign Corrupt Practices Act (The Economist, 2016). This is just one example of how Western influence is helping the region become less corrupt. Usually the first institutions to adopt these more transparent methods are in the private sector.

In Table 5.7, the reader can see that while public institutions receive a regional non-weighted rank of 107, private institutions receive a 92. Since

TABLE 5.7 Selected Global Competitive Index Component Ranks

Country	Public Institutions	Private Institutions	Difference between Public and Private	Corporate Ethics	Quality of Management Schools
Argentina	112	118	6	130	39
Brazil	110	99	−11	126	95
Chile	37	31	−6	39	27
Colombia	126	75	−51	113	63
Costa Rica	47	52	5	46	21
Dominican Republic	129	121	−8	132	97
Ecuador	132	115	−17	125	91
El Salvador	136	127	−9	128	114
Guatemala	114	82	−32	93	46
Honduras	127	77	−50	92	110
Mexico	125	90	−35	117	67
Nicaragua	115	117	2	111	62
Panama	77	64	−13	87	89
Paraguay	130	131	1	134	126
Peru	123	91	−32	121	90
Uruguay	34	37	3	35	57
Venezuela	137	133	−4	137	68
Latin America	123	91	−32	117	74
China	36	63	27	49	50
U.S.	20	17	−3	19	6

Source: The World Economic Forum (2018).

Note
Ranks are out of 137 economies.

there are three different components on the table, it is ranked in alphabetical order of country. While we will delve further into the components of the Global Competiveness Index in Chapter 7, we selected the components of *Public Institutions*, *Private Institutions*, and *Corporate Ethics* in order to illustrate that the private sector institutions are superior to the public sector institutions in nearly every country – sometimes significantly so Column three shows the difference between the rankings of the public and private sectors, where a positive sign illustrates cases where the public sector is better than the private sector. Colombia and Honduras are two extreme cases of divergence between the two sectors. The potential investor would be wise to deal with private institutions in those countries in particular. Chile (and to a lesser extent, Uruguay) stands out for both its public and private institutions, yet even it is not near the ranks of the United States. The Chinese investor may find doing business with the public sector easier in Latin America than the West does due to its relative proximity in ranks about the public institutions in a number of countries.

The fourth column of Table 5.7 delves a bit deeper into private institutions to examine the corporate ethics ranks of Latin America among its own countries and the rest of the world. Not surprisingly, Chile and Uruguay hold the best positions in the region. Indeed, the correlation between the private institutions ranking and the corporate ethics ranking is 0.92, meaning that they move strongly together. Whether good corporate ethics *cause* strong private institutions or vice versa is a matter of debate. What is not debatable is that a country cannot have one without the other. The quality of corporate ethics and private institutions go hand in hand. Latin American countries would do well to work on them simultaneously and include public institutions in their efforts.

Political Risk Management

Political risk in Latin America should be a major concern for investors in the region. Defining political risk as the effect that a government could have on the Doing Business framework in the country could be the precise guide for developing business in Latin America. As seen in different chapters of this book, the economic risk leads to poor performance, affecting monetary policy and the economic development in the region. Political risk represents the question "How much can government affect business?"

The first indicator for understanding political risk in Latin America is the credit rate of the nation. The credit rate is related to the interest rate that the government receives when issuing debt by bond or other monetary mechanism. If a country has a high risk, the interest rate will be higher. The opposite applies if the country has a low risk. Discerning this fact could be one of the best pieces of advice an investor can take.

Figure 5.2 demonstrates the relationship between political risk and credit risk. Along the y-axis is the credit risk, where the countries that are higher on the y-axis are in a better credit situation. Essentially, they will get a lower

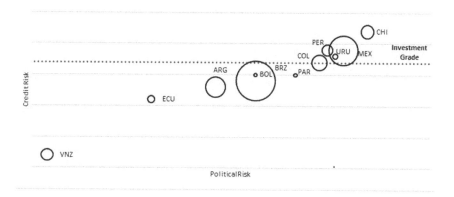

FIGURE 5.2 Political by Credit Risk

interest rate when they issue bonds, which is an advantage. Chile, Peru, Mexico, and Uruguay are at the top of this figure. The horizontal dotted line represents a hurdle in the investment world known as *investment grade*.

Many large investment portfolios around the world can only invest in investment grade countries or funds. Thus, when a country reaches investment grade along the y-axis, it stands to receive a flood of investment and will consequently have access to cheaper money. As one can imagine, when a country reaches this level, it is keen on remaining above it.

This is where political risk enters the equation. The political risk represented on the x-axis is correlated with credit risk. As with the y-axis, the farther to the right on Figure 5.2 a country is positioned, the lower its political risk. It stands to reason that the higher the political risk, the higher the credit risk. The worst-case scenario for a country is to be high on both types of risk, as indicative of countries in the bottom left portion of this figure. Venezuela is currently in this region. When the first version of this book was written, the data for 2012 placed Argentina next to Venezuela (actually in a slightly worse position). Since then Argentina is moving up and to the right. This scenario is the subject of the case study in this chapter because it sums up the relationship between political risk, credit risk, and what it means to the investor thinking about investing in the region.

Another important aspect when analyzing political risk is the confidence that citizens have in their institutions. For example, the institution that the citizens trust the most in Latin America is the church, followed by the armed forces, then television. The information gathered by Latinobarometro demonstrates that the least trustworthy institution is the congress. This is important because the congress makes relevant decisions on the future of the country; therefore, the lack of confidence is a major problem when doing business. Furthermore, this lack of confidence with the congress has not changed over the past decade.

Figure 5.3 demonstrates the level of trust placed in the church, armed forces, television, labor unions, private sector, and congress on a scale from 1–5, where 1 equals "none" and 5 equals "a lot." While over 40% of citizens have a lot of trust in the church, only 6% trust the congress a lot. In fact, none of the other four institutions have even 20% "trust a lot" levels. With that detail, one can answer questions such as: what country's citizens trust their congress the most? (answer: Costa Rica and Honduras), or what country's citizens trust their labor unions the most? (answer: Brazil and Panama). The figure also shows which institutions are gaining or losing the most trust over the past decade.

The lack of trust has driven the citizens of Latin America to think of dictatorship and/or authoritarianism as a plausible solution. Venezuela demonstrated in the 2013 presidential election that although the government is not as transparent as it could be, it has a connection with most of the population given the victory of the late Hugo Chavez's right-hand man, Nicolas Maduro. This type of

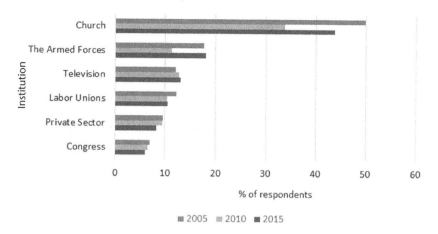

% of respondents

■ 2005   ■ 2010   ■ 2015

FIGURE 5.3   Institutional Trust

government perpetuating a certain type of politics is becoming more and more constant in Latin America. In the last edition of this book we listed a number of examples, but since it is constantly changing, we challenge the reader to do a current search for sitting presidents that may be positioning themselves to stay in power (e.g., Evo Morales of Bolivia).

Rule of Law and Other Obstacles to Doing Business

The rule of law is the principle that law should govern a country, as opposed to being governed by individual government officials. It primarily refers to the influence and authority of law within society, particularly as it constrains the behavior of government officials. The Rule of Law indicator by the Worldwide Governance report within the World Bank represents the confidence that society has in law enforcement institutions as well as the likelihood that laws will be enforced (see Figure 5.4). The data is presented in percentiles based on rank. 214 countries were included in the ranking used to calculate the percentiles, where a higher number is better.

As a benchmark, the United States is in the 92nd percentile, closely follow by Chile, then Uruguay. With the notable exception of Costa Rica and Panama, Central America is particularly poor in terms of rule of law. Not surprisingly, the near authoritarian regimes of Venezuela and Bolivia seem to have politicians "above the law."

Operating within the rule of law is important because it loosely translates to protection of property rights. In countries where the rule of law is strong, investors can make wise investment decisions based on long-term planning because they are confident that governments won't seize their property for political gain. This scenario has happened in countries such as Venezuela and Argentina,

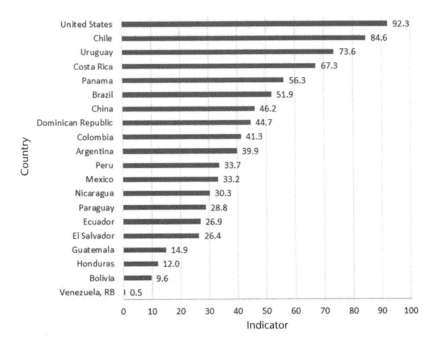

FIGURE 5.4 Rule of Law Indicator

resulting in a quick drop in foreign direct investment. Indeed, the robustness of the rule of law and the level of foreign direct investment are highly correlated. This correlation is especially strong when an investor is considering investing in a project that has a long-term maturity. An example is the mining sector. It often takes over ten years for a mine to break even on its initial capital investment. This could mean two or greater terms of office for a president in Latin America. While in one year a country may have a pro-business president (e.g., Macri in Argentina) and everything appears to be good, the following election could result in a swing toward populism, resulting in the expropriation of natural resources assets.

With that risk in mind, if one is considering investing in countries that are on the bottom half of Figure 5.4, then they would be wise to do so in sectors that have short-term payoffs. Another option that gives one an ability to reduce the risk of a low rule of law is to have a local partner. Governments are less likely to interfere with the business dealings of locals than those of foreign interests.

As mentioned in the previous few paragraphs, intricately tied to the rule of law are property rights. Table 5.8 demonstrates the ranking of property rights throughout the world. As usual, the lower the number, the better the rank. Since there are three components of the Table, it is sorted alphabetically.

Instead of focusing on Venezuela, which is at the bottom of this list as well, let's turn to Ecuador, which is the second worst country for property rights in

TABLE 5.8 Property Protection Ranks

Country	Property Rights	Intellectual Property Protection	Reliability of Police Service	Diff. b/t Property Rights and Police
Argentina	108	89	120	12
Brazil	64	63	103	39
Chile	34	56	24	−10
Colombia	88	74	114	26
Costa Rica	38	33	57	19
Dominican Republic	91	82	132	41
Ecuador	127	108	94	−33
El Salvador	121	123	135	14
Guatemala	87	83	127	40
Honduras	97	81	131	34
Mexico	84	67	134	50
Nicaragua	125	121	84	−41
Panama	39	38	66	27
Paraguay	112	109	129	17
Peru	107	105	130	23
Uruguay	37	41	83	46
Venezuela	137	137	137	0
Latin America	91	82	120	29
China	50	49	60	10
U.S.	20	14	22	2

Source: World Economic Forum (2018).

Note
Ranks are out of 137 economies.

Latin America. Ecuador has a particularly poor ranking because it has been dis-placing indigenous groups to make way for mining operations (Malo, 2016). This will be a case study in Chapter 4 which focuses on doing business in sus-tainable ways, including with indigenous people.

In many ways similar, yet different, the case of Nicaragua is also tied to mining. Yet, it is not the large mining companies that are threatening to take the land of indigenous peoples in Nicaragua. It is the Nicaraguans themselves as they are lured by the possibility of finding gold and lumber (Robles, 2016). Whether the investor is considering buying a vineyard in Argentina or starting a coffee plantation in El Salvador (which are both popular), one must take into consideration property rights. Coupled with the rule of law, if the two together are promising, then the venture will be more valuable than otherwise.

The second column in Table 5.8 shows the affiliation of the specific type of property rights with intellectual property. While this is different than the prior two examples, it still falls under the rule of law umbrella. It shouldn't surprise the reader that property rights and intellectual property protection rankings are correlated 0.94. Countries that value property rights in general tend to also value intellectual property rights. This is especially relevant for firms such as Google, Dell, and Hewlett Packard that wish to base part of their development and customer support in Latin America. They wisely select countries such as Brazil and Panama to set up their operations.

The final column of Table 5.8 pertains to whether the country can actually enforce property rights. Even if a country has stringent laws pertaining to intellectual property rights, if they are not enforceable, then they are relatively meaningless. While the correlation between reliability of police service and property rights isn't as highly correlated as intellectual property rights and overall property rights, they are still positively correlated. This means that the countries that rank well on property rights tend to do well in enforcing them. A couple of countries deviate from this trend, resulting in imperfections in the correlations.

We added a column that simply subtracts the rank of property rights from reliability of police service in order to examine where the large deviations exist. If the number in that last column is positive and large, then there exists a separation between what the country espouses to do in terms of property rights and enforcement. One should be particularly wary of the countries that have differences of 40 or greater. For example, Mexico has relatively strict property rights as part of law, but it is notoriously weak in enforcing them. The same is the case with Uruguay and Brazil. On paper, they appear to be a great place to do business. However, by digging deeper into the enforcement area, alternative conclusions may exist. Thus, a would-be investor should not rely on a single rubric when analyzing where to do business in Latin America. Instead, attempt to triangulate one's position and gather as much information as possible before making a final decision, because as the overall row on Latin America attests (with a difference score of 18), it is better at making laws than enforcing them.

Conclusion

This chapter began with an overview of the complex political climate in Latin America. While the names of the presidents and other relevant individuals will change since this writing, many of the scenarios will not. For example, poverty and inequality will still be at the forefront of many politicians' agendas.

We went into detail about how and why poverty and inequality affect the political processes in Latin America. The level of poverty in general is decreasing as the shift in the population from the rural countryside to the urban areas continues. There is still room for this shift to continue, but in many cities such as Sao Paulo, Mexico City, Lima, and Rio de Janeiro, space is becoming a problem. The next part of that section discussed the specific situation of urban poverty. At first glance, one might assume that if the citizens move away from the poor conditions of the countryside, then their lives will improve. Yet anyone that has visited or at least seen a favela in Latin America knows that in some cases it is better to be poor in the countryside than in the city. At the very least, the violence is much lower in the countryside.

With crime in mind, we moved to the next section of the chapter. The homicide rates tell a frightening story. Latin America has many of the most violent countries in the world. This doesn't just affect to which countries universities choose to send their students on study abroad, but also where companies chose to send their employees.

After an eye-opening discussion of crime in the region, we shift to corruption and transparency. While it has long been known that corruption is especially robust in Latin America, the current trend of exposing and prosecuting those that participate in the illegal act is both astonishing and commendable. It seems that as people move out of poverty into the middle class and start paying taxes, they demand that their money isn't squandered on padding wallets of politicians. There have been an unprecedented number of riots in Latin America calling for justice. It remains to be seen whether the judicial branches are able to fulfill their mandates of upholding the rule of law.

Upholding the rule of law has been particularly challenging in the Leftist countries where the regional strongman seems to be able to control all aspects of government and, in many cases, business. Fortunately, the private sector institutions are adjusting to worldwide trade practices that are more transparent, not to mention efficient. Hopefully the public sector will follow the lead of the private sector. If this were to happen, doing business in the region will become less politically risky, resulting in improved prospects in the region.

The Case of Venezuela

Although the business environment of Venezuela is far from ideal, there remains some potential. The largest opportunity for Venezuela is its oil reserves. They are the largest known reserves in the entire world. In April of 2017, it was confirmed that Nicolas Maduro would retain control of the country's vast oil industry and its reserves. Unfortunately, much of Venezuela's oil resources are currently inaccessible due to the high costs of obtaining it as well as other economic difficulties.

Because he has control of the country's oil resources, it is up to Maduro to find a way to fund – and basically save – Venezuela. It seems that Maduro needs to find a way to show good faith in how he moves forward in the industry because foreign investors are struggling to find patience in dealing with him and his government. Investors will be much more eager to invest in Venezuela and its oil if progress is seen. The problem lies within making that progress. China and Russia have both involved themselves in giving loans to the struggling country, which may be the key to the its progression. While these loans will leave the country with even more debt than already exists, it seems this is one of the very last chances the country has.

Another threat the country is facing is its extremely large number of nationalized businesses and industries. These nationalizations were started when Chavez was in power. Today, the country owns over 500 businesses, and most them are losing money. In a study performed by the nonprofit Transparency International they identified at least 511 different companies that are either majority or wholly owned by the Venezuelan government (Wyss, 2017). These companies range from anything from dairy, medicine, petroleum, aerospace, hotels, and more. They also discovered that 70% of these businesses are losing money, which may be contributing to the country's overall economic crisis. In 2016, these businesses lost a combined total of more than US$129 billion. This comes at a time when it is more important than ever for the government to be as smart as it can be with its money. This nationalization of businesses has made it less appealing for foreign investors to start business ventures in the country for fear of their company and profits being taken over by the state. An example of this is portrayed in a case study of the nationalization of the Venezuelan oil industry (Childress, 2017). This case study describes how in the 1990s, Venezuela hoped to accelerate the development of the oil industry in the country since they were sitting on massive reserves of oil but lacked the technology and methods to efficiently develop the industry. They planned to achieve this development through a program called the Apertura Petrolera. This program would involve incentivizing foreign investors to help with the country's oil industry development. Huge international developers, such as ConocoPhillips and ExxonMobil Corp., went through with the program and brought new technology and expertise with them. However, when Hugo Chavez came to power, he introduced new measures that hurt these foreign investors, such as an increase in royalties and taxes paid to the state. Then in 2007, the government under Chavez passed a measure that would involve a nationalization program to transfer ownership of these projects to the state. Some companies agreed to these measures and negotiated with the government's demands; however, others such as ConocoPhillips and ExxonMobil Corp. sued the Venezuelan government for billions of dollars. In 2014, Exxon won its case for a much lower settlement while Conoco is still awaiting its awarded payment. This is just one example of how the nationalization of industries has not only hurt foreign investors but Venezuela as well. If foreign investors continue to diminish and nationalized companies continue to lose money, this will prove to be a major threat to the wellbeing of the country and anyone looking to do business there.

Political History of Venezuela

In order to understand the politics of Venezuela, a brief history discussion is in order. In 1989, a member of the Democratic Action Party, Carlos Andres

Perez, was elected president. During his term he launched an austerity program with IMF loans and promoted economic reforms based on a free market (The Editors of Encyclopedia Britannica, 2016). As a result of his reforms, hundreds died in street violence during large strikes and protests. He was removed from office in 1993, and shortly after in 1994, he was arrested for embezzlement and misuse of public funds. Some consider this the beginning of the mistrust between Venezuela and the Western-backed IMF that continues to this day.

This then begins the era of Hugo Chavez, which is where the current situation of Venezuela started. He was elected in 1998 while the country was disillusioned and tired of established parties. He launched a Bolivarian Revolution, named for Simon Bolivar – a hero of South American Independence. Key aspects of this revolution were nationalism, centralizing the country's economy, and having a strong military which actively worked on engagements in projects for public interest (Nelson, 2017). In his first year as president, Chavez received an approval rating of 80%, which was a response to his promises to end corruption, increase social policies funded from oil profits, and redistribute the country's oil fortune. Through his popularity, he was also able to create a new constitution of Venezuela. In this constitution, he gave himself total power of all three branches of government. He also called for new elections for every single elected official in the country, which was carried out in 2000. During this election, Chavez was elected to a six-year term and was also able to establish a large enough majority in the National Assembly to pass a law enabling him to enact laws by decree alone. While many people were originally drawn to Chavez by his alternative to the two-party system and his promises of advocating for the lower class, during his rule, some began to grow weary of his increasingly radical actions and policies. He also alienated the country from the U.S. with anti-U.S. sentiments and an alignment with Cuba. By 2002, his approval rating fell as low as 30%. He remained in power after multiple coup attempts and was re-elected in 2005. After this election, he began to forge ahead with his plans for "21st century socialism" and nationalized many of the country's key industries such as oil, electricity, and telecommunications. By 2011, 96% of Venezuela's exports were oil related, compared to 77% when Chavez came to power. After a battle with cancer, including many surgeries in Cuba, Hugo Chavez died in 2013.

The effect of Chavez's rule still has an impact on Venezuela today. The country went from being independent on oil to completely dependent on oil during his presidency. This was a fine spot to be in when oil prices were booming; however, in recent years, oil prices have been falling. Regardless, this leaves the country in an extremely dangerous and vulnerable position, which places all their dependence on the oil sector. Also, due to the immense nationalization of businesses and industries in the country under Chavez, the country has been passed over for foreign investment, and many local companies have moved to other nearby countries. In 2011, out of the US$150 billion that was invested by foreigners in Latin America, only US$5 billion was invested in Venezuela. This is because foreign investors do not want the political risk of their companies being taken over by the government and losing profit. Finally, under Chavez, Venezuela became one of the most violent countries in the world. In 2011, the murder rate per 100,000 citizens was 45; at the beginning of his presidency, this rate was 25. A major part of this violence can be attributed to unrest and the poor economic situation. Overall, these conditions have made Venezuela an increasingly difficult and dangerous place to do business for not only foreign companies but locals as well.

Following Chavez's death, his appointed successor, Nicolas Maduro, was elected by a very narrow margin in 2013. However, the opposing party did not believe these results. In this same year, the ruling Socialist Party and its allies won local elections by a 10% margin. During Maduro's rule, in 2014, oil prices dropped, leading to hyperinflation in the country. This economic crisis also made it impossible for Maduro to continue the costly social programs started by Chavez which had been funded by oil revenues. Due to this and many other problems being faced by the country, Maduro's popularity is waning, which brings us to the current political situation that was discussed earlier in this chapter.

At this point, it is up to the potential investor to determine if and when the current regime will fall. If it does fall, will the people demand a more market-focused president similar to what happened in Argentina?

References

BBC News (2018). "Brazil Corruption Scandals: All You Need to Know." www.bbc. com/news/world-latin-america-35810578/, accessed May, 2018.

CEPAL, U.N. (2012). "Poverty Continues to Fall in Latin America, But Still Affects 167 Million People." www.cepal.org/en/pressreleases/poverty-continues-fall-latin-america-still-affects-167-million-people, accessed March, 2018.

CEPAL, U.N. (2013). *Social Panorama of Latin America*. Santiago, Chile.

CEPAL, U.N. (2015). "Poverty Rates." http://interwp.cepal.org/sisgen/ConsultaIntegrada. asp?idIndicador=182&idioma=i, accessed March, 2018.

CEPAL, U.N. (2017). "Social panorama of Latin America 2016/2017." www.cepal.org/ en/publications/41599-social-panorama-latin-america-2016, accessed March, 2018.

Childress, Patrick (2017). "Case Study: The Nationalization of the Venezuelan Oil Industry." *Pardon Our Interruption*, August 7, 2017.

Dwyer, R. (2016). "Dominican Republic Guide 2016: Political Stability." *Euromoney*. www.euromoney.com/article/b12knnns8wvj58/dominican-republic-guide-2016-political-stability, accessed June, 2017.

Freedom House (2018). "Democracy in Crisis." https://freedomhouse.org/report/ freedom-world/freedom-world-2018, accessed May, 2018.

Fund for Peace (2017). "Fragile States Index." http://fundforpeace.org/fsi/data/, accessed February, 2018.

Jaitman, Laura (2017). "The Costs of Crime and Violence." *Interamerican Development Bank.* https://publications.iadb.org/bitstream/handle/11319/8133/The-Costs-of-Crime-and-Violence-New-Evidence-and-Insights-in-Latin-America-and-the-Caribbean.pdf, accessed March, 2018.

Malo, Sebastien (2016). "U.N. Experts Slam Ecuador over Forced Closure of Land Rights Group." *Reuters.* www.reuters.com/article/us-un-ecuador-landrights/u-n-experts-slam-ecuador-over-forced-closure-of-land-rights-group-idUSKBN14J1TW, accessed February, 2018.

Messner, J. (2017) "Fragile States Index Annual Report 2017." *Fund for Peace.* http://fundforpeace.org/fsi/2017/05/14/fragile-states-index-2017-annual-report/9511717 05-fragile-states-index-annual-report-2017/, accessed March, 2018.

Nelson, Brian A (2017). "Hugo Chávez." *Encyclopædia Britannica*, November 22, 2017.

Robles, Frances (2016). "Nicaragua Dispute Over Indigenous Land Erupts in Wave of Killings." *New York Times.* www.nytimes.com/2016/10/17/world/americas/nicaragua-dispute-over-indigenous-land-erupts-in-wave-of-killings.html, accessed December, 2017.

Spillan, J. E., Virzi, N., & Garita, M. (2014). *Doing Business in Latin America: Challenges and Opportunities.* New York: Routledge.

The Economist (2016). "Brazil's Gargantuan Corruption Scandal Goes Global." www.economist.com/news/21712445-american-authorities-reach-record-bribery-related-settlement-two-huge-companies, accessed January, 2018.

The Economist (2018). "Democracy Index 2017." www.eiu.com/topic/democracy-index, accessed January, 2018.

The Editors of Encyclopedia Britannica (2016). "Carlos Andrés Pérez." *Encyclopædia Britannica*, April 14, 2016.

The World Bank (2018a). "Urban Poverty: An Overview." http://web.worldbank.org/WBSITE/EXTERNAL/TOPICS/EXTURBANDEVELOPMENT/EXTURBAN POVERTY/0,,contentMDK:20227679~menuPK:7173704~pagePK:148956~piPK:21 6618~theSitePK:341325,00.html, accessed April, 2018.

The World Bank (2018b). "Intentional Homicides." https://data.worldbank.org/indicator/VC.IHR.PSRC.P5, accessed March, 2018.

The World Bank (2018c). "Worldwide Governance Indicators." http://info.worldbank.org/governance/wgi/#home, accessed March, 2018.

The World Economic Forum (2018). "Global Competitiveness Report." http://reports.weforum.org/global-competitiveness-index-2017-2018/competitiveness-rankings/, accessed April, 2018.

Wyss, Jim (2017). "Venezuelan Government Controls More than 500 Businesses – and Most Are Losing Money." *Miami Herald,* March 14, 2017.

6

THE ECONOMIC CLIMATE

Overview

When the first edition of this book was written, Brazil, as part of the BRICs, was the star and perceived future of Latin America's economy. Since then, problems in Brazil that were discussed in the previous chapter helped slide the country into its worst recession in history. Fortunately, the recession there finally ended in 2017 (Leahy, 2017). Low oil prices as well as a somewhat reduction in commodity demand from China have not helped the nation. Currently, millions of Brazilians risk their recently acquired middle-class status. On the other hand, while foreign investors might be weary of Brazil, Argentina has finally addressed the stranglehold that U.S. investors had on their bond market. The result has been an influx of hard currency that the country can spend.

In this chapter, we present a detailed overview of the economic climate that exists in Latin America. From a macroeconomic and a microeconomic point of view, we discuss the dynamic economic environment that has existed since the mid-1990s, approximately where we left off in Chapter 3. Thus, we now discuss the present economy and what we believe the economic future of the region offers for business. Specifically, this chapter builds on Chapter 2 by going into more detail on GDP, trade, and inequality. While we discussed a number of historical issues that affected Latin America's economy in Chapter 3, in this chapter one can see how those issues are resonating in today's context.

It should be noted that entire semesters are taught just focusing on the economic development of Latin America. While we will elucidate many components affecting the economy in this chapter, for a more detailed discussion, we recommend *The Puzzle of Latin American Economic Development* by Patrice Franko (2007).

After analyzing inflation and GDP, we will address trade and globalization. We end the chapter with a discussion on how these macroeconomic issues affect the people of Latin America. Finally, we look at the rising middle class in Brazil to illustrate changes in its economic climate.

Economic Liberalization

Inflation Targeting

A few graphs will help to illustrate the progress that has been made in the area of price stability. As mentioned in Chapter 3 of this text, after decades of application of Keynesian economics, Latin America began the 1980s with double digit inflation. The lost decade of the 1980s left the region in an economic mess. Figure 6.1 demonstrates how bad things became for Latin America.

As per other chapters in this book, we added China and the United States for comparison reasons. Figure 6.1 shows that annual interest rates peaked at close to 40% in 1990 in Latin America. While still high by comparison in the early 1990s, at least they came down substantially with dramatic policy shifts towards inflation targeting. Compared to the United States in the same period it might appear to have been a wild ride doing business in Latin America due to its huge instability in inflation.

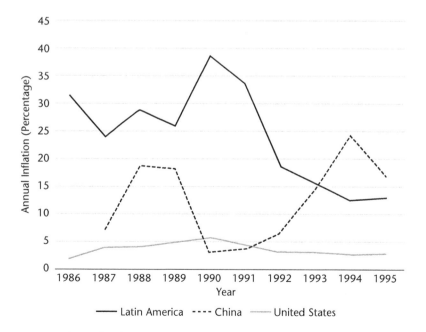

FIGURE 6.1   Annual Inflation

Figure 6.2 tells a different story of inflation in Latin America. One can see that the median inflation rate fell to under 10% in the late 1990s and stayed there. While there are exceptions, which we will discuss next, inflation appears to be largely under control in Latin America. Figure 6.1 shows a region out of sync with the rest of the world. Figure 6.2 illustrates how much closer it has become to being in line with the two biggest economies in the world. As of 2016, the median inflation rate is at its lowest, just under 4%.

As to be expected when analyzing a region as a whole, the median numbers mask a few outliers on inflation rates. Brazil, Argentina, and Venezuela stand out in their bouts with inflation. Note that the y-axis in Figure 6.3 is much larger than in the two previous figures. Argentina and Brazil had unmanageable rates above 1,000% at the end of the 1980s and early 1990s. During those times, prices changed by the day. Imagine owning a grocery store during those times. Attempting to change out stickers on every item every day to deal with the increase in prices would have given any manager fits.

We included Venezuela in this figure of outliers because it is entering similar territory of inflation above 200% for 2016. Indeed, Venezuela has by far the highest inflation rate in Latin America and is second only to South Sudan for the world's worst inflation ranking. Estimates for 2017 are around 4,000%. We don't have an exact figure because their government has not published inflation data for more than two years (Gupta, 2018). As of the publication date of this book, prices are nearly doubling every month in Venezuela. The case on Venezuela in the previous chapter highlights the political situation in the country, which exacerbates the inflation problem.

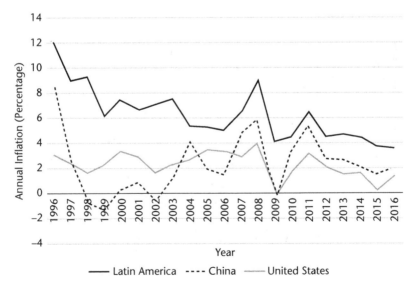

FIGURE 6.2 Annual Inflation

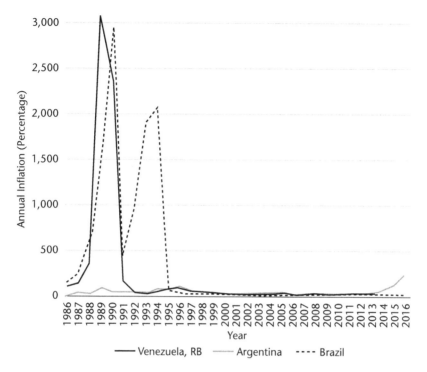

FIGURE 6.3   Annual Inflation

A lesson that is scattered throughout this book and illustrated in Figure 6.3 is that while it is important to understand the similarities of Latin American countries, there are also many differences. Therefore, one should seek a deeper understanding of the region by examining its countries individually.

Gross Domestic Product

In Chapter 2, we presented the GDP and GDP per capita for each country in Latin America at two points in time, 2006 and 2016. Figure 6.4 tells a different story by illuminating how Latin America did as a whole during the most recent recession of 2008–2009. While it is often discussed that Latin America fared better than countries from the West during the recession, Figure 6.4 helps shed light on the situation. It is true that Latin America's growth rate didn't get as low as that of the United States. Yet the growth rate in the region actually dropped more (5.9% vs. 2.5%) during the period. Per the opening statement of this chapter, prior to the recession, the economies in countries such as Brazil were large and growing at an astounding pace. To say that a negative growth rate of similar magnitude to that of the West is not relevant would underestimate the recession's negative impact on the region.

After a rough 2016, Latin America is expected to grow again in 2017 and 2018. Still, with a global environment that remains rather neutral to growth in the region, policy makers will need be cognizant to protect its most vulnerable nations (The World Bank, 2017b). The recovery should be led by Brazil and Argentina, partially due to their market size. Carlos Vegh, World Bank Chief Economist for Latin America and the Caribbean, suggested that Latin America will need to rely on internal growth made possible by labor reforms and increased infrastructure spending (The World Bank, 2017b). Mr. Vegh also focused on central bank independence to encourage growth, but not at the expense of inflation. To not pay attention to lessons from the past on inflation would be foolhardy.

Albeit not represented in Figure 6.4, we can delve deeper into the recession of 2009 at the individual country level in order to examine "what if" scenarios. For example, Argentina and Mexico had the lowest growth rate in the region at −6.3 and −4.9, respectively. Removing them from the regional average would have brought the GDP change for the recession of 2009 to essentially flat at zero. But since they are the second and third largest economies in all of Latin America, their large drops in GDP pulled down the entire region.

On the other hand, Uruguay *grew* by over 4% during the recession – the most in the region. As discussed earlier in this book, while many countries in Latin America were trading amongst the region or primarily with the United

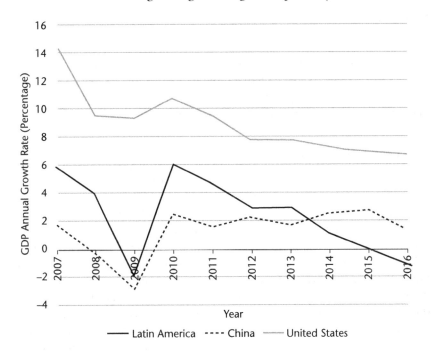

FIGURE 6.4 GDP Annual Inflation Growth Rate

States, Uruguay began an effort to "decouple" from its neighbors (The Eco-nomist, 2018a). It entered new industries like software and exported them to new markets.

Trade

Now that we have seen that the value of goods and services produced in Latin America is back to positive growth, we turn to examine how much the region is trading and with whom. Table 6.1 lists the value of imports and exports by country for two periods of time and the percentage change.

Beginning with imports, every country in Latin America except for Vene-zuela has increased the value of goods over the decade examined. Four of the countries – Bolivia, Panama, Peru, and Paraguay – have more than doubled the value of goods imported over the decade through 2016. Latin America as a

TABLE 6.1 Imports and Exports of Goods and Services (US$ billions)

Country Name	Imports			Exports		
	2006	*2016*	*% Change*	*2006*	*2016*	*% Change*
Argentina	40.5	73.6	82	53.6	69.7	30
Bolivia	3.8	10.8	189	4.8	8.3	74
Brazil	129.2	217.8	69	159.2	224.3	41
Chile	45.4	68.2	50	67.8	70.3	4
Colombia	33.4	58.5	75	28.7	40.1	40
Costa Rica	10.6	18.3	74	9.8	18.2	85
Dominican Republic	13.7	20.7	52	10.8	18.0	67
Ecuador	13.7	18.9	37	14.2	19.4	37
Guatemala	12.7	18.8	48	7.5	13.4	78
Honduras	8.4	12.5	49	6.1	9.2	51
Mexico	278.5	418.3	50	266.4	399.5	50
Nicaragua	3.8	7.5	99	2.1	5.2	144
Panama	13.0	27.4	110	12.0	24.7	106
Peru	18.8	43.0	128	27.1	43.1	59
Paraguay	5.2	10.8	108	6.3	11.4	83
El Salvador	8.6	10.5	23	4.8	6.7	40
Uruguay	6.2	10.6	71	5.9	11.2	89
Venezuela, RB	40.6	20.2	–50	67.0	27.2	–59
Latin America	686.0	1,066.4	55	754.0	1,019.9	35
China	782.8	1,950.4	149	1,023.1	2,200.0	115
U.S.	2,247.3	2,735.8	22	1,476.3	2,214.6	50
World	14,599.0	20,453.0	40	14,879.0	20,819.0	40

Source: The World Bank (2018c).

Note
Venezuela's amounts are based on estimates from the CIA World Factbook (2018).

region has increased its imports by over 50%, which is faster than the United States' and the world's growth of 22% and 40%, respectively. The biggest import into Latin America is petroleum, which is coming from the United States (World Integrated Trade Solution, 2018).

Importing oil in Latin America is a complicated topic. Because the region has tremendous reserves of petroleum, one would expect it to be a net exporter of oil. There are two issues that plague the region regarding petroleum. First, the production of oil has been hampered by state-run oil companies' inefficiencies in managing their production. Second, Latin Americans tend to send their oil to the United States for refining and then must import it back. The United States has become the world's top exporter of refined products thanks to increasing oil production, declining consumption, and a ban on crude exports. Latin America is now absorbing half of all U.S. oil product exports (Viscidi, 2015).

Latin American countries have long debated whether they have the ability and funds to build their own refining plants or take advantage of surplus capacity in the United States. Although new refineries would bring good jobs to the region along with energy security, their ability to compete without some policy changes is in doubt. Lisa Viscidi, the director of the Energy, Climate Change, and Extractive Industries Program at the Inter-American Dialogue, suggests Latin American policymakers should try to reduce demand by cutting fuel subsidies, imposing fuel economy standards, and creating stronger regulatory and fiscal incentives to promote alternative transportation (Viscidi, 2015). While this may curtail the petroleum import imbalance, it comes at a cost. Whether governments are willing to endure the cost just as they're starting to grow again remains to be seen.

Mexico stands out in terms of imports due to comprising approximately 40% of all imports for the region. Much of this has to do with its free trade agreement with the United States and Canada (i.e., NAFTA). As of the writing of this book, NAFTA is in the midst of a possible renegotiation.

While still on the topic of a NAFTA renegotiation, we can shift right in Table 6.1 to exports. Were NAFTA to be eliminated, it has been estimated that Mexico would fall into recession by 2019 since about 80% of its exports go to the United States and Canada (73% and 7%, respectively) (Navarro, 2018). Yet Mexico is not simply accepting new terms of trade that do not benefit it. It has recently joined the Trans Pacific Partnership discussed in Chapter 2. They have also been negotiating a free trade agreement with the EU, with plans on engaging more with the Chinese as well (Navarro, 2018).

Before shifting to with whom Latin America trades, it is noted that the rate of growth of Latin American exports has been slower than its imports. While its percentage of overall world imports has grown faster than the rest of the world, its exports have not. That said, the region still has a trade surplus, unlike the United States. Latin America represents about 5% of the world's imports and exports. Not surprisingly, China's increase in both imports and exports has been triple that of Latin America over the past decade.

Finally, the case of Chile should be addressed since it was the only country that had export growth of less than 10% in the past decade. Chile's exports grew at 4% over the period. The country's exports are heavily dependent on copper, of which Chile is the world's largest exporter. From 2011 to 2016 the price of copper was cut in half (Statistica, 2018). Since then, the price has started to rebound, and we encourage the reader interested in the exports of Chile to follow the link to the World Bank in order to update Table 6.1. As the reader will see in the next chapter, Chile is a very competitive country in the region, and these export numbers should not be the sole reason for not considering doing business there.

With Table 6.2 we shift the focus from overall trade by country to which specific country is most important to each Latin American country in terms of trade.

The United States is the top importer from and exporter to Latin America, which is partially due to its proximity, historical ties, and sheer market size. However, China which is the largest exporter to seven countries in Latin America and the largest importer from three, is gaining influence in the region. China currently has bilateral Free Trade Agreements with three countries in the region (Peru, Chile, and Costa Rica) and is considering FTAs with Colombia and Panama (Reuters, 2017). The negotiations for Panama's agreement are set to begin June of 2018, and if they are successful could further weaken the United States' dominance in the region.

Further evidence of China's advance in the region can be found on the World Integrated Trade Solution database, referenced in the Table 6.2 (World Integrated Trade Solution, 2014). Seven countries imported the most from China in 2016. Only five years ago, there were just two countries that imported the most from China (Panama and Paraguay). The United States lost three of them: Brazil, Chile and Peru. All three are very large markets. Brazil lost the other two: Bolivia and Uruguay. Additionally, three other countries are close to having China as their main supplier of imports: Ecuador, Nicaragua, and Venezuela. All three of these countries are turning to China instead of the United States as their primary import provider. Needless to say, if Mexico were to be added to this list, the sphere of trade influence in the region from the United States to China will be effectively transformed.

Another interesting aspect of the table is Uruguay's largest destination for exports. The destination of 19% of the goods from Uruguay is the country's Free Trade Zones, and then Brazil (DLA Piper, 2016). These zero-tax zones are one of the most attractive features of the Uruguayan economy. They allow foreign investors to operate in them without paying any taxes or customs. Investors are also permitted to freely exchange foreign currency with less regulatory steps than would be necessary outside of the zones. Although the

TABLE 6.2 Top Trading Partners of Latin American Countries (US$ billions)

Country	For Imports	Value	For Exports	Value
Argentina	Brazil	13.6	Brazil	9.0
Bolivia	China	1.7	Brazil	2.4
Brazil	China	30.7	China	35.6
Chile	China	14.1	China	17.1
Colombia	U.S.	12	U.S.	10.2
Costa Rica	U.S.	5.7	U.S.	4.1
Dominican Republic	U.S.	7.5	U.S.	4.6
Ecuador	U.S.	3.8	U.S.	5.4
El Salvador	U.S.	3.7	U.S.	2.6
Guatemala	U.S.	6.5	U.S.	3.7
Honduras	U.S.	3.3	U.S.	2.0
Mexico	U.S.	195.9	U.S.	318.7
Nicaragua	U.S.	0.9	U.S.	2.4
Panama	China	2.9	U.S.	2.3
Paraguay	China	2.6	Brazil	3.0
Peru	China	8.2	China	8.5
Uruguay	China	1.5	Free Trade Zones	1.3
Venezuela★	U.S.	4.5	U.S.	9.5

Source: World Bank (2016).

Notes
★ Venezuela's amounts are based on estimates from the CIA World Factbook: www.cia.gov/library/publications/the-world-factbook/geos/ve.html.
The U.S. is the top importer from and exporter to Latin America which is partially due to its proximity and historical ties. However, China which is the largest exporter to seven countries in Latin America and the largest importer from three, is gaining influence in the region. China currently has bilateral Free Trade Agreements with three countries in the region (Peru, Chile, and Costa Rica) and is considering FTAs with Colombia and Panama. The negotiations for Panama's agreement are set to begin June of 2018, and if they are successful could further weaken the U.S.'s dominance in the region.
Another interesting aspect of the table is Uruguay's largest destination for exports. The destination of 19.42% of the goods from Uruguay is the country's Free Trade Zones. These zero-tax zones are one of the most attractive features of the Uruguayan economy. They allow foreign investors to operate in them without paying any taxes or customs. Investors are also permitted to freely exchange foreign currency with less regulatory steps than would be necessary outside of the zones. Although the country's value of imports from its top exporting trading partner is the second smallest in the region and value of exports to its top importing trading partner is the smallest in the region, Investors should not discount trade in this small country, as it has the largest GDP per capita (see Table 3. GDP) in Latin America.

country's value of imports from its top exporting trading partner is the second smallest in the region and value of exports to its top importing trading partner is the smallest in the region, investors should not discount trade in this small country. Per Table 2.1 in Chapter 2, Uruguay has the largest GDP per capita in Latin America.

Globalization

An element that is affecting trade within the region is its level of globalization. Table 6.3 illustrates that level per the KOF Index of Globalization. After the country list, the first column shows each country's rank in the world for 2015. The following columns represent the overall change in the past 10 years along with the change in each of the components.

Overall globalization in Latin America has increased slightly over the last decade. Argentina is an exception to this trend. The country saw an overall change of –3%, the worst decline other than Venezuela, mainly due to the economic globalization indicator. More specifically, the financial globalization element decreased significantly between 2011 and 2012 and has not recovered. This decline is mainly a result of increased investment regulations. For example, in late 2011 the Argentine government passed a law limiting the amount of land foreigners can own (U.S. Department of State, 2014). Another example is that several Double Taxation Agreements were revoked in 2012, which have complicated efforts to doing business there (U.S. Department of State, 2014).

The largest increase in any one indicator was in Colombia where the social globalization indicator rose by 28%. This increase was primarily due to the improvement of the information globalization component which includes elements such as internet usage. Colombia's internet usage increased around 400% over the last decade which can be compared to Chile whose internet usage grew around 100% in the same time frame (The World Bank, 2017a).

Therefore, although usage has impressive growth in the region, the growth in Colombia far exceeded the average. Another contributing factor to this technology increase could be the Colombian government's push for technology through their US$10 billion Vive Digital plan of investment and subsidization (Villegas, 2014).

Composition of Production

This section of the chapter looks at how trade and globalization have shifted the composition of production in Latin America. Figures 6.5 and 6.6 illustrate the structure of GDP by sector for each country at two points in time, 1995 and 2015.

For the most part, over the last two decades, both Latin America and the rest of the world have become less agrarian as defined by a lower percentage of GDP originating from the agricultural sector. In 1995, Latin America as a region was generating about 12% of its GDP from agriculture. By 2015, the number had been reduced to roughly 8%. Nearly every country reduced their dependence on agriculture revenue.

One exception however, is Argentina who had a larger share of their GDP deriving from this sector in 2015 compared to 1995. Part of the reason for the

TABLE 6.3 Change in the KOF Index of Globalization, 2005–2015

Country	Overall World Rank 2015	Overall % Change	Economic % Change	Political % Change	Social % Change
Argentina	79	–3	–36	15	1
Bolivia	94	–2	–19	16	–1
Brazil	95	2	–19	18	3
Chile	43	0	–12	12	2
Colombia	84	17	11	8	28
Costa Rica	61	3	–7	10	6
Dominican Republic	87	3	5	9	–4
Ecuador	93	–1	–21	13	1
El Salvador	67	5	–1	10	6
Guatemala	78	1	–8	2	9
Honduras	83	14	15	8	19
Mexico	51	8	4	15	5
Nicaragua	92	7	–1	14	10
Panama	53	5	4	11	3
Paraguay	74	5	–10	19	7
Peru	59	7	–2	14	10
Uruguay	46	1	0	2	0
Venezuela, RB	114	–6	–32	6	2
Latin America	79	3	–4	11	4
China	88	3	–13	15	4
U.S.	23	1	–7	10	0

Source: KOF Swiss Economic Institute (2018).

Notes
Ranks are out of 185 countries.
Overall globalization in Latin America has increased slightly over the last decade. Argentina is an exception to this trend. The country saw an overall change of –3%, the worst decline on than Venezuela, mainly due to the economic globalization indicator. More specifically, the de jure financial globalization element decreased significantly between 2011 and 2012 and has not recovered. This decline is mainly a result of increased investment regulations. The "Regime for Protection of National Domain over Ownership, Possession or Tenure of Rural Land" passed in late 2011 which limited companies from the same country to 4.5% ownership of productive land. It also limited individual companies to 2,470 acres of total land. In addition, several Double Taxation Agreements were revoked in 2012, and the country set forth other protectionist regulations.
The largest increase in any one indicator was in Colombia where the social globalization indicator rose by 28%. This increase was primarily due to the improvement of the de jure information globalization component which includes elements such as internet usage. Colombia's internet usage increased around 400% over the last decade which can be compared to Chile whose internet usage grew around 100% in the same time frame. Therefore, although usage has impressive growth in the region, the growth in Colombia far exceeded the average. Another contributing factor to this technology increase could be the Colombian government's push for technology through their US$10 billion Vive Digital Plan of investment and subsidization. (Villegas, 2014).

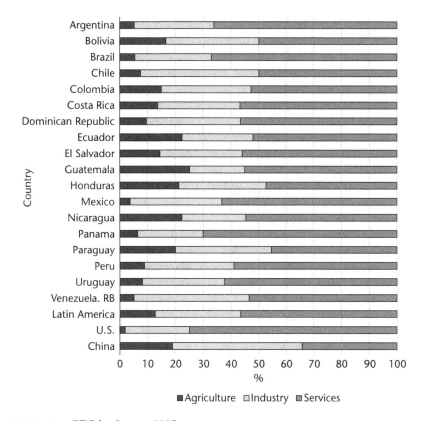

FIGURE 6.5 GDP by Sector, 1995

increase is that the agribusiness sector was low in 1995 with previous regimes such as that of Isabel Martínez de Perón increasing taxes on exports and instituting harsh exchange controls. These measures lead to strikes and loss of production. In 1991 in the middle of a financial crisis, Argentina decided to peg the Argentine peso to the U.S. dollar. This did not help agriculture as much as other sectors, but it did stabilize the economy for a time. This strategy made Argentina more cost competitive with India in service sectors such as programming, so the service sector increased comparatively for a time (Smith, 2002). However, Argentina fell back into recession. As a remedy, the government devalued the Argentinian Peso against the U.S. Dollar which along with rising commodity prices made agricultural exports more attractive (The Economist, 2001). Since 2003, the portion of Argentina's total GDP captured by the agricultural sector has been decreasing.

In summary, there has been a major shift of where value added (according to GDP) occurs in Latin America. The move out of agriculture to services was about a 6% shift over a 20-year period, compared to a 3% shift for the United States. With nearly 56% of GDP in services, it's even higher than China's 50%. Special attention should be focused on Brazil, Costa Rica, and Panama since

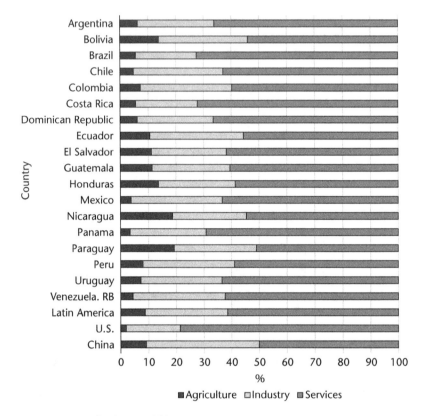

FIGURE 6.6 GDP by Sector, 2015

these three countries get the most GDP as a percentage from the services indus-try. One need only visit Sao Paolo in Brazil or Panama City, Panama to see the sophisticated financial services industries at work. Costa Rica has tapped into the vastly expanding outsourcing of services industry and is currently ranked first in the region for high value-added services (Cinde, 2018).

Impact on Human Development

While the percentage of GDP by sector is pertinent to an understanding of the economic climate of a region, it's also important to know how many people are working in them. As demonstrated in Figures 6.7 and 6.8, just because a certain percentage of GDP comes from a sector does not mean that the percentage of people employed there is the same. This move of people from agriculture to industry (manufacturing) to services is important because it usually comes with increased income. As mentioned throughout this book (and later in this chapter), poverty and inequality reduction must be cornerstone of Latin America's human development effort.

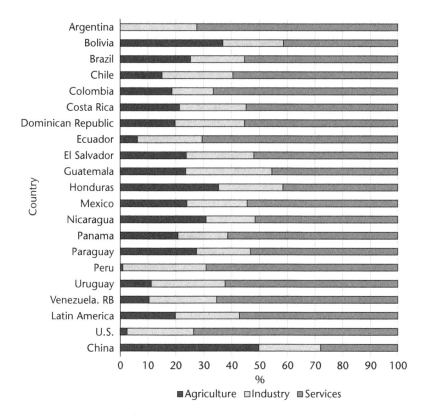

FIGURE 6.7 Percentage of Individuals Working by Sector, 1995

As with previous figures, Figures 6.7 and 6.8 represent the two periods in time of 1995 and 2015. We maintained these ranges in order to allow enough time for significant changes to manifest themselves and also for comparison purposes with GDP change.

At first glance, Latin America as a region has reduced its numbers of people employed in the agriculture sector from approximately 20% to 18%. This does not coincide with the reduction in the same sector in terms of GDP (6%). In order to understand why this is the case, we move to the individual country level distributions by sector. Notice that Guatemala, Honduras, and Bolivia all have about 30% of their workforce in the agriculture sector. This is partially due to the relatively large indigenous portion of their populations that are working small plots of land. This is different than the agriculture fields in Argentina where more modern machinery (e.g., tractors and combines) can allow a single farmer to cultivate thousands of acres of land per year. One can see that from a productivity perspective, Argentina produced a higher percentage of its GDP in 2015 in the agriculture sector than it had workers. The opposite is true of Guatemala, Honduras, and Bolivia.

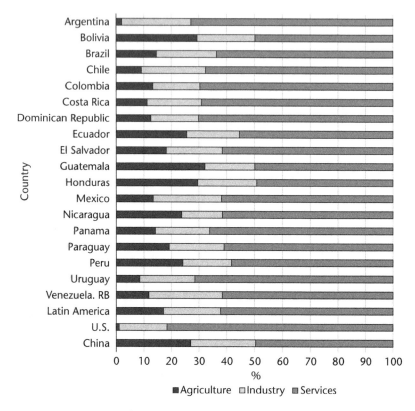

FIGURE 6.8   Percentage of Individuals Working by Sector, 2015

The apparent lack of productivity also seems apparent in China, which also has nearly 27% of its workers producing 8% of its GDP. This is partially due to the fact that almost all farmland in China is owned by village collectives, which are notoriously inefficient (The Economist, 2018c). Yet, at the time of the writing of this book, land reform was gaining traction in China (The Economist, 2018c). That should result in consolidation of land, and bigger farms – perhaps nothing compared to Argentina's or Brazil's, but enough to change the landscape per se.

Inequality

Now that we have seen in what sectors the workers in each country of Latin America work and the shift from agriculture to services industries, we shift to whether the changes are affecting the region's inequality. The Gini coefficient compares the income or wealth distribution of a population to a perfectly equal distribution. A perfectly equal distribution is one where every citizen of a country (or city) has equal wealth. The index ranges from zero (perfect equality) to one, where one person has all of the wealth of a country.

TABLE 6.4 Inequality in Latin America: Gini Index, 2006–2016

Country	2006	2016	% Change
Argentina	47	42	−9
Bolivia	57	45	−21
Brazil	56	51	−8
Chile	48	48	−1
Colombia	54	51	−5
Costa Rica	49	49	−1
Dominican Republic	52	45	−13
Ecuador	52	45	−14
Guatemala	55	48	−12
Honduras	58	50	−13
Mexico	48	43	−9
Nicaragua	49	46	−5
Panama	55	50	−8
Peru	51	44	−13
Paraguay	53	48	−10
El Salvador	46	40	−12
Uruguay	46	40	−14
Venezuela, RB	47	n/a	−
Latin America	51	46	−10

Source: The World Bank (2017d).

Notes
For this figure, the median available index was used over each 15-year span. If none, existed that year was excluded from consideration.
"Gini index measures the extent to which the distribution of income (or, in some cases, consumption expenditure) among individuals or households within an economy deviates from a perfectly equal distribution. A Lorenz curve plots the cumulative percentages of total income received against the cumulative number of recipients, starting with the poorest individual or household. The Gini index measures the area between the Lorenz curve and a hypothetical line of absolute equality, expressed as a percentage of the maximum area under the line. Thus, a Gini index of 0 represents perfect equality, while an index of 100 implies perfect inequality." (World Bank, 2017d)

We did not include the United States in this comparison because the U.S. Census Bureau usually reports Gini coefficients based on pre-tax numbers, whereas many calculations for foreign countries use post-tax numbers, which often include redistribution of wealth from rich to poor and tend to lower the Gini coefficient. Comparing the pre-tax number in one country with the post-tax number in another is somewhat meaningless (Lamb, 2012). We also did not include China since the most recent data is from 2012. The Latin America numbers are medians.

In general, Latin America has seen a decrease in the Gini index of about 10% over the past decade, meaning lower inequality in the region. While it is the only region where inequality decreased during the 2000s, according to UNICEF, it was still the region with the highest Gini index in the world.

Indeed, seven countries in Latin America are in the top 20 countries list worldwide. Yet, at least it's decreasing. This decrease is primarily the result of better education which has produced a higher skilled labor force along with an increase in targeted welfare programs.

Until recently, there was concern in Mexico about its Gini index because it had stayed about the same for the past few years. Inequalities were also growing across states and sectors. Those divergences in income and informality have negative externalities on poverty and therefore inclusiveness (OECD, 2017). This inequality increase was partially due to the financial crisis in 2008. However, less obvious causes include a decrease in low-skilled jobs and a decrease in conditional welfare programs. Mexico's rising inequality proves problematic for foreign businesses hoping to invest, as increases in the Gini coefficient have been linked to increases in violence, in particular the drug related violence that plagues the country (Woody, 2016). If this violence persists, it may become increasingly unprofitable to do business in certain states within Mexico. Fortunately, 2016 results were better with a coefficient of 43.

The countries that have made the biggest strides over the past decade are Bolivia, Ecuador, and Uruguay. With a 21% reduction in inequality in a decade, it should be no surprise that Bolivia's president, Mr. Morales is poised to run for a fourth term (The Economist, 2017). Inequity reduction is a powerful tool for political aspirants. A similar situation has happened in Ecuador, where after ruling for 10 years, a former leftist president, Mr. Correa, will attempt to run again. He expected his successor, Mr. Moreno, to carry on his program of "21st-century socialism" (The Economist, 2018b). This amounted to spending lots of money on social programs and infrastructure and subjecting independent institutions like the press and the courts to control by the president (The Economist, 2018b). Yet, with a decrease in oil revenues, this formula will be difficult to implement. This problem has also been exacerbated in Venezuela, Brazil, and to a lesser extent, Colombia.

The countries that have basically stalled in their efforts to reduce inequality are Chile and Costa Rica. Part of the problem in Chile is a lack of access to a high-quality education at an affordable price. If more people in Chile could get a good high school or even university degree, they could earn more and reduce the inequality of the nation. Tax reform could make this happen, but the very rich in Chile are opposed to it (Council on Hemispheric Affairs, 2011). Chilean economist Claudio Sapelli points out that inequality levels are lower in younger generations (Council on Hemispheric Affairs, 2011). Thus, there is hope that the overall inequity index should improve. Two things are contributing to the lack of improvement in inequality in Costa Rica. First, redistribution via taxes is low due to the country's small size. Second, high unemployment and informality of jobs are both rising, especially for women (OECD, 2016). We will focus on how the informal economy affects the economic climate of Latin America in the next section. Costa Rica still isn't as bad as Brazil and Colombia, but at least the latter two countries are reducing inequality faster. Albeit, per the aforementioned paragraph, we do not know how much longer Brazil and Colombia can keep it up. A closer look at the data can be found at the World Bank's website (The World Bank, 2018a). The year over year data suggests that the two countries have maintained a steady improvement in the Gini index.

Informal Economy

Informal employment is defined by the International Labor Organization as employment in the informal economy as a percentage of total non-agricultural employment (The World Bank, 2018b). It basically includes all jobs in unregistered and/or small-scale private unincorporated enterprises that produce goods or services meant for sale or barter. Self-employed street vendors, taxi drivers and home-base workers are all considered enterprises. However, agricultural and related activities, households producing goods exclusively for their own use (e.g., subsistence farming, domestic housework, care work, and employment of paid domestic workers), and volunteer services rendered to the community are excluded. Table 6.5 provides the percentage of workers employed in the informal sector for select countries.

Unfortunately, we do not have access to data for a few of the biggest countries in the region such as Brazil, Mexico, and Venezuela. Additionally, about half of the countries were missing data going back a decade, so we altered the date range to be between 2010 and 2016 in order to look at changes by country. The number for Latin America is a median of the countries in the list, and not weighted.

TABLE 6.5 Informal Employment

Country	2010	2016	% Change
Argentina	48	47	−1
Bolivia	77	78	1
Chile	41	38	−2
Colombia	62	57	−6
Costa Rica	33	37	5
Dominican Republic	51	53	3
Ecuador	57	51	−6
El Salvador	66	63	−3
Guatemala	76	74	−3
Honduras	71	74	3
Paraguay	70	66	−4
Peru	70	58	−12
Uruguay	39	24	−15
Latin America	62	57	−6

Source: The World Bank (2017e).

Increasing the number of workers in the formal economy is important because they pay taxes, have access to social protection (e.g., health care), and tend to be able to bargain better with employers (e.g., collective bargaining). The challenge of decent work conditions among informal workers can be viewed within the framework the traditional labor protection systems. The employment relationship is the foundation on which labor protection system is traditionally framed. When this is not clear, the mechanisms it offers (e.g., labor law, collective bargaining agreements, labor inspection and mediation, labor courts) are also hard to access. Furthermore, where workers are also scattered with no fixed premises, their interests are more difficult to aggregate through trade unions (International Labour Organization, 2015).

A couple of things stand out from the Table. First, the total number of people employed in the informal economy is high at around 60%. Thus, there is still much room for improvement. With that in mind, 9 of the 13 countries we have information have improved over a period of 6 years. And roughly 6% have shifted out of the informal economy overall in Latin America. Although, some countries such as Costa Rica are losing ground in their efforts to shift their workforce to the formal sector.

Next, we turn to Peru and Uruguay, which reduced their informal employment percentages by 12% and 15%, respectively. In Peru, simply cross-checking information between the labor and tax administrations through an e-payroll system has led to a sharp rise in formalization (International Labour Organization, 2014). The case of Uruguay is more impressive not only because they lead the region in only having 24% of their labor force in the informal economy, but also in reducing that percentage the most over a six-year period.

Uruguay's transition to a more formal economy is partially made possible by a "Monotax." This is a mechanism that provides a way to facilitate procedures and lower the burden on small businesses. Specifically, it allows some categories of microenterprises and self-employed to pay their taxes and social insurance contributions through simplified bureaucratic measures. This facilitates compliance and ensures the social protection of entrepreneurs and employees (International Labour Organization, 2015).

While the case of Uruguay has been discussed before in this book, it is worthwhile to point its successes here as well and how they got there. For example, recently the government has invested in raising productivity. Public spending on science and technology increased by 73% in real terms between 2007 and 2015 (The Economist, 2018a). The next step may be to loosen their rigid labor markets in order to bring in more foreign investment. On the other hand, it may be these rigid labor markets that keeps their people in the formal economy.

Conclusion

This chapter on the current economic climate in Latin America focused on two main themes: economic liberalization and its impact on human development in the region. We describe various components of each and how one might use that information to improve their chances of successfully engaging in business there.

Not to infringe on the economic history discussed in Chapter 3, we began this chapter by going back to the 1980s in order to get an understanding of how bad inflation was in Latin America. Doing business in that environment would have been challenging at best. Per the current situation with inflation in Venezuela, we can observe a country in crisis. For the vast majority of countries in the region, the menacing issue of inflation has been eliminated. This has paved the way for outside firms to confidently move into the nations of Latin America.

With that problem solved, we shifted to see how the region responded economically to the influences of the world economy. For example, while the financial crisis of 2009 was painful for Latin America, it was able to bounce back quickly in terms of GDP growth. Unfortunately, many countries in the region have not been able to sustain those growth rates. The savvy business investor should pay attention to where and why certain countries are growing and others not.

Next, we examined how much goods and services each country in Latin America trades. Further analysis demonstrates the primary trading partners of each country. There has been a striking shift of influence from the United States to China. This can be partially explained by looking at the degree each country has globalized in the past decade.

At that point we shifted away from macroeconomic topics to focus on the people of the region and how the economic climate was affecting them. First, more people are moving away from agriculture jobs to services industries. As always in this book, there are exceptions to this trend, depending on the country. Each country should be analyzed individually when considering doing business in Latin America.

The "people" component of the chapter ended by digging into how the problem of inequality has shifted over a decade. Every country in the region has done better than a decade ago. The shift from the informal economy to the formal economy is partially the reason. As more people move into the middle class, they have more demands – not just of things they want to buy but also things they want changed in their countries. The case of Brazil illustrates the process for both.

Now that the current economic climate has been reviewed, we turn our focus to why some countries in Latin America are more competitive than others.

The Case of Brazil

Over the past decade, many Brazilians have risen into the middle class. This achievement is the result of the various governmental policies, growth dynamics, and a reduction in the unemployment rate. The rise in the middle class has impacted the country in many positive ways. For example, more people making more money results in an increase in tax revenue. The expansion also means increased spending and a rise in domestic demand. This class is also able to afford better health services and a quality education for their children, which increases their likelihood of getting formal sector employment. In addition, the Brazilian banking sector is expected to grow as the new middle class requires more banking services. The growing middle class has also helped to improve the general welfare of the entire population by demanding better public services. Citizens that pay taxes generally expect better public services from their governments. As we are currently witnessing in Brazil, they don't like to have their tax money squandered on corruption.

Notably, women are making up more of the middle-class labor force. Currently, Brazilian women make up about 43% of the total labor force, which is about 10% higher than in 1990 (The World Bank, 2017c). Many of these women are well educated and landing jobs in leading firms. For example, approximately half of the boards of directors in Brazil have at least one woman (30% Club, 2017).

Brazil's rising middle class leads to many investment opportunities in different markets. Some of the largest markets that go along with a growing middle class include automobiles, household appliances, and electronics. Ten years ago, it was common to see people washing clothes by hand. Now they heat up their food in a microwave while the washing machine does the work. Further, retail and entertainment markets all profit from a rise in the middle class. Many products that are common in the United States are now becoming a ubiquitous part of middle-class life in Brazil.

Another change that goes hand in hand with a rise in middle class is a rise in the formal sector. Brazil has a wide range of formal and informal sectors of its economy. For example, there are many established stores that look like retail stores in Western countries alongside street vendors and outdoor markets. The rise in the formal sector is good for potential investors that may want to expand their brand into Brazil.

Having more formal sector businesses will also help Brazilian society as more income will be taxed. This money can then be spent on important initiatives such as infrastructure improvements. One of the concerns with the decreasing informal class, however, is the potential loss of jobs for members of low income communities. As mentioned earlier in this chapter, Brazil already has the highest income inequality index in Latin America, so as the informal sector shrinks, there could be a chance that lesser educated workers would become unemployed. This will be a challenge that Brazil will continue to face as its economy grows.

The rise in the Brazilian middle class also brings hope that innovation will occur in the country. As Chapter 10 illustrates, entrepreneurship and innovation are critical to the economic climate of the region. Brazil has its own version of Silicon Valley in Campinas, a metropolitan area of around 3.6 million near São Paulo (Wikipedia, 2018). What is unique about Campinas as compared to other tech friendly cities in Latin America is the support that it gets from universities around the area. Universities help sponsor different innovative products that come out of the Campinas Valley. There is also a large emphasis on the peer-review process, so inventors can help each other make their ideas come to life (Wadhwa, 2012). Indeed, the rise of Campinas embodies a growing middle class made up with an engaged, young workforce that is prepared to compete with (and buy from) the rest of the world.

Finally, as Brazil's technology and retail industries continue to grow, Brazil's e-commerce industry will continue to boom. Large international e-commerce sites like Amazon.com and Alibaba will have many opportunities in Brazil. Not only is Brazil the fourth largest internet market in the world with over 140 million users, but Brazilians also spend more time online than other BRIC countries (PagBrasil, 2018; Singh, 2013). Thus, the market from mobile phones and laptops to app providers and online stores are ready for business.

References

30% Club (2017). "Global Board Diversity Analysis, 2016." https://30percentclub.org/assets/uploads/UK/Third_Party_Reports/2016_GBDA_DIGITAL_FINAL.pdf, accessed, January, 2018.

Central Intelligence Agency (2018). "World Factbook." www.cia.gov/library/publications/the-world-factbook/geos/ve.html, accessed March, 2018.

Cinde (2018). "A dynamic multifunctional site for complex business processes." www.cinde.org/en/sectors/services, accessed March, 2018.

Council on Hemispheric Affairs (2011). "The Inequality Behind Chile's Prosperity." www.coha.org/the-inequality-behind-chiles-prosperity, accessed June, 2017.

DLA Piper (2016). "Uruguay – Free Trade Zones: An Overview." www.latamlawblog.com/2016/10/uruguay-free-trade-zones-an-overview/, accessed January, 2018.

Emarketer.com (2013). "2013 India Digital Future in Focus." *ComScore Media Matrix*. www.comscore.com/Insights/Presentations-and-Whitepapers/2013/2013-India-Digital-Future-in-Focus, accessed August, 2013.

Franko, P. M. (2007) *The Puzzle of Latin American Economic Development*. Lanham, Maryland: Rowman & Littlefield.

Gupta, Girish (2018). "Venezuela Annual Inflation at More Than 4,000 Percent: National Assembly." *Reuters.* www.reuters.com/article/us-venezuela-economy/venezuela-annual-inflation-at-more-than-4000-percent-national-assembly-idUSKBN1FR2FH, accessed March, 2018.

ILO (2014). "Recent Experiences of Formalization in Latin America and the Caribbean." *Notes on Formalization.* Produced by the Program for the Promotion of Formalization in Latin America and the Caribbean (FORLAC).

International Labour Organization (2014). "Recent Experiences of Formalization in Latin America and the Caribbean." www.ilo.org/global/docs/WCMS_245882/lang--en/index.htm, accessed May, 2018.

International Labour Organization (2015). "Report of Transition to the Formal Economy." www.ilo.org/employment/Whatwedo/Eventsandmeetings/WCMS_456553/lang--en/index.htm, accessed June, 2018.

KOF Swiss Economic Institute (2018). "Globalization Index." www.kof.ethz.ch/en/forecasts-and-indicators/indicators/kof-globalisation-index.html, accessed April, 2018.

Lamb, Evelyn (2012). "Ask Gini: How to Measure Inequality." *Scientific American.* www.scientificamerican.com/article/ask-gini, accessed April, 2018.

Leahy, J. (2017) "Brazil emerges from its worst ever recession." *Financial Times,* September 1, 2017.

Navarro, Andrea (2018). "What Might Happen to Mexico If Nafta Gets Wiped Away." *Bloomberg.* www.bloomberg.com/news/articles/2018-03-30/what-might-happen-to-mexico-if-nafta-gets-wiped-away-quicktake, accessed May, 2018.

Organisation for Economic Co-Operation and Development (OECD) (2016). "Costa Rica Policy Brief." www.oecd.org/countries/costarica/costa-rica-towards-a-more-inclusive-society.pdf, accessed February, 2017.

Organisation for Economic Co-operation and Development (OECD) (2017). "OECD Economic Surveys Mexico." www.oecd.org/eco/surveys/Mexico-2017-OECD-economic-survey-overview.pdf, accessed December, 2017.

PagBrasil (2018). "Brazil, One of the Biggest E-Commerce Opportunities in the World." , accessed February, 2018.

Reuters (2017). "China, Panama to Begin Talks on Free-Trade Deal in June 2018." www.reuters.com/article/us-china-panama/china-panama-to-begin-talks-on-free-trade-deal-in-june-2018-idUSKBN1E205K, accessed February, 2018.

Singh, Amarpal (2013). "2013 India Digital Future in Focus." *comScore.* www.comscore.com/Insights/Presentations-and-Whitepapers/2013/2013-India-Digital-Future-in-Focus, accessed January, 2018.

Smith, Tony (2002). "Peso's Devaluation Gives Argentina Cost Advantages." *New York Times.* www.nytimes.com/2002/10/24/business/peso-s-devaluation-gives-argentina-cost-advantages.html, accessed October, 2017.

Statistica (2018). Average Annual Market Price of Copper From 2009 to 2017. www.statista.com/statistics/533292/average-price-of-copper/, accessed May, 2018.

The Economist (2001). "Argentina in a fix." www.economist.com/node/541226, accessed January, 2017.

The Economist (2017). "Evo Morales Finds a Way to Run for Re-Election." www.economist.com/news/americas/21731949-bolivias-constitutional-court-gives-president-decision-he-wants-evo-morales-finds-way?zid=309&ah=80cf288b8561b012f603b9fd9577f0e, accessed January 2018.

The Economist (2018a). "Uruguay's Record-Setting Economic Growth Streak." www.economist.com/news/americas/21739793-how-small-country-outperforms-its-neighbours-uruguays-record-setting-economic-growth-streak, accessed April, 2018.

The Economist (2018b). "Ecuador's President Lenín Moreno Tries to Bury The Legacy of his Predecessor." www.economist.com/news/americas/21736365-referendum-designed-stop-rafael-correa-making-comeback-ecuadors-president-len-n, accessed March, 2018.

The Economist (2018c). "Why China Needs Bigger Farms." www.economist.com/news/china/21734394-despite-huge-improvements-maos-dire-day-farming-china-still-woefully-inefficient-why, accessed April, 2018.

The World Bank (2016). "Top Trading Partners." https://wits.worldbank.org/Default.aspx?lang=en, accessed March, 2018.

The World Bank (2017a). "Individuals using the Internet." https://data.worldbank.org/indicator/IT.NET.USER.ZS?end=2015&locations=CO-1W-CL&start=2005, accessed March, 2017.

The World Bank (2017b). "Growth vs. Inflation: A Difficult Balance for Latin America and the Caribbean." www.worldbank.org/en/news/press-release/2017/10/12/growth-inflation-difficult-balance-latin-america-caribbean, accessed January 2018.

The World Bank (2017c). "Labor Force, Female." https://data.worldbank.org/indicator/SL.TLF.TOTL.FE.ZS?locations=BR, accessed January, 2018.

The World Bank (2017d). "Inequality Index." https://data.worldbank.org/indicator/SI.POV.GINI, accessed December, 2017.

The World Bank (2017e). "Informal employment." https://data.worldbank.org/indicator/SL.ISV.IFRM.ZS, accessed December, 2017.

The World Bank (2018a). *Gini Index*. https://data.worldbank.org/indicator/SI.POV.GINI?locations=CL-CR, accessed July, 2018.

The World Bank (2018b). "Informal Employment." https://data.worldbank.org/indicator/SL.ISV.IFRM.ZS, accessed May, 2018.

The World Bank (2018c). "Imports and Exports of Goods and Services." https://data.worldbank.org/, accessed March, 2018.

U.S. Department of State (2014). "2013 Investment Climate Statement – Argentina." www.state.gov/e/eb/rls/othr/ics/2013/204592.htm, accessed January, 2018.

Villegas, Luis (2014). "Technology is driving change in Colombia." *Boston Globe*. www.bostonglobe.com/opinion/2014/09/19/technology-driving-change-colombia/Fz3eABonGaoQD4JO54EDPK/story.html, accessed May, 2017.

Viscidi, Lisa (2015). "The US Energy Boom & Refining Markets in Latin America. The Dialogue." www.thedialogue.org/resources/filling-the-gap-how-the-us-energy-boom-is-shaping-refining-markets-in-latin-america/, accessed December, 2017.

Wadhwa, Vivek (2012). "Why the Next Mark Zuckerberg May Come from Brazil." *Washington Post*. www.washingtonpost.com/national/on-innovations/why-the-next-mark-zuckerberg-may-come-from-brazil/2012/03/20/gIQA3X2ZRS_story.html?noredirect=on&utm_term=.1bd1d1624f2a, accessed January, 2018.

Wikipedia (2018). "Campinas." https://en.wikipedia.org/wiki/Campinas, accessed August, 2018.

Woody, Christopher (2016). "An Ominous Economic Trend May Be Returning to Latin America, and It Could Have Deadly Consequences." *Business Insider*. www.businessinsider.com/inequality-and-violence-in-latin-america-2016-2, accessed December, 2017.

World Integrated Trade Solution (2014). "Peru Exports, Imports and Trade Balance by Country and Region." https://wits.worldbank.org/CountryProfile/en/Country/PER/Year/2011/TradeFlow/EXPIMP, accessed December, 2017.

World Integrated Trade Solution (2018). "Latin America & Caribbean Trade at a Glance: Most Recent Values. 2018." https://wits.worldbank.org/CountrySnapshot/en/LCN/textview, accessed January, 2018.

7

GLOBAL COMPETITIVENESS

Overview

This chapter extends the previous one by more specifically focusing on the competitiveness of the region per the Doing Business Index and the World Competitiveness Report. We present the Doing Business Index in order to get more than one perspective on how competitive the region is. We analyze both the current state of the region as well as trends in the various components of the report. While the World Trade Organization seems to have reached its limits regarding tariff reductions on a global basis, bilateral and smaller regional trade blocks are blooming in the region. Even in countries with relatively small markets, innovation via export processing zones (i.e., Panama) continues to generate a robust income for the region. The recent expansion of the Panama Canal should also enhance the competitiveness of products moving to and from the Far East and the Western Hemisphere. As a regional leader according to the World Competitiveness Report, the case for this chapter will focus on Panama and what it has done better than others in the region.

Doing Business in Latin America

The Doing Business Project by the World Bank provides objective measures of business regulations and their enforcement across 190 countries (The World Bank, 2018a).[1] If Latin America were a country, it would be in around the 98th position (see Table 7.1). This means the region as a whole is below the half way point. If we compare it to the United States or even China, we can see that the region has considerable room for improvement. Of the 10 aspects for measuring the climate for doing business, we selected four to focus our attention. First, we

TABLE 7.1 Rankings of Selected Indicators from Doing Business Index

Country	Overall	Starting a Business	Getting Electricity	Paying Taxes	Trading Across Borders
Mexico	49	90	92	115	63
Chile	55	65	44	72	68
Peru	58	114	63	121	92
Colombia	59	96	81	142	125
Costa Rica	61	127	21	60	73
El Salvador	73	140	88	61	43
Panama	79	39	18	180	54
Uruguay	94	61	50	106	151
Guatemala	97	139	36	100	79
Dominican Republic	99	116	108	149	59
Paraguay	108	146	104	127	120
Honduras	115	150	144	164	115
Argentina	117	157	95	169	116
Ecuador	118	168	85	145	102
Brazil	125	176	45	184	139
Nicaragua	131	138	100	159	74
Bolivia	152	179	101	186	89
Venezuela, RB	188	190	186	189	187
Latin America	98	139	87	144	91
China	78	93	98	130	97
U.S.	6	49	49	36	36

Source: The World Bank (2017a).

Notes
Ranks are out of 190 economies. Sorted based on the Overall column.

chose starting a business since that is were there were the most reforms in the past 15 years. Second, we chose getting electricity because it is the best ranked pillar in the region and the second-best improvement over the prior year. Next, we selected paying taxes because it has the worst ranking in the region. Finally, we chose trading across borders because it had the most reforms last year.

Regarding getting electricity, on average, the region's economies perform well. For example, the average time for an entrepreneur to connect to the electricity grid in the Latin America is 66 days compared to the global average of 92 days. On the other hand, the region underperforms in the areas of paying taxes (144) and starting a business (139). On average, 28 tax payments are required per year to comply with legal tax obligations compared to an average of 11 payments in OECD high-income economies (The World Bank, 2018b).

In the past year, the bulk of the business reforms were implemented in the Doing Business indicators of Trading Across Borders (5), Registering Property (4), and Getting Electricity (4) (The World Bank, 2018b). El Salvador implemented four reforms, the most by a single economy in the region. Other notable reformers included the Dominican Republic (with 3 reforms) and Costa Rica (with 2 reforms). Examples of reforms they implemented include: El Salvador made paying taxes easier by implementing an online platform. It also made exporting and importing easier by increasing the number of customs officers at the Anguiatú land border. The Dominican Republic reduced the time to start a business and improved the reliability of electricity (The World Bank, 2018b).

Competitiveness of Latin America

The World Economic Forum orchestrates a major project to construct indicators to measure conditions promoting productivity. These conditions are based on the assumption that making people better off is accomplished by increasing their output with fewer inputs. The result of this project is the Global Competitiveness Index (GCI) that is produced annually and covered by newspapers throughout the world. It recognizes that countries at different stages enhance productivity for different reasons (see Table 7.2). For example, growth in less sophisticated economies is driven by basic factor conditions. Once countries improve the primary levels of health, education, and infrastructure, in the second stage, growth is derived from improving efficiency. Finally, when the gains from efficiency enhancers reach diminishing returns, to continue to improve productivity countries in the third stage must focus on improving business sophistication and innovation (Franko, 2007).

In her book on the economic history of Latin America, Dr. Franko points out that although all factors matter to all countries, countries such as Bolivia and

TABLE 7.2 Classification by Each Stage of Development

Stage 1: Factor Driven	Transition from Stage 1 to 2	Stage 2: Efficiency Driven	Transition from Stage 2 to 3	Stage 3: Innovation Driven
Haiti	Honduras Nicaragua Venezuela	Brazil Colombia Dominican Ecuador El Salvador Guatemala Mexico Paraguay Peru China	Argentina Chile Costa Rica Panama Uruguay	U.S.

Source: World Economic Forum (2018).

Note
Bolivia was excluded this year due to insufficient data.

Nicaragua would be more successful by targeting factor policies such as primary education (Franko, 2007). When she last published the book, she was using the most recent data at the time from the 2006 GCI report. At that time, Colombia and Peru were in the transition between factor-driven and efficiency-driven competitiveness. Now they have progressed into the efficiency-driven category and would benefit from focusing on efficiencies in the goods and labor markets.

Per Table 7.2, one can see that the majority of the countries in Latin America are in the second of three stages of development. We included Haiti in the table as an example of a country that is still in the first stage. Next, Honduras, Nicaragua, and Venezuela are in the transition stage from stage one to two. And five countries are in the transition stage from stage two to three: Argentina, Chile, Costa Rica, Panama, and Uruguay. Finally, we added China and the United States for comparison purposes.

The Global Competitiveness Index

The World Economic Forum defines competitiveness as the set of institutions, policies, and factors that determine the level of productivity of a country (Schwab, 2018). The level of productivity, in turn, sets the level of prosperity that can be reached by an economy. The productivity level also determines the rates of return obtained by investments in an economy, which in turn are the fundamental drivers of its growth rates. In other words, a more competitive economy is one that is likely to grow faster over time (Schwab, 2018).

The GCI offers impartial information that allows leaders from the public and private sectors to better understand the main drivers of growth. The index permits a country level analysis to identify the primary challenges and barriers to growth. We encourage the interested reader to research countries of interest at the website of the World Economic Forum. The information is very well presented and easy to access. While we are not going to go into the detail of the individual country reports in this book, we are going to look at each country by indicator. As throughout this book, we will look for patterns and trends, and the possible reasons why they exist. Before looking at the overall GCI, a paragraph on its methodology is in order.

A detailed explanation of the methodology begins on page 317 of the GCI (Schwab, 2018). The GCI includes a weighted average of 114 indicators for growth and are grouped into 12 categories. The weights are assigned based on how important they are to one of the three stages (see Figure 7.1). For example, infrastructure is weighted more than innovation for countries that are in stage one. The 12 categories are referred to as pillars and listed in order from basic requirements up to the more advanced requirements. The four pillars of the basic requirements subindex are institutions, infrastructure, the macroeconomic environment, and health and primary education. Next, the efficiency enhancers subindex is comprised of higher education and training, goods and labor market

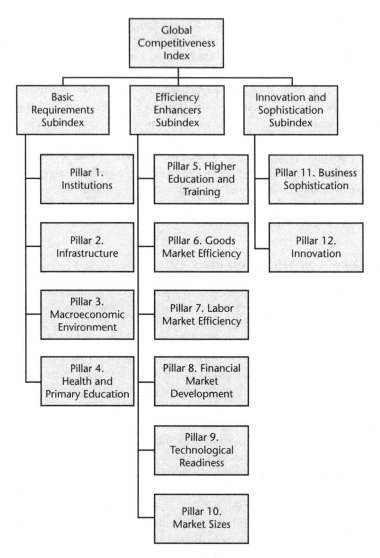

FIGURE 7.1   Global Competitiveness Index Components

efficiency, financial market development, technological readiness, and market size. Finally, business sophistication and innovation make up the final subindex. Although it reports each of the 12 pillars separately, they are not independent. If a country does very well on one pillar, it is likely to have positive spillovers to other pillars. The same goes for doing particularly poor on a pillar having negative effects on other pillars.

After looking at the overall ranking of the GCI (Table 7.3), we will look at each pillar separately in the order of relevance from basic to the most advanced.

TABLE 7.3 Overall GCI

Country	2007	2017	Δ in Rank
Chile	26	33	−7
Costa Rica	63	47	16
Panama	59	50	9
Mexico	52	51	1
Colombia	69	66	3
Peru	86	72	14
Uruguay	75	76	−1
Brazil	72	80	−8
Guatemala	87	84	3
Argentina	85	92	−7
Nicaragua	111	93	18
Honduras	83	96	−13
Ecuador	103	97	6
Dominican Republic	96	104	−8
El Salvador	67	109	−42
Paraguay	121	112	9
Venezuela	98	127	−29
Bolivia	105	n/a	n/a
Latin America	84	84	0
China	34	27	7
U.S.	1	2	−1

Source: World Economic Forum (2018).

Note
Ranks are out of 137 economies and sorted best to worst for 2017.

When describing each pillar, we start with the actual description from the most recent GCI since the team at the World Economic Forum built the index and we do not want to misinterpret the meaning of each pillar.

After two years of recession in many countries in the region, the slow response of exports revealed the competitiveness challenges in the region. Large gaps between the best and worst countries in all of the pillars of competitiveness persist, especially in institutions, infrastructure, labor market efficiency, and innovation. The wide range of performance exhibited in the region also contributes to regional inequality (Schwab, 2018). Latin America's poor performance and the region's lack of progress in closing gaps with global leaders are associated with low productivity, high informality, insufficient export diversification, and growth that is insufficient to create employment and fund the growing demand for more and better public goods (Schwab, 2018). These are all issues that have been expanded upon throughout this book.

As Latin America attempts to consolidate the social gains it has made in the past decade (e.g., a record reduction in poverty and a growing middle class) it must strengthen its ability to adapt to changing international conditions and rediscover new sources of sustainable growth based on a coherent competitiveness agenda that enables entrepreneurship and new innovative businesses to emerge. The results in the GCI can help guide the identification of priorities and stimulate public-private collaboration (Schwab, 2018).

Overall, we can see in Table 7.3 that the median rank for Latin America has not changed in the past decade. Note that a ranking is relative, since a country could technically improve on its score on a component and have a worse rank at the same time due to changes in other countries' scores. Thus, both could be considered when getting into the detail of the GCI. That said, we don't have aggregate scores for Latin America as a whole, and thus will save the more detailed analysis for the individual country level scores.

Beginning with the biggest improvement in overall ranking, Nicaragua and Costa Rica moved up the most. This pulled Nicaragua up from the stage one category to the transition category to stage two. A similar effect happened for Costa Rica, albeit at a higher category. It is also worth noting that a decade ago there were no Latin American countries on their transition to stage three. So, while some countries have taken steps back in their competitiveness, others have risen.

The countries the lost the most ground in the rankings were El Salvador and Venezuela. While El Salvador was already in the transition stage a decade ago, Venezuela with the worst competitiveness ranking in the region has dropped down from stage two to the prior transition stage. Venezuela is currently one of the least competitive countries in the world. This is likely correlated to their poor ranking in the Doing Business Index displayed in Table 7.1.

First Pillar: Institutions

The institutional environment of a country depends on the efficiency and the behavior of both public and private stakeholders (Schwab, 2018). The legal and administrative framework within which individuals, firms, and governments interact determines the quality of the public institutions of a country and has an important bearing on competitiveness and growth. It influences investment decisions and the organization of production and plays a key role in the ways in which societies distribute the benefits and bear the costs of development strategies and policies. Good private institutions are also important for the sound and sustainable development of an economy. The 2007–2008 global financial crisis, along with numerous corporate scandals, has highlighted the relevance of accounting and reporting standards and transparency for preventing fraud and mismanagement, ensuring good governance, and maintaining investor and consumer confidence.

The data in Table 7.4 would suggest that Latin America does particularly poorly managing its institutions. In fact, with a median rank of 116, this is the

TABLE 7.4 Institutions

Country	2007	2017	Δ in Rank
Uruguay	46	34	12
Chile	29	35	–6
Costa Rica	52	48	4
Panama	66	74	–8
Brazil	104	109	–5
Guatemala	91	111	–20
Argentina	123	113	10
Nicaragua	108	115	–7
Peru	106	116	–10
Colombia	79	117	–38
Honduras	89	120	–31
Mexico	85	123	–38
Ecuador	125	128	–3
Dominican Republic	107	129	–22
Paraguay	129	131	–2
El Salvador	84	133	–49
Venezuela	131	137	–6
Bolivia	124	n/a	n/a
Latin America	98	116	–19
China	77	41	36
U.S.	33	20	13

Source: World Economic Forum (2018).

Note
Ranks are out of 137 economies and sorted best to worst for 2017.

worst pillar of the 12 in the GCI. The bad news gets worse when one looks at the change over the past decade. 14 of the 18 countries in Latin America score above 100 of the 137 countries in the world in this indicator. Unfortunately for those wanting to do business in Latin America, nearly every country in the region has got worse in the past decade. Notable exceptions are Uruguay for being more transparent and Argentina with its shift in leadership at the presidency that reflects renewed trust in public institutions. At this point in the book, it should come as no surprise that the subcomponents of corruption, security, and public-sector performance are three of the five elements that make up the institutions pillar. We have covered these issues in depth throughout this book, and the GCI reinforces the problem with their ranking of Latin America.

Some countries such as Mexico would be doing much better were not for its particularly poor rank in the institutions pillar. Efficiency in government spending got worse in both score and rank. Private institutions also got worse due to poor corporate ethics and responsibility. While this pillar looks particularly bleak, it should be noted that hope exists that a change is possible in Latin

America. The "operation car wash" of identifying corrupt organizations and individuals is sweeping through Latin America (BBC, 2018). What is so different about this scandal is that presidents of the largest firms and nations are being held accountable. Many are currently serving jail time after paying record fines. If this shift towards transparency can maintain its current trajectory, doing business in Latin America will look completely different in a decade from now. Indeed, Brazil recovered 11 positions from last year on this pillar, showing the effects of the perception of successful proceedings to curb corruption within its institutions.

Finally, while the information on Table 7.4 appears grim, and there is currently change taking place in the region, the fact that the most basic pillar for competitiveness is the region's worse is troubling. It may behoove the risk averse investor to target the four countries on the top of the list: Uruguay, Chile, Costa Rica, and Panama. As mentioned at the opening of this chapter, we will go into much more detail on Panama in the case at the end of the chapter.

Second Pillar: Infrastructure

The second of the four basic requirements for a competitive economy is infrastructure. The sheer size of Latin America along with the geographical elements such as the Andes mountain range and Amazon rainforest make the infrastructure particularly important in this part of the world. Extensive and efficient infrastructure is critical for ensuring the effective functioning of the economy (Schwab, 2018). Effective modes of transport – including high-quality roads, railroads, ports, and air transport – enable entrepreneurs to get their goods and services to market in a quick and safe manner. This facilitates the movement of workers to the most suitable jobs. Economies also depend on electricity supplies that are free from interruptions and shortages so that businesses and factories can work unimpeded. Finally, a solid and extensive telecommunications network allows for a rapid and free flow of information (Schwab, 2018). Fixed line and mobile phone subscriptions increase overall economic efficiency by helping to ensure that businesses can communicate, and decisions are made by business people. Note that this does not include the internet, which is in the more sophisticated ninth pillar. We are still in the basic requirements.

In Table 7.5, we see that Panama is at the top of the ranking, up 13 slots to number 37. Three primary reasons exist why Panama is so high. First, the Panama Canal and its port authority are world class, ranked as the sixth best port infrastructure in the world. Second, Copa airlines, which is the primary airline servicing Central America is based in Panama City. So, many business travelers that want to get in and around that part of the region often go through Panama City. At the time of this writing, Panama is expanding its airport to improve flying into the region. Therefore, we expect Panama to continue to hold this

TABLE 7.5 Infrastructure

Country	2007	2017	Δ in Rank
Panama	50	37	13
Chile	31	41	−10
Uruguay	64	45	19
Mexico	61	62	−1
Costa Rica	95	65	30
Ecuador	97	72	25
Brazil	78	73	5
El Salvador	51	77	−26
Argentina	81	81	0
Guatemala	70	84	−14
Peru	101	86	15
Colombia	86	87	−1
Nicaragua	116	92	24
Dominican Republic	79	101	−22
Honduras	75	104	−29
Venezuela	104	117	−13
Paraguay	126	118	8
Bolivia	118	n/a	n/a
Latin America	80	81	−1
China	52	46	6
U.S.	6	9	−3

Source: World Economic Forum (2018).

Note
Ranks are out of 137 economies and sorted best to worst for 2017.

ranking on this pillar in the future (or even improve). Finally, mobile phones are everywhere in Panama. At 172 subscriptions per 100 people, Panama ranks 6th in the world for mobile phone penetration. On a recent study abroad trip, we recall heading up a river in the middle of the jungle in a primitive dug-out canoe while the young Embera tribesman called ahead to the village on his mobile phone to inform them we were on our way.

Costa Rica has climbed 30 slots in the past decade partially due to its very high mobile phone penetration (similar to Panama), ranking it 12th in the world. On the other hand, its roads are atrocious, ranked 123rd in the world, and worse than every other country in Latin America except Paraguay. While there are plans to improve the roads in Costa Rica, progress has been slow (Chacon, 2016). This means that moving goods and people from side to side in the country is slow and expensive. Roads are not the only problem Paraguay has regarding infrastructure. Being one of two land locked countries in Latin America, means that it needs very good roads and air infrastructure. It ranks last in Latin America on both.

Third Pillar: Macroeconomic Environment

The stability of the macroeconomic environment is important for business. Although it is true that macroeconomic stability alone cannot increase the productivity of a nation, it is also recognized that macroeconomic frenzy harms the economy (Schwab, 2018). Further, the government cannot provide services efficiently if it must make high-interest payments on its past debts. Running fiscal deficits limits the government's future flexibility to react to business cycles. Inflation rates restrict the efficiency of firms due to high borrowing costs. And because firms need to borrow money in order to invest in innovative technology, the economy cannot grow in a sustainable manner unless the macro environment is stable.

Even with Brazil, Argentina, and Venezuela pulling Latin America down on the macroeconomic environment pillar, it is still arguably one of the region's best performing factors. The government not being able to balance its budget is hurting Brazil. And unless the current president can push through changes in the pension system, it will continue to struggle on this pillar. Inflation over 10%

TABLE 7.6 Macroeconomic Environment

Country	2007	2017	Δ in Rank
Panama	52	11	41
Chile	12	36	−24
Peru	78	37	41
Paraguay	117	42	75
Mexico	35	43	−8
Dominican Republic	91	49	42
Nicaragua	115	51	64
Honduras	71	52	19
Guatemala	86	54	32
Colombia	63	62	1
Costa Rica	111	79	32
El Salvador	67	85	−18
Ecuador	27	91	−64
Uruguay	99	95	4
Brazil	126	124	2
Argentina	64	125	−61
Venezuela	70	134	−64
Bolivia	49	n/a	n/a
Latin America	71	54	17
China	7	17	−10
U.S.	75	83	−8

Source: World Economic Forum (2018).

Note
Ranks are out of 137 economies and sorted best to worst for 2017.

is a negative issue for Argentina. And Venezuela has both of those issues even worse than Brazil and Argentina.

Six countries are in the top 50 in the world on the macroeconomic pillar. Paraguay has risen 75 slots in a decade, which is a remarkable feat. As one might surmise from the last section on infrastructure, Paraguay is not spending very much on it. The upside to this is low government debt, which ratings companies reward them for. Both items have been improving for Paraguay. At some point, the country will have to decide on which pillar is more important for their competitiveness. Ideally, they strike a balance by increasing infrastructure spending, or even encouraging private firms to initiate projects such as toll roads and airports not owned by the government.

Fourth Pillar: Health and Primary Education

The final pillar of the basic requirements index is access to health care and a primary education. A healthy workforce is paramount to a country's competitiveness and productivity. Workers who are ill cannot function to their potential

TABLE 7.7 Health and Primary Education

Country	2007	2017	Δ in Rank
Costa Rica	50	35	15
Ecuador	90	61	29
Argentina	54	64	−10
Chile	70	66	4
Uruguay	58	70	−12
Mexico	55	76	−21
Panama	57	79	−22
Nicaragua	100	86	14
Colombia	64	88	−24
Honduras	92	89	3
Peru	95	93	2
Brazil	84	96	−12
Venezuela	76	99	−23
El Salvador	80	100	−20
Paraguay	89	104	−15
Dominican Republic	102	105	−3
Guatemala	97	106	−9
Bolivia	91	n/a	n/a
Latin America	82	88	−6
China	61	40	21
U.S.	34	29	5

Source: World Economic Forum (2018).

Note
Ranks are out of 137 economies and sorted best to worst for 2017.

and obviously be less productive. Poor health leads to significant costs to business, as sickness increases absenteeism and decreases efficiency. Thus, countries need to invest in the health care of their citizens. In addition to health, this pillar considers the quality and quantity of the *basic* education received, which is a fundamentally basic need in today's economy. The efficiency of each individual worker is dependent on it.

While nearly every country in the region has fallen lower in this pillar, a few countries such as Costa Rica and Ecuador are preventing them from getting particularly low. On the health side, Ecuador does well managing malaria. On the education side, while the quality of the primary education is not good (ranked 85th in the world) it makes sure students attend (98% enrollment rate).

On the other hand, the quality of primary education in Guatemala is particularly poor. They are ranked 130th in the world and last in the region. Poverty, corruption, violence and racism all have negative impacts on the primary education system in Guatemala, where the trend is towards less children attending primary school (Galicia, 2016). The effects of this trend could have long-term effects on the countries' competitiveness in the region. Business people that can not hire employees with even basic skills are not likely to establish a business there. This is part of the reason multinational firms from around the globe choose Panama and Costa Rica in Central America instead of Guatemala, El Salvador, and Honduras to set up their regional hubs.

Fifth Pillar: Higher Education and Training

Once a country has established the basic requirements for competitiveness, it usually shifts focus to efficiency enhancers and the six pillars within it (see Figure 7.1). As mentioned earlier in this chapter, this is where the majority of Latin American countries are currently rated in the GCI. Quality higher education and training is crucial for economies that want to move up the value chain beyond simple production processes and products (Schwab, 2018). Regardless of whether countries are becoming more or less globalized, countries need to develop a well-educated workforce that can perform complex tasks and adapt rapidly to their changing environment and the evolving needs of the production system. This pillar measures secondary and tertiary enrollment rates as well as the quality of education as evaluated by business leaders (Schwab, 2018). The World Bank defines tertiary education as including universities as well as trade schools and colleges. The extent of staff training is also taken into consideration because of the importance of vocational and continuous on-the-job training in order to maintain and upgrade skills.

As mentioned, this pillar is made up of the quantity and quality of higher education, and on-the-job training. All three are weighted equally as one-third of the pillar. Higher education and training is one of the few pillars that have improved in Latin America over the past decade (see Table 7.8). 12 of the 18 countries improved over the time span with notable exceptions being Brazil and Panama. It is not that a large percentage of Brazil's people do not attend secondary (99.7% enrollment rate) and tertiary (50.6% enrollment rate) institutions, but rather that the quality level in both are so low (ranked 125th and 131st, respectively). Exacerbating the issue is that wealthier families tend to send their children to much better private schools for secondary education, which pays off later when they get accepted into the competitive (and nearly free) federal universities. Naturally, this adds to the inequality we have demonstrated in this book. Panama's issue is the quality of their math and science education system (ranked 112th). This is one of the few pillars Panama has not improved in the past decade and should be a concern as it attempts to reach the highest level of competitiveness because innovators need to be highly educated. That said, Panama knows this is a problem and has expanded its international ties and domestic spending in a bid to strengthen its education system (ICEF Monitor, 2016). It is also focusing on skills gaps in the labor market by expanding the quantity and quality of its education system. An example of an excellent

TABLE 7.8 Higher Education and Training

Country	2007	2017	Δ in Rank
Chile	42	26	16
Costa Rica	50	31	19
Argentina	51	38	13
Uruguay	67	53	14
Venezuela	85	58	27
Colombia	69	66	3
Ecuador	111	77	34
Brazil	64	79	−15
Mexico	72	80	−8
Peru	84	81	3
Panama	73	88	−15
Dominican Republic	99	93	6
Guatemala	101	99	2
Honduras	96	102	−6
El Salvador	92	104	−12
Paraguay	112	107	5
Nicaragua	108	110	−2
Bolivia	91	n/a	n/a
Latin America	85	80	5
China	78	47	31
U.S.	5	3	2

Source: World Economic Forum (2018).

Note
Ranks are out of 137 economies and sorted best to worst for 2017.

program being offered is at the City of Knowledge in Panama City (Ciudad del Saber, 2018). University students from all over the world meet there to visit innovative businesses that have set up shop there. The City of Knowledge is a good example of how a country took an old asset (U.S. Army base) and turned it into something that makes it more competitive.

An altogether different problem exists for many of Central America's countries. For instance, both Nicaragua and El Salvador are ranked nearly last in the world for both quality of the education system and quality of math and science education (Lakhani, 2015). High poverty levels lead to child labor and ultimately drop outs.

The opposite is the case for Chile, which has a huge (88.6%) tertiary education enrollment rate (ranked seventh in the world). In 2013, Michelle Bachelet's presidential campaign was partially based on a pledge to make higher education tuition-free for all students from families in the lower 70% of the income distribution by 2018, and tuition-free for all students regardless of income by 2020 (Delisle & Bernasconi, 2018). President Bachelet won the election based partly on that proposal. The program had to be cut back a bit with the price of copper dropping, which is the primary export for the country and a large source of income. The policies of Chile should go a long way towards reducing inequality as a young generation gets access to tertiary education. Another point worth applauding Chile on the pillar is its rank for quality of management schools (27th in the world, 2nd in Latin America to Costa Rica). It is not coincidental that Santiago, Chile is home of many multinational enterprises that are looking for a base of operations in South America.

Sixth Pillar: Goods Market Efficiency

Countries with efficient goods markets are well positioned to produce the right mix of products and services given their particular conditions, as well as to ensure that these goods can be most effectively traded in the economy. Healthy market competition, both domestic and foreign, is important in driving market efficiency, and thus business productivity, by ensuring that the most efficient firms, producing goods demanded by the market (Schwab, 2018). Market efficiency also depends on demand conditions such as customer orientation and buyer sophistication. For cultural or historical reasons, customers may be more demanding in some countries than in others. This can create an important competitive advantage, as it forces companies to be more innovative and customer oriented and thus imposes the discipline necessary for efficiency to be achieved in the market (Schwab, 2018). As one can tell by the language of this pillar, we are moving towards more sophisticated factors that will help with innovation.

As with pillar six, this pillar essentially consists of three components: domestic and foreign competition, and how demanding buyers are. A score of 98 puts the region towards to bottom of the ranking and the fourth worst pillar out

TABLE 7.9 Goods Market Efficiency

Country	2007	2017	Δ in Rank
Chile	28	39	−11
Panama	54	41	13
Guatemala	62	48	14
Costa Rica	52	63	−11
Mexico	61	70	−9
Peru	67	75	−8
Uruguay	73	77	−4
Paraguay	116	86	30
Honduras	87	98	−11
Colombia	85	102	−17
El Salvador	56	109	−53
Dominican Republic	100	115	−15
Nicaragua	111	117	−6
Brazil	97	122	−25
Ecuador	123	128	−5
Argentina	115	133	−18
Venezuela	124	137	−13
Bolivia	125	n/a	n/a
Latin America	86	98	−12
China	58	46	12
U.S.	12	7	5

Source: World Economic Forum (2018).

Note
Ranks are out of 137 economies and sorted best to worst for 2017.

of the 12. And it is getting worse. When a country moves towards dictatorship such as the case in Venezuela, there will not be any competition (Horsey, 2017). This is why Venezuela is ranked last, not only in the region, but in the entire world. The country ranks over 130 in nearly all of the 16 subindex issues. While the situation is different in Argentina, the prior socialist government effectively taxed the incentive to invest out of businesses for years. As the case on Argentina in Chapter 3 attests, we believe this is changing for the better. Now the government is implementing reforms that specifically target distortions effecting market efficiency (Schwab, 2018).

Guatemala with the third best rank in the region has the largest market in Central America, and perhaps surprisingly, the Guatemalan market is competitive and price-sensitive. Business people expect good after-sales service and support (US Commercial Service, 2017). Hopefully, the country can get a grip on its business costs of organized crime (pillar one) in order to stop its decrease in competitiveness levels that have happened over the past decade (see Table 7.3).

Seventh Pillar: Labor Market Efficiency

Along with goods market efficiency, the labor market also needs to be efficient for a country to be productive and competitive. The efficiency and flexibility of the labor market are relevant for ensuring that workers are allocated to their most effective use in the economy and provided with incentives to give their best effort in their jobs. Labor markets must therefore have the flexibility to shift workers from one economic activity to another rapidly and at low cost, and to allow for wage fluctuations without much social disruption (Schwab, 2018). Efficient labor markets must also ensure clear strong incentives for employees and promote meritocracy at the workplace equally for men and women. Taken together these factors have a positive effect on worker performance and the attractiveness of the country for talent, two aspects of the labor market that are growing more important as talent shortages loom (Schwab, 2018).

This pillar is concerned with flexibility and the efficient use of talent (weighted 50% each). Unfortunately, this pillar is even worse than the last one, and continues to deteriorate. It is the second weakest pillar in the region, only

TABLE 7.10 Labor Market Efficiency

Country	2007	2017	Δ in Rank
Chile	14	49	−35
Peru	87	64	23
Costa Rica	18	69	−51
Panama	70	76	−6
Colombia	74	88	−14
Nicaragua	97	101	−4
Guatemala	81	102	−21
Mexico	92	105	−13
Paraguay	114	106	8
Brazil	104	114	−10
Dominican Republic	86	117	−31
Uruguay	89	121	−32
Honduras	61	124	−63
El Salvador	41	125	−84
Ecuador	116	126	−10
Argentina	129	132	−3
Venezuela	123	137	−14
Bolivia	121	n/a	n/a
Latin America	88	106	−18
China	55	38	17
U.S.	1	3	−2

Source: World Economic Forum (2018).

Note
Ranks are out of 137 economies and sorted best to worst for 2017.

trailing institutions (pillar one). Once again, Venezuela is the worst in the world, but all but five countries are ranked above 100 in the world. Even more startling is that only two countries out of the 18 we are analyzing improved in the past decade. Peru has jumped 23 positions to be second in the region. The only thing it is still particularly poor at is hiring and firing practices, where strikes and rigid labor laws limit flexibility. On the other hand, Peru businesses have the second most (to Chile) flexibility in wage determination of any country in the region. The country also does well in attracting and retaining talent, where it only trails, Panama, Costa Rica, and Chile in Latin America. Perhaps Peruvian businesses focus on talent acquisition and retention due to the country's very poor education, which was mentioned above (Posada, 2016).

Eighth Pillar: Financial Market Development

An efficient financial sector allocates the resources saved by a nation's population, as well as those entering the economy from abroad. The allocations go to the entrepreneurial or investment projects with the highest expected rates of return rather than to the politically connected (Schwab, 2018). Because business investment is critical to productivity, economies require sophisticated financial markets that can make capital available for private-sector firms. This capital comes in the form of loans from a sound banking sector, well-regulated securities exchanges, venture capital, and other financial products. In order to fulfill all those functions, the banking sector needs to be trustworthy and transparent. Finally, financial markets need appropriate regulation to protect investors and other actors in the economy at large (Schwab, 2018).

Returning back to what Latin American countries do well, Table 7.11 shows that half of the countries in Latin America are ranked higher than China on a pillar. This is one of only a few cases where China has not completely pulled away from Latin America in terms of competitiveness. The two stars are Panama and Chile, which both have very robust financial markets and have each improved their position by nine slots over the past decade. At this point, along with Guatemala, the scores are identical. The main difference is that Guatemala is improving much faster (up 69 positions; the most in Latin America) than the other two nations due to its soundness of banks, legal rights index, and affordability of financial services. All three of which are pertinent to a competitive financial environment.

Alternatively, Ecuador has done poorly on this pillar for a long time. This is because financial services are hard to access and expensive. This is likely correlated with the poor access to venture capital, which certainly is not likely coming from abroad with a rank of 127 on the legal rights index.

TABLE 7.11 Financial Market Development

Country	2007	2017	Δ in Rank
Panama	23	14	9
Chile	26	17	9
Guatemala	87	18	69
Colombia	72	27	45
Peru	46	35	11
Mexico	67	36	31
Honduras	81	38	43
Costa Rica	70	39	31
El Salvador	62	57	5
Uruguay	89	60	29
Paraguay	95	82	13
Brazil	73	92	−19
Dominican Republic	108	99	9
Nicaragua	92	100	−8
Ecuador	99	113	−14
Argentina	114	121	−7
Venezuela	104	122	−18
Bolivia	106	n/a	n/a
Latin America	84	57	27
China	118	48	70
U.S.	11	2	9

Source: World Economic Forum (2018).

Note
Ranks are out of 137 economies and sorted best to worst for 2017.

Ninth Pillar: Technological Readiness

The technological readiness pillar measures the responsiveness with which an economy adopts existing technologies to enhance the productivity of its industries. Specifically, there is an emphasis on a country's capacity to fully leverage information and communication technologies in daily activities and production processes for increased efficiency and enabling innovation for competitiveness (Schwab, 2018). Whether the technology used has or has not been developed within national borders is irrelevant for its ability to enhance productivity. The central point is that the firms operating in the country need to have access to advanced products and the ability to absorb and use them (Schwab, 2018). Among the main sources of foreign technology, foreign direct investment (FDI) often plays a key role, especially for countries at a less advanced stage of technological development.

This pillar has two parts; information technology and its adoption. A few key subindex measures are how many internet users does a country have, and what is its bandwidth. With an increased reliance on internet technology (e.g., Skype) to have virtual meetings, few things are more frustrating for business people than when one keeps losing a connection due to low or unreliable bandwidth. Further, what access do firms in each country have to the latest technology is pertinent to doing business in Latin America. Table 7.12 shows that Latin America does okay on this pillar but is losing ground; especially in the Dominican Republic. In the Dominican Republic, they continue to have problems with getting FDI and technology transferred to them. And while internet speeds have more than doubled in Uruguay and tripled in Chile (at the other end of Table 7.12) over the past five years, they are basically the same in the Dominican Republic in the same time frame.

Albeit not amazing, Uruguay does have the best rank (33rd) in the region on the number of fixed-broadband internet subscriptions (27%). E-commerce businesses in particular should look for the countries that have the most people using broadband, and what that connection speed is trending towards. In 2011, the Uruguay government invested big in broadband to help it connect to the United States via Brazil through a new submarine cable (Nixon, 2015).

TABLE 7.12 Technological Readiness

Country	2007	2017	Δ in Rank
Uruguay	67	36	31
Chile	42	38	4
Costa Rica	56	45	11
Brazil	55	55	0
Panama	61	63	−2
Colombia	76	65	11
Argentina	78	66	12
Mexico	60	71	−11
Peru	80	86	−6
Dominican Republic	64	87	−23
Ecuador	100	92	8
El Salvador	85	95	−10
Guatemala	81	96	−15
Honduras	98	99	−1
Paraguay	128	103	25
Nicaragua	120	108	12
Venezuela	79	109	−30
Bolivia	126	n/a	n/a
Latin America	79	86	−8
China	73	73	0
U.S.	9	6	3

Source: World Economic Forum (2018).

Notes
Ranks are out of 137 economies and sorted best to worst for 2017.

We predict that this type of focused investment by the public and private entities will pay off for many years to come due to the increased innovation and competitiveness in Uruguay.

Tenth Pillar: Market Size

The final efficiency enhancer pillar is market size. The size of the market affects productivity since large markets allow firms to exploit economies of scale. Traditionally, the markets available to firms have been constrained by national borders (Schwab, 2018). In the era of globalization, international markets have become a substitute for domestic markets, especially for small countries. Thus, exports can be thought of as a substitute for domestic demand in determining the size of the market for the firms of a country. By including both domestic and foreign markets in the measure of market size, they give credit to export-driven economies and geographic areas (such as the European Union) that are divided into many countries but have a single common market (Schwab, 2018).

TABLE 7.13 Market Size

Country	2007	2017	Δ in Rank
Brazil	10	10	0
Mexico	13	11	2
Argentina	23	32	−9
Colombia	30	37	−7
Chile	47	44	3
Peru	53	48	5
Venezuela	51	52	−1
Ecuador	68	66	2
Dominican Republic	63	68	−5
Guatemala	74	73	1
Panama	93	79	14
Costa Rica	69	80	−11
Paraguay	90	87	3
Uruguay	89	89	0
El Salvador	86	91	−5
Honduras	94	95	−1
Nicaragua	97	103	−6
Bolivia	96	n/a	n/a
Latin America	69	68	1
China	2	1	1
U.S.	1	2	−1

Source: World Economic Forum (2018).

Notes
Ranks are out of 137 economies and sorted best to worst for 2017.

While the free trade areas in Latin America are not as open as the EU, we saw in the last chapter that there are a number of free trade agreements in Latin America and the number is expanding. Therefore, the export market is weighted at 25%, and the domestic market at 75% for this pillar.

Per the description above, market size is pretty straight forward. Countries with bigger GDPs tend to do the best on this pillar. This is also why we chose to focus on those countries in this book. If a firm that is considering entering a country in Latin America can compete in one of these countries high on the list, then the sheer market potential should steer them there. This is part of the reason for the massive FDI flows into Brazil and Mexico.

Finally, while we will advocate for Panama's impressive competitiveness in the case at the end of this chapter, it is unlikely to surpass Chile as the region's most competitive country due to market size differences. Something rather poor would have to happen in Chile for this to happen, which does not help us do business in Latin America.

Eleventh Pillar: Business Sophistication

There are two pillars that comprise the highest level in the CGI: Business soph-istication and innovation. Business sophistication concerns two elements that are intricately linked: the quality of a country's overall business networks and the quality of individual firms' operations and strategies (Schwab, 2018). These factors are especially important for countries at an advanced stage of develop-ment once the more basic sources of productivity improvements have been exhausted. The quality of a country's business networks and supporting indus-tries, as measured by the quantity and quality of local suppliers and the extent of their interaction, is important for a variety of reasons. When companies and suppliers from a sector are interconnected in geographically proximate groups, called clusters, efficiency is heightened, greater opportunities for innovation in processes and products are created (Schwab, 2018).

The countries at the top of Table 7.14 have realized that if they want to compete and move into the highest level of countries operate (stage 3, see Table 7.2), then they must decide on what they can be really great at and then form clusters to help each other. This has long been understood in Japan, United States, China, and South Korea, which not coincidentally produce the most patents in the world (Science Business, 2017). Three of these countries are all innovation driven countries (stage 3), China withstanding. And we believe it is just a matter of time until China progresses to this stage with its current govern-ment support to innovate more.

Since we will discuss Chile's competitiveness in the case in Chapter 10 and Panama in the case in this chapter, we will focus on Costa Rica and Mexico for the business sophistication pillar. There has been quite a bit of variance in Costa Rica's score on this pillar over the past decade. The country has been able to

TABLE 7.14 Business Sophistication

Country	2007	2017	Δ in Rank
Costa Rica	38	35	3
Panama	49	44	5
Mexico	54	49	5
Chile	32	50	−18
Guatemala	61	53	8
Brazil	39	56	−17
Colombia	65	64	1
Argentina	75	78	−3
Peru	63	80	−17
Uruguay	86	83	3
Dominican Republic	87	85	2
Honduras	84	88	−4
El Salvador	78	104	−26
Ecuador	93	105	−12
Paraguay	122	114	8
Nicaragua	110	129	−19
Venezuela	96	133	−37
Bolivia	125	n/a	n/a
Latin America	77	80	−4
China	57	33	24
U.S.	7	2	5

Source: World Economic Forum (2018).

Notes
Ranks are out of 137 economies and sorted best to worst for 2017.

build a competitive advantage in the exports of services based on information and communication technologies (Leon, 2017). Alternatively, Mexico has invested heavily in research and development to become a significant country for high-tech value chains (Leon, 2017). There is a long discussion of how Mexico has developed a competitiveness lab in the GCI referenced throughout this chapter (p.30 of their report). It is a great example of how a country is using the GCI to specifically focus on improving its competitiveness. With trade between the United States and Mexico in question, the timing could not be better for Mexico to focus on maximizing its productivity. If not for trading with the United States, then with other nations.

Twelfth Pillar: Innovation

The last pillar of the GCI focuses on innovation. Innovation is particularly important for economies as they approach the frontiers of knowledge, and the possibility of generating more value by integrating and adapting exogenous technologies tends to disappear (Schwab, 2018). In these economies, firms must design and develop cutting-edge products and processes to maintain a competitive edge and move toward even higher value-added activities. This progression requires an environment that is conducive to innovative activity and supported by both the public and the private sectors. It means sufficient investment in research and development, especially by the private sector; the presence of high-quality scientific research institutions that can generate the basic knowledge needed to build the new technologies; extensive collaboration in research and technological developments between universities and industry; and the protection of intellectual property (Schwab, 2018).

Table 7.15 shows that this is one of the few pillars that no country did particularly well. This is not to have been expected since no country in Latin America is really in this stage. But as well demonstrated at the beginning of this chapter, five countries are now in the transition zone between stage two and stage three. While it will be particularly difficult for Costa Rica and Panama to reach the third stage due to market size restrictions, Chile, Argentina, and

TABLE 7.15 Innovation

Country	2007	2017	Δ in Rank
Costa Rica	35	43	−8
Chile	45	52	−7
Panama	87	55	32
Mexico	71	56	15
Argentina	91	72	19
Colombia	72	73	−1
Brazil	44	85	−41
Guatemala	83	88	−5
Uruguay	80	93	−13
Honduras	101	108	−7
Ecuador	118	111	7
Peru	100	113	−13
Dominican Republic	106	120	−14
Paraguay	130	127	3
El Salvador	109	130	−21
Venezuela	99	131	−32
Nicaragua	124	133	−9
Bolivia	128	n/a	n/a
Latin America	99	101	−2
China	38	28	10
U.S.	1	2	−1

Source: World Economic Forum (2018).

Notes
Ranks are out of 137 economies and sorted best to worst for 2017.

Mexico, will certainly have their sites on that goal of an innovation driven economy. We do not want to dismiss Costa Rica and Panama. If they can continue to improve their export services market, they would be able to partially overcome the liability of a small domestic market.

Regional Comparison

Now that we have analyzed all 12 of the GCI, we conclude with an analysis of selected regions in order to show how Latin America is faring in competitiveness with other parts of the world. Note that the "overall" row is not the median of each of the 12 pillars, but the median score of each country's overall score in the region. This only really matters for the East Asia and Pacific region since the medians of the pillars in a region are very close to the country medians.

The purpose of this comparison is not to show who Latin America is "beating" or "losing" to, but rather to initiate a discussion of what it needs to do in order to generate more productive investments. We know Latin America's institutions are for the most part failing the region's effort to be more competitive. On the other hand, the macroeconomic environment and financial markets look pretty good. In general, before the region can truly get behind improving the efficiency enhancing factors, it must take care of the problems with institutions and infrastructure.

Conclusion

In this chapter we provided two sources of information in order to delve into Latin America's ability to do business and compete. As with other parts of this book, the results were both complicated and mixed, depending on which country was the focus.

We tend to adhere to the regional analysis in the GCI that starts by acknowledging the GDP for the region is finally out of recession. The region was not ready for the end of the commodities boom and their loss of export income. Even though exchange rates favored exports during this time, it was not enough to prevent a stall in the economy. This increased the strain on the region's ability to invest in the pillars that could make it more competitive, such as infrastructure.

The GCI prescribes that as Latin America strives to consolidate the social gains it has made in the past decade (e.g., a record reduction in poverty and a growing middle class) it must strengthen its capacity to adapt to changing international conditions and rediscover new sources of sustainable growth based on a coherent competitiveness agenda that enables entrepreneurship and new innovative businesses to emerge (Schwab, 2018). While we are not sure that the region is ready to invest heavily in innovation, we do concur that poverty

TABLE 7.16 GCI Pillar Median Ranks by Region

Indicator	Latin America	North America and Europe	East Asia & Pacific	Middle East & North Africa	South Asia
Macroeconomic Environment	54	39	26	66	79
Financial Market Development	57	46	40	70	78
Market Size	68	55	27	53	49
Higher Education and Training	80	29	47	71	99
Business Sophistication	80	31	32	69	79
Infrastructure	81	32	43	57	100
Technological Readiness	86	27	60	67	109
Health and Primary Education	88	25	31	63	93
Goods Market Efficiency	98	35	33	58	91
Innovation	101	35	28	66	70
Labor Market Efficiency	106	44	38	119	108
Institutions	116	47	41	49	83
Overall	84	36	27	65	87

Source: World Economic Forum (2018).

Notes
Ranks are out of 137 economies.

reduction and a growing middle class have benefited hugely by the growth in the region.

Its possible that public and private policy makers use the GCI to develop strategic plans based on what a country can realistically produce over a given period of time. And if these leaders can coordinate across the region so as to not waste money in order to improve efficiency, all the better.

The Case of Panama's Competitiveness

The case of Panama's competitiveness is unique for a number of reasons. Resorting the 12 indicators of the CGI by the order of their position in the three stages helps us interpret the country better than sorting by rank.

Further, it is helpful to compare them with the only other Central American country even close to them in the rankings, Costa Rica. First, for the overall subindex of the basic requirements, Panama scores much better holding the 37th rank in the world compared to Costa Rica's 53rd. Other than Chile (36th), no other country in Latin America is even close to Panama. The Table displays that Panama is in the top seven in all four pillars. While its roads aren't wonderful, the rest of its infrastructure is, as with its macroeconomic environment. Both are top in the region. Its biggest problem in the basics category is its primary education system. We discussed why this is the case in that section of this chapter.

Indeed, Panama is only below the half way mark in Latin America in higher education and market size. We discussed their issue with market size

TABLE 7.17 Panama

Indicator	2007	2017	Δ in Rank	Rank in Region
Institutions	66	74	−8	4
Infrastructure	50	37	13	1
Macroeconomic Environment	52	11	41	1
Health and Primary Education	57	79	−22	7
Higher Education and Training	73	88	−15	11
Goods Market Efficiency	54	41	13	2
Labor Market Efficiency	70	76	−6	4
Financial Market Development	23	14	9	1
Technological Readiness	61	63	−2	5
Market Size	93	79	14	11
Business Sophistication	49	44	5	2
Innovation	87	55	32	3
Overall GCI	59	50	9	3

Source: World Economic Forum (2018).

Notes
Ranks are out of 137 economies and sorted best to worst for 2017.

being one difficult to alter, yet the country struggles with its education system. On the other hand, the financial district in Panama City is a site of wonder. No other area of Central America looks anything like it. Especially not in Costa Rica.

Finally, what makes us most enthusiastic about Panama is its potential to use its high levels of business sophistication to generate innovative service solutions. Not only could this be in the financial services sector, but Panama has strategically incentivized foreign multinationals to operate out of massive free trade zones. This has brought many good jobs to the country, increasing the size of the middle class. And as their middle class grows, so do their demands for more interesting goods, and the people that can provide them. La Rana Dorada micro-brewery is one such case (The Rana Dorada, 2018).

The craft beer scene in Panama remains small, but one of the major players right now is without a doubt La Rana Dorada (The Golden Frog). Run by an American and serving an even ratio of locals, tourists, and expats, the brewery aims to bring more variety to the beer drinking culture in Panama. With a wave of micro-breweries opening across Europe and North America, master brewer Brad Kraus discusses in a YouTube video the trend in Latin America (The Rana Dorada, 2012). Mr. Kraus has worked in the United States, Peru, Chile, and most recently at a very successful brewery in Colombia. Yet he has given that up to pursue his dream of running a top brewery in Panama. And if you are fortunate enough to take one of his free tours, you will see that he is very happy with how things are going.

From a beer blog covering the company, we get more of their story. The La Rana Dorada Pub on Via Argentina opened first in September of 2010. After a couple successful years in that location, they opened the brewery across town in February of 2012. The site is at the entrance of Casco Viejo, the historic part of Panama City that still displays colonial facades and streets of brick. Designated a World Heritage site in 2003, Casco is going through a rapid renovation. It's not only the heart of tourism in Panama City, but also the place where many residents like to head for dinner and drinks (Ackley, 2012). On our most recent trip to Panama, the company had recently acquired a warehouse in order to handle the increased demand.

We believe that the case of La Rana Dorada illustrates how what may seem like developed world tastes (microbeers) can turn into major business opportunities for an expanding middle class, such as the one in Panama.

References

Ackley, David (2012). "Panama: La Rana Dorada." www.localbeerblog.com/2012/05/panama-la-rana-dorada.html, accessed March, 2018.

BBC (2018). "Brazil Corruption Scandals: All You Need to Know." www.bbc.com/news/world-latin-america-35810578, accessed May, 2018.

Chacon, Ricardo (2016). "Is Infrastructure Costa Rica's Achilles' heel?" *Infrastructure Intelligence*. www.infrastructure-intelligence.com/article/aug-2016/infrastructure-costa-rica%E2%80%99s-achilles%E2%80%99-heel, accessed February, 2018.

Ciudad del Saber (2018). "Ciudad del Saber." http://ciudaddelsaber.org/en, accessed August, 2018.

Delisle, Jason, & Bernasconi, Andres (2018). "Lessons from Chile's Transition to Free College." *Brookings Institute*. www.brookings.edu/research/lessons-from-chiles-transition-to-free-college/, accessed March, 2018.

Franko, P. M. (2007). *The Puzzle of Latin American Economic Development*. Lanham, Maryland: Rowman & Littlefield.

Galicia, Patricia (2016). "Guatemala's Social Problems. Development and Cooperation." www.dandc.eu/en/article/poverty-corruption-and-racism-guatemalas-primary-schools-reflect-countrys-social-problems, accessed November, 2017.

Horsey, David (2017). "Venezuela's Descent into Dictatorship Shows Democracy Can Be Lost." *Los Angeles Times*. www.latimes.com/opinion/topoftheticket/la-na-tt-venezuela-democracy-20170801-story.html, accessed March, 2018.

ICEF Monitor (2016). "Panama's Rising Economy Funding New Investments in Education and English Training." http://monitor.icef.com/2016/01/panamas-rising-economy-funding-new-investments-in-education-and-english-training/, accessed February, 2018.

Lakhani, Nina (2015). "Poverty in Nicaragua Drives Children Out of School and Into the Workplace." *Guardian*. www.theguardian.com/global-development/2015/may/19/poverty-nicaragua-children-school-education-child-labour, accessed January, 2018.

Leon, Lorena (2017). "Beyond Chile, Costa Rica and Mexico, Latin America's Innovation Potential is Largely Untapped." *The Conversation*. http://theconversation.com/beyond-chile-costa-rica-and-mexico-latin-americas-innovation-potential-is-largely-untapped-80032, accessed March, 2018.

Nixon, Patrick (2015). "Why Uruguay is LatAm's Fiber Broadband Leader." www.bnamericas.com/en/features/telecommunications/why-uruguay-is-latams-fiber-broadband-leader, accessed December, 2017.

Posada, Cecilia (2016). "Economic Slowdown in Peru." *Pedersen & Partners*. www.pedersenandpartners.com/news/economic-slowdown-peru-how-are-employers-reacting-el-portal-del-capital-humano, accessed January, 2017.

Schwab, Klaus (2018). "The Global Competitiveness Report, 2017–2018." *World Economic Forum*. http://www3.weforum.org/docs/GCR2017-2018/05FullReport/TheGlobalCompetitivenessReport2017%E2%80%932018.pdf, accessed May, 2018.

Science Business (2017). "New Analysis of Tech Clusters Puts Europe in the Shade." https://sciencebusiness.net/news/80303/New-analysis-of-tech-clusters-puts-Europe-in-the-shade, accessed August, 2017.

The Rana Dorada (2012). *La Rana Dorada Micro-Brewery*. www.youtube.com/watch?v=9cntQeXx7eI, accessed October, 2017.

The Rana Dorada (2018). "The Rana Dorada." www.laranadorada.com/la-rana-dorada.html#hacer, accessed February, 2018.

The World Bank (2018a). "Doing Business." www.doingbusiness.org/, accessed January, 2018.

The World Bank (2018b). "Doing Business Fact Sheet: Latin America and the Caribbean." www.doingbusiness.org/~/media/WBG/DoingBusiness/Documents/Fact-Sheets/DB18/FactSheet_DoingBusiness2018_LAC_Eng.pdf?la=en, accessed May, 2018.

U.S. Commercial Service (2017). *Doing Business in Guatemala*. https://build.export. gov/build/groups/public/@eg_gt/documents/webcontent/eg_gt_101917.pdf, accessed January 2018.

World Economic Forum (2018). "Global Competitiveness Report." http://reports. weforum.org/global-competitiveness-index-2017-2018/competitiveness-rankings/, accessed April, 2018.

8

ESTABLISHING A BUSINESS

Introduction

This chapter is a culmination of the previous chapters with a focus on pulling them together in order to form a strategy for entering the Latin American market. The chapter focuses on issues such as securing financing, selecting an entry mode type, and supply chain management. As previously established, Latin America is a large market with high growth potential that is increasingly important to the world economy. The region's GDP of over US$7 trillion-accounts for over 8% of global GDP, and by 2017 its real GDP growth rate is expected to surpass that of all other regions except the Middle East and North Africa (Obiols, 2017).

A positive economic growth expected in the region for the coming years. With strong domestic demand, economic openness, combined with substantial infrastructure investments (Aguilar, 2014) and improvement of private consumption, there is solid indication of strong momentum for doing business in the region (Momentum, 2017). The continuous development of construction, automotive maintenance, and aviation sectors in Latin America are driving the demand of building hardware.

Latin America can be considered a dynamic and fast-growing region in the world. Unfortunately, many companies are not in position to take advantage of this growing opportunity. Companies that anticipate and understand their business environment will innovate accordingly. This action will allow them to outpace those who simply react to unstable and changing markets. Some organizations welcome innovation, while many others fall behind. In the future, more firms will intensify their capacity and take advantage of the results that innovation can provide (Arnal, 2014). Latin America is a modern marketers delight.

It has been projected that by 2020 10% of the world economy will be generated in Latin America (Kelly, 2015). Additionally, Latin America is the fourth largest mobile market in the world. This means that with social media adoption surpassing the U.S., it is situated on the cutting edge of the digital revolution (Kelly, 2015).

Corporate Strategy

A primary function of a business is to generate a sustainable profit that can promote growth, development and long-term success. The achievement of these goals is inherently associated with the corporate strategy. Each business must develop a plan of action that will move the organization towards achieving the goals and objectives that are set forth in their business plan. The strategy sets forth the actions that managers need to take along the path towards goal attainment. This process can be complex for multinational enterprises (MNEs) or simple for vendors selling goods on the streets of a Latin American country. Understanding the characteristics of three of the most dominate businesses in Latin America is an important step in establishing a business and developing a business strategy for success.

Businesses in Latin America can be classified into three major categories:

1   Multinationals are typically large, established organizations, that have well-structured organization charts, and are typically financially solid. Such companies include: (a) CEMEX cement in Mexico, (b) LaTam airline in Chile, (c) Temex chemical in Mexico, (d) Indra communications solutions in Brazil, and (e) Belcorp Group cosmetics in Peru. All of these companies have large operations, sales volumes, and profits. Their business environments cross-borders and thus are exposed to many places of the world. These companies have strong reputations, both domestically and abroad.

2   Small and Medium Size (SME) businesses are the second category of business types. There are literally thousands of these businesses scattered all over Latin America. Every city and town has many of these businesses concentrated in the urban area and scattered in the rural sections of Latin America. They can range from the mom and pop store to a 300-employee hardware store. They are vital to the economy of each country and provide the daily necessities each community needs to survive.

3   The informal business or the itinerant vendors. These business people can also be squatters. They set up and tear down their business each day. There are a massive number of them scattered all over; often side-by-side selling the identical product or service. This type of business is extremely competitive because there are so many of them and their prices are so low. Most people involved in the informal market are on a survival budget meaning they live day to day. Surprisingly, many of them are astute

business people and are very knowledgeable of how to sell products to their customers. In some cases, they had viable large-scale ideas but could not tolerate the long delay in formally establishing their business, so they resorted to the informal sector. Alternatively, the Central Markets of each city have many vendors that have an appearance of informality, however since they are housed in a large regulated public space, they are not, in absolute terms fully informal. They generally do not have to set up and break down each day nor do they move to other locations like the street vendors generally do.

All of these categories of business have, albeit quite different, a strategic plan. Since international opportunities are much more complex than domestic markets, managers need to plan prudently (e.g., be strategic). Corporate strategy means competitively creating and obtaining value of its products and services in particular markets. These strategic plans are the vehicles used to achieve goals and objectives. "Almost all successful companies engage in long-range strategic planning and position themselves to take advantage of worldwide trends. MNEs report that strategic planning is essential both to content with increasing global competition and to coordinate their international operations" (Deresky, 2014, p.176). While strategy has become an integral part of a business' DNA, it is only temporary because it changes over time. New trends, disruptive events and shifting competitive positions are always happening. Managers must constantly read and reread their environments in order to determine the best strategy that can create and capture the value of their products and services.

Multinationals – Multilatinas

Latin America is among the world's most challenging regions in which to do business. Nevertheless, corporations, some headquartered within the region and some outside it, have been courageous and entrepreneurial. Many profiting from Latin America's vast market potential. While, a reappearance of unrest in such major markets as Argentina, Brazil, and Venezuela has recently diminished some companies' regional ambitions, Latin America's MNEs remain ready. Firms will only succeed, however, if they adjust their objectives to the territory's real opportunities.

During the decade of the 1990s, foreign MNEs seemed relentless in their efforts to invest in and conquer this culturally rich land of more than 500 million people. Since most of the people were upwardly mobile consumers, and the industrial markets were showing great promise, why would an MNE not invest? Between 1991 and 2001, the ownership of the 500 largest companies in Latin America changed dramatically, with non-Latin MNE ownership growing to 39% from 27%. The growing foreign competition forced local Latin American companies to merge and magnify their exposure into other Latin American countries. This process changed them into more vigilant companies after the stock market failure in 2000. With the currency devaluations, growing political turmoil, and the likelihood of defaults on debt obligations had to a large extent lessened both the rate and the value of foreign investment in Latin America.

Thomson Financial pointed out that in the year 2000, there were 166 merger and acquisition (M&A) deals initiated by MNEs, for a total value of US$102.6 billion. Two years later, the total value of M&A activity non-Latin MNEs was only US$38.9 billion. Poor financial performance led some MNEs to reduce their Latin operations. The "multinationalization" of businesses in Latin America set off new avenues for growth for all types of companies. This flurry of MNE development required new and different strategies for both the MNEs and the multilatinas (MNEs based in Latin America) (Martinez, de Souza & Liu, 2003).

TABLE 8.1 28 of the Top Latin American Multinationals

Company	Country	Sector
CEMEX	Mexico	Cement
LATAM	Chile	Airlines
JBS GROUP	Brazil	Food
SOUTH AMERICAN STEAM	Chile	Shipping
TENARIS	Argentina	Steel Metallurgy
AVIANCA-TACA	Colombia	Airlines
MEXICHEM	Mexico	Petrochemical
AJEGROUP	Peru	Beverage Liquor
TEMEX	Mexico	Telecom
GERDAU	Brazil	Steel
GRUMA	Mexico	Food
AMERICAN MOBILE	Mexico	Telecom
MASISA	Chile	Manufacturing
ARAUCO	Chile	Paper Pulp
CENCOSUD	Chile	Retail
NEMAK	Mexico	Automotive Auto Parts
PROBE	Chile	Software Data
SIGMA	Mexico	Food
ARTECOLA	Brazil	Chemistry
CMPC	Chile	Paper Pulp
NARFRIG	Brazil	Food
INDRA	Brazil	Multisector
COPA AIRLINES	Panama	Airlines
ALFA GROUP	Mexico	Multisector
ISA	Colombia	Electricity
FEMSA	Mexico	Beverages
BELCORP GROUP	Peru	Chemistry
GRUPO BIMBO	Mexico	Food

Source: Hunkar (2014).

As long as the economic environment is growing, and the political situation is stable, MNEs will continued to gain overall share in Latin American markets in major consumer and industrial sectors that now is called multilatinas (Martinez et al., 2003). Table 8.1 lists a collection of multilatinas that are popular and thriving in many parts of Latin America. Their existence has enriched the respective economies and provided opportunities for many people to have economically stable lives. In some cases, it has raised the quality of life because there are more goods and services available than would otherwise be there.

Besides having local domestic markets, Latin American multilatinas and multinationals also have found many lucrative export markets in and outside of the region. The export markets are significant and provide huge opportunities for economic and business development. Distinguishing between domestic and export driven business is becoming an increasingly important to vendors in Latin America. The subsequent table summarizes the major markets outside of Latin America:

Table 8.2 clearly indicates that while exports to the Americas or neighboring countries in the region are a significant portion of the exports, the exports to China is an area to watch because it may grow in the future. Obviously exports to the U.S. are important because it is the largest market in the hemisphere. Be it as it may, Latin American countries are growing their export business and it indicates another opportunity area for business development and growth.

Multilatinas produce less innovation and are not managed as well as multinationals. Additionally, they are less productive than similar multinationals from other regions (Lederman, Messina, Pienknagura & Rigolini, 2014).

Multinational corporations have had considerable positive impact on Latin American economies over the last few years. The positive impacts from technology transfers, knowledge spillovers, and linkages are significantly more robust than the negative impacts from greater competition in product and factor markets. The maximum potential of multinational corporations has yet to be fully realized. Unfortunately, multinational partners in Latin America perform

TABLE 8.2 Major Export Destination for Goods Made in Respective Countries (Percentage)

Country	U.S.	China	Americas
Argentina	6	9	33
Brazil	12	19	20
Chile	13	28	18
Colombia	31	6	32
Mexico	82	1	5
Peru	15	23	17

Source: Gendreau & McLendon (2017).

like local firms, meaning very little investment in innovation. As such, Latin America is not drawing the most innovative multinationals. This is because the obstacles that local firms encounter to innovate are also act obstacles to innovation for foreign firms operating in the region. Multinationals are also more inclined than local firms to submit an application for a patent, trademark, or copyright. They are also more likely to collaborate in innovation projects with other organizations. They are also more motivated to invest in R&D; and adopt foreign technologies. The productivity gains from knowledge spillover from multinational corporations in Latin America are not being fully realized. This is in part due to the low levels of R&D by foreign companies functioning in Latin America. Multilatinas numbers are small and are primarily concentrated in three countries (Brazil, Chile, and Mexico) (Lederman et al., 2014).

In many cases the multilatinas fail to transfer knowledge to the home economy through their involvement in global value chains. The absence of integration is worsened because most of the cross-border activity of multilatinas occurs in the large countries in the region (Brazil, Chile, and Mexico). These countries make up 70% of total multilatinas' revenue. Only approximately 15% of multilatinas' revenues originate from outside Latin America (Lederman et al., 2014).

The obvious policy test for governments and businesses is related to structural characteristics of the enabling environment for innovative entrepreneurship. This take in not only laws and institutions but also infrastructure and the

FIGURE 8.1   Picture of Multinational Corporation in Guatemala

quality and quality of human. The rise of multilatinas has not changed the landscape. By and large the multilatinas conduct less research than their peers from other regions. The large greater part of their business is assembled in Brazil, Mexico, and Chile. They therefore miss the opportunities presented by greater integration, both regionally and globally (Lederman et al., 2014).

Small and Medium Size Enterprises (SMEs)

SMEs are more vulnerable to the uncertainties than the MNEs, which are established and have many more resources at its disposal. To strategically compete in world markets, SMEs need to employ several important strategies to be successful. First, they need to acquire the proper current technology that connects them with the world. Second, they need to be agile. Agility is an absolute, so they need to be able to turn their business around almost instantly. Third, they need to constantly innovate. Being ahead of the competition in products, services and process is an imperative. Finally, and probably most importantly is the recruitment of talented employees. No strategy can be successfully implemented without properly trained employees (Oxford Economics, 2017). In the present world of intense competition, a company cannot survive unless it has the appropriate human capital and technology. In reality, Latin American firms need to invest more in technology to level the playing field. Presently, only 31% of all Latin American Small and Medium sized businesses have gone beyond using technology to bring in the digital economy. To remain competitive at both global and local level LA Firms need to prioritize technology adoption to improve internal and external efficiencies (Mueller, 2017).

Informal Markets

Informal marketers are survivors. They create business when business does not appear to exist. Even though this category of business is the closest to poverty, it is usually honest, diligent entrepreneurship against enormously intense competition. Each day, seven days a week these business owners labor for very low wages to survive. It is the next step to poverty, but it is a livelihood. The managers of these businesses have to be one step ahead of their completion using agility, innovation and persistence. Each day they have to think about a new strategy to lure customers to their business, to their products and to their style of business. Owners of these businesses are striving for success just as those of SMEs and MNEs. The primary differences are size, resources and sophistication. The end point is the same; make a profit (see Figure 8.1).

Table 8.3 summarizes the pervasiveness of informal employment that exists among many of the Latin American countries. The informal economy and employment is strong and thriving in many of the Latin American countries.

TABLE 8.3 Informal Employment Rate by Country – Non-Agricultural – Informal Jobs as a Percentage of Total Employment

Costa Rica	30.7
Uruguay	33.1
Brazil	36.5
Panama	40.4
Argentina	46.8
Ecuador	49.3
Mexico	53.8
Colombia	54.5
Paraguay	63.8
Peru	64.0
El Salvador	65.6
Honduras	72.8
Guatemala	73.0

Source: Gonzalez (2015).

The characteristics of the Informal Market are evident in all of their physical arrangements. Generally, they are open air and operate in structures without walls. They are tightly squeezed together only an arms length away to a competitor or fellow vendor. The vendors usually arrive at their business place early in the morning and leave late at night. They are in survivor mode seven days a week. There contribution to society is important not only that it allows the vendor and his/her family to eek out a livelihood but also gives community another alternative for purchasing goods.

While one would observe that Latin American informal markets have high levels of employment, one can also observe that China has issues with

FIGURE 8.2 Example of an Informal Market Setting in Latin America

informal employment too. Joann Vanek et al., 2014 discovered that the total informal employment rate for non-agricultural jobs was approximately 22%. This seems to be lower than most of the rates listed in the preceding table, but one can possible explain that to the enormous growth that China has been making in the last 25 years. Additionally, even though China is growing rapidly, it has 1.2 billion people who would indicate that there just are not enough formal jobs to go around and hence some people have to resort to the informal sector to make a living (Vanek, Alter, Carre, Heintz & Hussmaans, 2014).

Factors Affecting Business Strategies

There are two strategic areas that are to the long-term success of Latin American companies. First, businesses must invest in workforce development. In the global market, all companies in the Latin American private sector need to take the initiative in training a modern workforce. There are more than sufficient existing talent pools to fill the growing need for skilled workers and accelerate business growth. This effort will not only furnish workforce competencies but also produce well-paying jobs that will spur consumption, which leads to an economic growth cycle in the broader economy. Second, there is a need to protect natural resources through sustainable development practices. Many times, the environment is often one of the last things that businesses think about when they see an opportunity for rapid growth. To prevent such behavior in Latin America, companies need to incorporate Environmental, Social and Corporate Governance (ESG) concerns in their decision-making processes (Fleischmann, 2017).

Latin America is an entrepreneurial ecosystem with some of the world's most valuable natural resources. As such, Latin America is well positioned to rise in the 21st century economy. However, businesses must look after its natural resources and implement sustainable development measures to realize this promise. This realignment would promote business development and be an opportunity for Latin America to raise and meet the promise of the global economy (Fleischmann, 2017).

Investment, Finance and Start-up funding

Start-up funding for a business is difficult for any business anywhere in the world. However, in Latin America over the years it has been particularly difficult. Recently, however, pioneer venture capital firms have paved the way for others to find success. Examples of such firms are NXTP Labs in Argentina and Vox capital in Brazil. The success and failure of these venture capital firms have become models for many of the new early stage funding initiators. Entrepreneurs have been gaining experience and understanding how to acquire and dispense capital to start-ups. This experience has been spread among various Latin American countries in Buenos Aires, Santiago and Medellin. Early stage accelerators programs such as start-up Chile and Wayra have put the region on the map as an attractive place for start-ups. Global start-up network and Start-up boot camp are spreading to Latin America. Seestars is another entrepreneurial organization traveling around LA helping to fund start-ups (Lustig, 2017).

Financing Alternatives

The MNEs use the generally accepted financing methods that have been traditional for many decades: issuing of stock, debt financing and other traditional approaches to financing company operations. However, in the last few years other types of financing have emerged that have given companies broader financing opportunities and alternatives. Investment-based models depend on the assumption that the funders can logically expect a financial return based upon their investments, as they are purchasing a debt or equity security instrument. Throughout the Americas, the spread of investment-based models has led to diverse development. Several models have been reverberating more blatantly in some jurisdictions than others.

These investment-based models can be segmented into debt-based or equity-based transactions.

This is where companies either borrow money from financial institutions or achieve it through issuing more stock to the public. The online alternative financing industry has been growing in Latin America. Over two-thirds (71%) of Latin America and the Caribbean (LAC) online alternative business finance came from Chile (US$97.1 million) and Mexico (US$69.5 million). Chile led in debt-based finance (US$92.9 million) and non-investment-based business finance (US$2.8 million). Mexico led in equity-based business finance (US$4.9 million) (Ziegler, Reedy, Le, Zhang, Kroszner & Garvey, 2017). LAC in 2016 to a total market volume of US$35.2 billion. The 23% increase of investment from last year, 2016 as driven by growth across all regions and most market segments of the Americas (Ziegler et al., 2017).

In addition to financing for MNEs, small and medium-sized enterprises also need vital yet demanding financing. SMEs play a very important role in powering economic growth in many countries in Latin America. Over 90% of businesses in the region are categorized as SMEs. Unfortunately, a financing gap of close to US$250 billion exists to fund their activities (Mendoza, 2015). Historically, numerous barriers to funding have existed. Such things as lack of audited financial statements, credit history, and inability to access guarantees. Regular institutions that finance SMEs are being challenged to come up with novel ways to change and take advantage of changes that exist in the SME finance environment (Mendoza, 2015). An illustration of change is the Entrepreneurial Finance

Lab (EFL) that has been established and is operating in Mexico and Colombia. This was a brainchild that emerged at Harvard's Center for International Development. This idea uses psychometric scoring as a substitute for the traditional credit records. This is an innovative step forward for SMEs who need financing. Credit scores are important for getting financing. Fintechs are pioneering in different ways of financing such as crowd financing and peer-to-peer lending (Reaching the Last Mile, 2015).

Besides the local investment activity that has spurned business development there has been a significant amount of capital inflows to Latin America. The subsequent table illustrates the robustness of this capital investment in Latin American countries:

Table 8.4 clearly demonstrates that there is significant interest in investing in Latin America. With close to US$150 billion per year being invested in Latin America indicates that there it is a major area of business development and has many business opportunities awaiting investors.

Microfinance among Latin American businesses

Brazil was the first country in Latin America to pioneer micro finance services offerings. The positive experiences of micro enterprises in that country motivated the spread of micro finance across Latin America. As it grew as a concept, more formal institutions took on the idea and began to develop it more fully. For example, the Inter-American Development Bank (IDB) is an institution established to provide financing for small and *micro*-sized businesses. This is completed thru the Multilateral Investment Fund (MIF). This organization is the largest provider of grants for improving the competitiveness of micro and small enterprises in Latin America and the Caribbean. This agency through its affiliates has lent close to US$12 billion to over 10 million low-income clients (Microfinance, 2017). Microfinance provide a variety of services such as credit,

TABLE 8.4 Summarizes Capital Flows to Latin America (US$ billions)

Country	Year – 2015	Year – 2016(e)	Year – 2017(f)
Argentina	9.5	26.6	41.8
Brazil	56.5	20.0	34.4
Chile	5.0	5.8	4.3
Colombia	19.0	14.0	12.5
Mexico	34.9	36.6	28.1
Peru	10.1	7.3	8.3
Venezuela	22.5	2.3	2.8

Source: Gendreau & McLendon (2017).

Note
e = estimated, f = forecasted.

savings, insurance, money transfer and other non-traditional services. A typical client of a microfinance agency would be low-income people who cannot get funding from traditional banking entities. Generally, these people are self-employed entrepreneurs or people from microenterprises such as street vendors, artisan manufacturers and food providers (Microfinance, 2017).

Distribution and Focus – Supply Chain Management Issues

The ability to satisfy customers by meeting their needs is a requirement of all businesses that desire success. Good management and smart decision-making are fundamental to achieving this goal. One area of business operation across the world is the ability to get the right product or service, at the right quality, at the right time, at the right price, and in the right condition to the customer. This is a large challenge that companies work diligently to address every working day. Because there are so many rights to satisfy and so many other uncontrollable intervening variables (i.e., climate, crime, accidents, etc.) that could impact the delivery of the goods and services, supply chain management is a major operation that needs constant attention with appropriate facilities, equipment and management competencies. Absent these three elements, companies will not be able to operate a successful business in the global markets (Wisner, Tan & Leong, 2009).

Since there is a great potential for manufacturing across an array of industries in Latin America it has gained popularity as a supply chain partner because of several reasons: a. proximity to North America, b. large supply of natural resources, c. attractive labor costs, d. liberal trade policies, e. and ability to deliver quality goods rapidly and on time (Boccalandro, 2013).

While growth continues and suggests great opportunities, there are issues to be addressed. LA businesses need to adopt leading edge supply chain practices and devices in order to work in partnership with new global associates to compete effectively and profitably. Implementing advanced supply chain improvements has been slower in LA than in the U.S. and Europe due to less investment. This process needs to be sped up to be competitive.

In some LA businesses, resource-planning systems are out dated and over loaded causing them to be much slower reacting to the fast-paced global world's complex challenges. Many LA businesses are late in adopting new and modern technology that is needed in the management of supply chains (Boccalandro, 2013). While there are lags in supply chain modernization, there are also many LA companies that are implementing improvements in areas such as demand management, inventory replenishment, transportation, and sales and operations planning. All of these are crucial to the success of any supply chain management activity. They are absolute necessities for being in the competitive mix with other businesses be they Multinationals or SMEs.

Those companies who seek and adopt change and continue to improve their supply chain management processes will have a significant competitive edge.

Building new models for the addition of supply, demand and capacity is imperative. Making intelligent decisions that correspond to the shifts in customer demands is another imperative for LA businesses.

The construction of new distributions centers, building of strategic inventories and optimizing sourcing are key ingredients for meeting the ever-changing supply chain challenges that are part of the global business environment.

One major need among LA businesses regarding supply chain management relates to training and capability development. Companies need to recruit properly trained supply chain managers and develop continuous improvement training programs within their companies that will provide a continuum of suitably trained supply chain managers capable of meeting every changing global business environment and build winning supply chains in Latin American businesses.

Table 8.5 presents a perspective on where Latin American countries stand in relation to their peers in the LA region and worldwide. Germany leads the pack with a 4.23 ranking out of a total 5 as the highest possible score. Clearly Latin American countries are not scoring or ranking in the top of world performers. That means that there needs to be significant improvement. Only Panama and Chile are in any close competition and they are 1.66 and 1.75 respectively away from a perfect score of 5.

TABLE 8.5 Summarizes the Global Logistic Performance Rankings (LPI) for Latin American Countries

Country	Year	LPI Rank	LPI Score	Infrastructure
Panama	2016	40	3.3	3.3
Chile	2016	46	3.3	2.8
Mexico	2016	54	3.1	2.9
Brazil	2016	55	3.1	3.1
Uruguay	2016	65	3.0	2.8
Argentina	2016	66	3.0	2.9
Peru	2016	69	2.9	2.6
Ecuador	2016	74	2.8	2.5
El Salvador	2016	83	2.7	2.3
Costa Rica	2016	89	2.7	2.3
Colombia	2016	95	2.6	2.5
Paraguay	2016	101	2.6	2.5
Nicaragua	2016	102	2.5	2.5
Guatemala	2016	111	2.5	2.2
Honduras	2016	112	2.5	2.0
Venezuela	2016	122	2.4	2.4

Source: The World Bank (2016).

Other Supply Chain Management (SCM) Issues in Latin America

The potential is large, and the opportunities are huge in the area of SCM. Business entrepreneurs and managers need to think about some of the following issues as they think about investment in their supply chains:

1   Transportation is highly fragmented with many owners and operators. Lack of an efficient and effective transportation management system is required,

2   Infrastructure issues – some of the highways have poor surfaces, dangerous routes and limited capacity (i.e., Guatemala, Bolivia and Peru and rural areas of the countries). Latin America is constrained by inadequate infrastructure. Additionally, some of the countries do not have state of the art telecommunication/communication systems that are essential to efficient and effective SCM. This is especially existent in the rural areas.

3   Safety and security risks – while this is also a concern in developed countries, it is more pronounced in developing countries. Criminals blocking the highways so transports cannot pass by causing highway robberies, and hijacking. This is common in some of the Central American countries like Guatemala, El Salvador, Honduras, and Nicaragua. Some of this activity occurs in Bolivia, Colombia and Peru but not as frequent.

4   E-commerce has become a disruptive factor in the digital age. This has put more emphasis on efficient and effective supply chain management.

5   Implementations of the seven rights of supply chain management are accentuated even more intensely. These rights are as follow: (1) Right Product, (2) Right time, (3) Right Place, (4) Right Quantity, (5) Right Quality, (6) Right Condition, (7) Right Price (Srinivasan, Stank, Dornier & Petersen, 2014).

Changing the Business Environment

Latin America countries are working to ameliorate their business environments to make them attractive to Foreign Direct Investment and local business development. In the last year and one half from 2015 to 2017, 15 of the 32 Latin American countries have implemented reforms that move in a positive direction of making business easier to start and operate.

One of the most popular reforms that achieved the highest number of implementations was in paying taxes (8) and getting credit (5). Unfortunately, no reforms were registered in Registering Property or Enforcing Contracts. Costa Rica among the 10 top improvers worldwide. Costa Rica had three reforms. One in getting electricity easier, another in getting credit easier and the final one in allowing out-of-court enforcement.

Mexico and Peru were among the six economies in the region implementing multiple reforms in the past year. In addition, Brazil reduced the time for border and documentary compliance for exporting by implementing an electronic portal system.

Honduras made the biggest improvement globally in the area of Protecting Minority Investors (World Bank Doing Business, 2016).

Tables 8.6 and 8.7 provide a clear perspective on how Latin America rates in the world according to the rankings on elements for starting and doing business and ease of doing business. These are based on 189 countries in the world.

The foregoing tables give a clear perspective on the between starting a business and the ease of doing business. Both of these indicators are important for any investor who is serious about investing in any country in Latin America.

TABLE 8.6 Ranking on Element for Starting and Doing Business in Latin America

Element	Rank
Starting a Business	126
Resolution of Solvency	101
Enforcing Contracts	112
Trading across Borders	108
Paying Taxes	127
Protecting Minority Investors	112
Registering Property	101
Getting Credit	70
Getting Electricity	83
Dealing with Construction Permits	106

Source: The World Bank Flagship Report (2016).

TABLE 8.7 Economy Ranking according to Ease of Doing Business

Panama	44
Uruguay	61
Mexico	65
Colombia	84
Peru	97
Guatemala	101
Costa Rica	121
Nicaragua	123
El Salvador	125
Paraguay	135
Honduras	150
Argentina	157
Ecuador	166
Bolivia	178
Venezuela	186

Source: The World Bank Flagship Report (2016).

Physical Infrastructure

Infrastructure is a critical part of a country's economic system. Without suitable infrastructure the country cannot achieve satisfactory levels of productivity. Nor can it achieve levels of economic development that can sustain a reasonable quality of life for its citizens. The LA infrastructure has been identified by (Fay, Andres, Fox, Narloch, Straub & Slawson, 2016) as inadequate and a barrier to economic development. Over 60% of the region's roads are unpaved, compared to 46% in emerging economies of Asia and 17% in Europe. Latin American sanitation systems are very weak. It is estimated that two thirds of these sanitation systems are untreated and very unhealthy. The absence of clean water continues to be the second largest killer of children under five years old. Losses from the electrical systems and networks are among the highest in the world (The Economist, 2018). Latin America's expenditures on infrastructure are less than any other area of the world with the exception of Sub-Saharan Africa. While the infrastructure is not good, Chile and Uruguay are leaders in the region. Chile's roads are better than those of Belgium, New Zealand and Cuba. Uruguay's electrical system and telecommunication system is a lot better than that of the U.S. and Canada (The Economist, 2018). Economic development needs infrastructure, and infrastructure needs economic development. When infrastructure is weak, there is a loss of competitiveness, which hinders economic growth. There needs to be a more concentrated effort to improve infrastructure throughout the region. Governments have a very important role to play in setting the stage, identifying the needs, helping with the financing and making sure projects are completed. The private sector also has a responsibility by helping with various areas of development. Participating in the development of local financing markets for infrastructure bonds and other innovative ways of financing important projects. Having both public and private partners is a win/win situation (Kapowicz, Matheson & Vtyurina, 2016).

The bottom line is that Latin America's infrastructure is more of a hindrance than an asset for growth of the economy. There have been and continue to be opportunities to make the infrastructure better. Low interest rates help in the financing process and can at least help in different areas of the infrastructure improvement process. The market-oriented presidents in Brazil, Argentina and Peru have made it a priority to ameliorate their country's infrastructure. One of the great outcomes of the peace accord in Colombia is a provision that improvements in the infrastructure will be made (The Economist, 2018). It is interesting that China has taken a big interest in assisting with infrastructure development in Latin America. China is investing more in Latin America than the World Bank or the International Development Bank (IBD). China has invested US$21 billion in Brazil and has given Bolivia a loan of US$10 billion. Additionally, they have helped Argentina with a nuclear power plant. This type of foreign direct investment has pros and cons. It does say that Latin America is being recognized by the second largest economy in the world as a good investment (The Economist, 2018). Continual variances in country-to-country infrastructure prevent the development of real directions towards development. Over the long haul, infrastructure investment will promote sustained and inclusive economic development. Unfortunately, the average total investment as a percentage of GDP in LA has been low. Weak investment causes insufficient regional connections and a deficiency in basic necessities such as clean water, sanitation, power grids, power supply and telecommunication (Bulletin FAL, 2016).

Some infrastructure investment profiles show what is happening among some of LA's member countries:

1 Transport – Chile, Colombia Nicaragua, Panama, Peru and Bolivia have surpassed the region average for transport investment of 1.7% GDP.
2 Energy Investment:

a	Costa Rica	2.1% of GDP
b	Nicaragua	1.8%
c	Paraguay	1.6%
d	Uruguay	1.2%
e	Brazil	1.2%

3 Telecommunication – Central America and Panama have been recognized for heavy investment in this area

a	Nicaragua	1.6% of GDP
b	Honduras	1.2%
c	Costa Rica	1.1%
d	Panama	0.8%
e	El Salvador	0.8%
f	Guatemala	0.6% (Bulletin FAL, 2016)

The following Tables 8.8 and 8.9 outline very specifically the resource allocations, percentage of GDP allocated and timelines for the completion of the project. This perspective gives one a point of view regarding the progress or no progress LA is making regarding infrastructure improvements. Table 8.8 and 8.9 summarize some of the activity that is occurring in respective counties relative to infrastructure investments.

The foregoing table summarizes the large amount of money that is being spent on various infrastructure projects. Most of the country has long-term projects because of their size or because of the time frames prescribed by their respective governments. Viewing the end dates of the projects tell a whole lot about how long it will take to get some of the country's infrastructure up to speed. On face it looks like Latin American countries are spending significant

TABLE 8.8 Infrastructure Investment Projections in Latin America in Year 2015 (US$ billions)

Country	Estimated Investment	% of Total	Number of Projects	End Date of Project
Brazil	166,126	31.67	123	2025
Mexico	57,744	11.01	96	2020
Nicaragua	50,102	9.55	3	2020
Colombia	44,775	8.92	86	2038
Peru	44,024	8.39	63	2031
Chile	27,725	5.29	72	2024
Argentina	23,888	4.55	32	2022
Panama	16,524	3.15	18	2025
Guatemala	14,873	2.84	11	2019
Bolivia	13,379	2.55	46	2025
Paraguay	12,910	2.46	17	2021
Honduras	11,845	2.26	9	2030
Uruguay	10,257	1.96	13	2025
Venezuela	9,812	1.87	7	2017
Ecuador	6,362	1.21	21	2024
Costa Rica	4,082	0.78	15	2017
El Salvador	1,215	0.02	5	2032

Source: Adapted from Bulletin FAL (2016).

TABLE 8.9 Latin American and the Caribbean Transportation Infrastructure Projects

Type	Investment (US$ billions)	% of Total	Number of Projects	End Date
Roads	106,703	21.9	307	2038
Railways	105,902	21.7	48	2030
Internal waterways	65,640	13.4	10	2020
Maritime Ports	51,683	10.6	94	2025
Logistics Platforms	2,396	0.5	5	2017
Airports	32,277	6.6	57	2032
Urban Transit	123,518	25.3	115	2022

Source: Adapted from Bulletin FAL (2016).

amount on infrastructure but in many cases that is not translating into actual better life for the citizens of these countries. With all the corruption surrounding construction projects some may or may not get completed. Be it as it may, this is a great start and has real possibilities.

Both tables 8.8 and 8.9 demonstrate that the people of Latin America recognize the need to improve their infrastructure and that the renewing of the infrastructure is going to be good for business and economic development in the long run. Businesses who are interested in investing need to know this information for planning and investment purposes.

Latin America achieved nearly 60 points in the new Latin Trade Infrastructure Index. This metric evaluates conditions in the areas of transport, technology, electricity and water in 18 economies in Latin America and the Caribbean. The 60 points indicates a growth of 0.43 percentage points from last year or 2016. By and large the countries had very few changes in their index levels. The only exception would be Chile, which drop two spots. Bolivia on the other hand climbed two places in this year's index (Latin Trade Infrastructure Index, 2017).

This project in Figure 8.3 demonstrates the infrastructure development capabilities of some Latin American countries and the desire to move forward in modernizing and providing sustainable energy and power for the citizens of the respective countries.

Negotiation Patterns and Partners in Latin America

The word negotiation depicts a process of discussion where two or more parties strive to obtain a mutually acceptable agreement. This process is difficult when

FIGURE 8.3 Huanza Hydroelectric Project in Peru

it is conducted among people of the same background. As such when the negotiation process is moved to another culture (e.g., Latin America) the dynamics
and processes are much more difficult. Knowing how to negotiate with businesses in Latin America is a critical skill considered to be highly desirable for any
professional who is engaged in international business in Latin America. Cultural
differences produce many difficult issues in the negotiating process. Those who
are good at it are highly valued individuals. Ignorance of the native ways of
negotiating is a single most outstanding error associated with unsuccessful negotiations. (Zerin, 2014).

When business people negotiate in Latin America, they must be mindful of
several points:

1   The relationship is the main concern and at the core of all negotiations in
     Latin America. Latinos treat friends and even some business people like
     family. Socializing is a major element of the negotiation process. After the
     first meeting the Latin American negotiator will investigate his foreign
     counterpart and find out about his background. The Latin American will
     do this by asking around to friends, acquaintances and other business
     people. Making friends in negotiations is critical and one businessperson's
     friendship with one person can multiply into friendship with many people.
     This can lead to friends all over the country.
2   Be open-minded and alert. Latin culture places a lot on the appearance of
     macho or strong. The main advice in this case is keep cool and don't get
     hoodwinked by these tactics.
3   Nobody will tell you "No" when negotiating in Latin America. The
     Spanish and Portuguese languages are rich in words and phrases. Thus, one
     should pay particular attention to the context and wording when negoti-
     ating. Depending on the situation, some words can have different mean-
     ings. For example, yes may really mean no in a negotiation. Many Latin
     American negotiators will go a long way to avoid saying no.

Being aware of these customs and how to operate in different Latin American
environments is imperative. It is recommended that one who wants to seriously
negotiate in Latin America must find a trusted contact that knows the "ropes"
and can advise, consult, or coach the negotiators on how to get to "Yes" in the
negotiation process.

Being able to understand negotiation partners is influenced by one's understanding of the cultural dimensions in a country. Generally Latin Americans
approach negotiations from a win-lose style. This way to negotiate has pros
and cons. If Latin Americans have this negotiation style, then it is important
to gain their trust, a huge variable in Latin America, in order to move towards
a win-win end result. Achieving a win-win conclusion requires trade-offs on
both sides, something given and taken from each negotiator. Trying to realize

a win-win result will take more time, energy and costs. The negotiators need to determine whether they are negotiating for the short or long term (Becker, 2011).

A win-lose approach can also be used but each negotiator needs to understand the positive and negative consequences of this outcome. Either strategy (win-win, win-lose) is appropriate depending on the goals and objectives that each side wants to accomplish. Negotiations in Latin American countries need to factor in the cultural dimensions. Each country while having similar cultures in terms of language and other customs they may have a set of negotiation approaches that are driven by the culture. Those business people who are involved in the negotiations need to investigate the way Latin American business people negotiate. How does culture play in the negotiation process and what cultural factors need to be recognized in order to successfully negotiate in this region of the world?

To make the negotiation process more compatible, thorough, and professional each side needs to follow the steps listed below:

1   Preparation – careful preparation is an imperative activity. Thorough and in-depth groundwork must be done to be successful in negotiations,
2   Relationship building – as mentioned earlier, trust is a critical factor in negotiations. Building trust means understanding relationships and establishing relationships. This means knowing one's contacts in Latin America and begin building the trust.
3   Exchange – task related materials – once the relationships are established then each side needs to present their positions. They have to incorporate the win-win or win-lose strategies into this delicate negotiation process step.
4   Persuasion – this is where the difficult negotiating begins. Understanding that Latin America is primarily a high context culture where non-verbal communication is important can have an impact on this stage of the negotiation process. That is why preparation is so critical. There may be subtle elements of the culture that have a big effect on the ability to persuade a Latin American negotiator.
5   Concession or agreement – is there a win-win or a win – lose outcome? The tactics used to arrive at either outcome will depend on how well prepared each side is. Since Latin Americans from the start like to have a win-lose strategy then arriving at a win-win outcome may require much introspection on the costs and benefits of a hardline position or a trade off position (Deresky, 2014).

Managing the negotiation process requires skill. With so many factors interacting and being involved, the negotiators need to be flexible, knowledgeable, and innovative in their approaches to the negotiation process.

Contemporary business people living in the Digital age need to be aware of e-negotiations. With the speed of the internet and the versatility of the electronic messaging, this approach is another way to accomplish negotiations among businesses in Latin America. This approach has pros and cons. Managers who use this must understand how outcomes can be affected by using this method of negotiation. Not all countries in Latin America are totally ready for this methodology (Deresky, 2014).

Figure 8.4 is a glimpse of how each side has a position to present and sustain. They overlap and become a Venn diagram arrangement both entering each other's domain. Understanding these relationships is important to successful negotiations.

Corporate Social Responsibility in Latin American Businesses

Child Labor

The regional outlook report of 2016 indicates that 10.5 million children between 5 years and 17 years old or 7% of all the children in the region were engaged in child labor. This is two million less in 2016 than were engaged in 2012. It was found that children in this region perform dangerous tasks in agriculture and domestic work. Moreover, they are involved in the worst forms of child labor possible such as commercial sex exploitation that generally turns into human trafficking. Children of migrants and indigenous families are vulnerable to exploitation in awful types of labor conditions. It has been noted in official reports that significant progress has been made in reducing child labor in Argentina, Brazil, Chile, Colombia, Costa Rica, Chile, Guatemala, Panama, Paraguay and Peru. New rules and enforcement efforts have been the key ingredients for the reduction in vulnerability. Part of the effort was the allocation of funds to hire inspectors and enforce the laws has helped. Continued work to develop comprehensive legal protections to prevent and eliminate child labor problems is in process. Clearly, progress is being made because countries are taking the issue seriously (Child Labor, 2016).

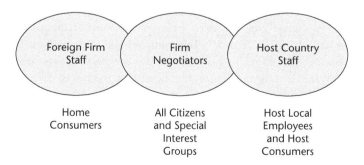

FIGURE 8.4 Stakeholders in Cross-Border Negotiations

Sweatshop Conditions

Sweatshop conditions are evident all across Latin America. From urban business managers who make employees were long hours with no pay and no job security to rural *campesinos* who have to work in the field cutting sugar cane for US $5.00 per day from dawn to dusk, six or seven days a week. These conditions exist and they are real. In many cases they have existed for decades and in other cases for centuries. Exploitation of the indigent, the indigenous and the marginal people is routine in many Latin American countries. The Oligarchs control the wealth and the *campesinos* do the work. One of the authors of this book has first had experience witnessing the way in which indigenous people are hired to work in homes, fields and businesses for very low wages, long hours and zero job security. Yet they have families that need the necessities like all others. So yes, sweatshop conditions exist in Latin American businesses. The question is to what degree? One example is that of a Bolivian woman working in a Brazilian factory that sews clothing. Her work place and her home are one in the same. One day she woke up and found her son sick with a cold. Because she could not miss work, which was just down the hall, she put a blanket on him and walked to her work several doors down the hall. She was required to work 11 hours per day, 6 days per week. No work meant no pay and hence no food for her son and her. Unfortunately, her dream of having a better life in Brazil was extinguished because he son died because she could not get him to a doctor for proper care. She had to work and loss of work time meant no money to eat. This is and example of the conditions that exist in not only Brazil but also other countries throughout Latin America (Lozada, 2013).

Bribery

The issue of corruption of which bribery is germane, is one of the first topics we discussed in Chapter 1 of this book. Yes, corruption is a very serious problem in Latin America. In Mexico and the Dominican Republic bribery is considered a major issue by 51% and 46% respectively. These are only two countries that have given some good evidence of the existence of bribery in their nation. Nearly one in three people across Latin America using public services have paid a bribe in the past year 2016–2017. This is a large number and it probably is not totally accurate because it is difficult to collect data on corruption (Transparency International, 2017). There is no question that significant amount of corruption exists in Latin American countries especially the less developed countries. However, we are seeing now that even the large more significantly developed countries like Brazil, Mexico Argentina and Chile are now showing real evidence of corruption, bribes and other forms of bad behavior.

Recently the major scandals in Brazil have focused and accentuated the issue of bribes among public and private organizations. The Odebrecht Construction

Co. involvement in paying bribes has reverberated across the region. The scandal has created a tumultuous environment where projects are going unfinished, politicians are running scared and public credibility is in jeopardy. In Mexico one of the major airport projects has been plagued with corruption allegations (The Economist, 2018). It appears that corruption is a scourge that has long and deep roots all over Latin America. While corruption is not totally curable, certainly there can be rules and laws put into place that at least minimizes it occurrence. Until that happens, which does not seem to be imminent, then corruption will continue to cause damage to the entire region.

Making the Choice of What?

To make a choice in Latin America, the first step is to accept that in the region every country is different in their capabilities as in their weaknesses. In Central America, a relatively small region, the decision of establishing a new business venture in Guatemala could be determined by its proximity with Mexico and the United States. Yet there are also concerns with violence and timelessness that affects the country. Alternatively, one may choose El Salvador because it is dollarized, which makes transactions easier. Finally, Costa Rica is attractive due to the size of the middle class.

South America also has a number of variables to consider when determining where to do business. Venezuela has been politically unstable since approximately the year 2013. Argentina has had difficult economic circumstances since the year 2001 and became worse in 2014, which have affected the investment climate. And Chile has remained stable since around 1997. These examples make it evident that Latin America is a region of contrasts.

When making a choice of where to enter, one needs to take into account the product to be introduced to the region and the investment you are planning to make. The problems when investing in Latin America could be summed up in two ways: (1) lack of knowledge of the market and (2) logistical problems. For both problems, asking questions such as would enlighten managers:

1   Why are we entering the market?
2   If we are entering the market to expand to other countries, do we know the Free Trade Agreements?
3   What is the economic and social situation in the country we are planning to enter?
4   What are the logistics problems that we are going to face?

The importance of answering these questions is to establish the opportunities and the issues of entering Latin America. To make an efficient choice, one has to analyze the information offered, the type of business that the company is going to develop, and the how the business is going to tackle the different challenges.

Conclusions

Establishing a business in Latin American requires a variety of skills and access to resources. By skills, we mean a thorough knowledge of the business and cultural environment. An investor or businessperson is entering into Latin America, with the ability to establish relationships among potential sources of business that can give objective feedback on potential investments. Moreover, the investor needs a network of contacts that can help analyze and determine the feasibility of making successful business operations. This chapter has outlined a host of essential areas that one would need to know about as one pursues the journey of investing in Latin America. Some of these areas are more important to know about than others. Clearly knowing about the financing structure, the types of business classes, the infrastructure and the elements of negotiation are essential areas that need careful understanding. Challenges and opportunities exist. Establishing a business in Latin America is a long-term project that needs an investment of time, energy, money and an ability to see situations and issues from different perspectives. If that can be done then, the process will be much easier and the outcomes more beneficial for all parties involved.

CASE

Peru represents a country with solid and sound economic growth over a long period of time. In the Latin American environment this is a unique trait that few countries display. Peru's GDP per capita totals to around US$6,000. Because of its unique history it attracts a large number of tourists from around the world. As such, the tourist industry is one that has large opportunities due to the several historic sites such as Machu Picchu, Sacred Valley, Colca Canyon, and the Saksaywaman. The tourist industry also benefits from Peru's multicultural cuisine specifically in Lima. It is not uncommon for tourists to come to Peru and enjoy the cuisine and nightlife of Peru and then fly out to the more remote historic sites in the same trip. Unlike other in Latin American countries, Peru's inflation rate has been steadily low. The inflation rate is only 3.6% today. Thus, Peru is among the fastest-growing economies and shows sustainable growth. Furthermore, moderate inflation rates support Peru's aspirations of a strong middle-class income country.

Peru offers many incentives to open up a small business. With GDP growth rates ranging between 2.5% and 8.5% in the past 7 years and public support mechanisms, Peru has evolved into a new start-up environment. In 2012, the government of Peru announced a budget of more than US$20 million for the start-up program. Former president Pedro Pablo Kuczynski pledged during his campaign in 2016 for small enterprises, while also reducing bureaucracy. Moreover, the cost of living in Peru is significantly lower compared to the United States, which has the potential to attract investors. Additionally, the barriers of opening up a business are relatively low. Considering that Peru is not enacting a required minimum capital and has several visa schemes that facilitate doing business as a foreigner.[1] The political stability that Peru has shown over the last decade is an advantage for businesses operating in Peru. With this positive platform in mind we can see that business continue to grow, develop and flourish. One of those businesses that have taken advantage of the positive economic environment for a long time is the AJE Group, of Peru. Peru has many industrial regions within its geographic boundaries. One area of Peru called Ayacucho is a region that was heavily damaged by the Shining Path guerilla conflict that occurred two decades ago. Because of this struggle many of the major beverage companies left the area. This created a major disparity in the market. As a result, the Ananos Family began to produce carbonated beverages named Kola Real. They began the business with an orange flavored drink. Initially they decided to direct their business towards the segments, which had been abandoned by the more popular brands. These leading brands generally centered their business on the customers who had the highest purchasing power. AJE Group's goal has been to provide high-quality products to people with limited resources. This has been the recipe for its success.

AJE Group has become a leading multinational Beverage company in Peru. It has 28 years of experience in production of soft drink with 8 global brands. All of these brands can be of service to the tourist industry. AJE is the fourth largest soft drink producer in the world. It has 23 brands sold in global markets and continued interest in its products among other markets around the world. It has 32 factories and facilities to produce the soft drink products. From 1911–1997 AJE expanded to major cities in Peru. It landed Cola Real Brand in 1997. It started its international expansion in 2000 to Venezuela and Ecuador. In 2002 it launched a bottled water brand called Cielo. In the same year AJE entered the Mexican. This was a major milestone in AJEs business history because Mexico has the highest per capita of consumption in the world. In 2005 Costa Rica, Guatemala, Nicaragua and Honduras became major markets for AJE. It established a major corporate office Spain in 2006.

Overall, AJE is in 23 countries with a Global but local focus. In 2013 AJE introduced the concept of using local partnerships to develop new international markets. The Local focus Business Model is allowing AJE to move into markets much more rapidly than before. This has allowed AJE to globalize their brands much more speed than before. AJE believes that those partners who accept its culture and brand allegiance can help advance the business's products and long run profit success. Partners have to have a thorough knowledge of the local markets and have enough financial strength to follow a growing distribution business. Clearly partners with experience in the beverage business are more desirable. Within this business model AJE provides global brand management, R&D, and technical assistance in manufacturing, marketing, distribution and purchasing power that allows them to focus on their core soft drink business. AJE is a true success story that took advantage of the positive business environment and continues to benefit from this venture.

Source: www.ajegroup.com

Note

1 Santarini, Maria (2017). "2017: Business Opportunities in Peru." *Bizlatinhub.com,* accessed February, 2017.

References

Aguilar, Omar (2014). "Latin America Rising: How Latin American Companies Have Become Global Leaders." https://www2.deloitte.com/global/en/pages/strategy/articles/latin-america-rising.html, accessed April, 2018.

An overview of Microfinance in Latin America (2012). https://lab.org.uk/an-overview-of-microfinance-in-latin-america, accessed January, 2018.

Arnal, Luis (2014). "New Report, The state of Innovation in Latin America, Organization & Culture, Reports." www.innovationmanagement.se/2014/10/15/new-report-the-state-of-innovation-in-latin-america/, accessed April, 2018.

Becker, Thomas (2011). *Doing Business in the New Latin America: Keys to Profit in America Next-Door Markets.* Westport: CT, U.S., Greenwood Publishing.

Boccanlandro, Antonio (2013). "A Renewed Look at Doing Business in Latin America." www.supplychain247.com/article/a_renewed_look_at_doing_business_in_latin_america, accessed January, 2018.

Bulletin FAL (2016). "Latin America's infrastructure investment situation and Challenges, Facilitation of transport and trade in Latin America," 374(3/2016). www.cepal.org/transport, accessed March, 2018.

Child Labor in Latin America and Caribbean (2016). "Regional Outlook." www.dol.gov/agencies/ilab/resources/reports/child-labor/latin-america-caribbean, accessed March, 2018.

Deresky, Helen, (2014). *International Management: Managing Across Borders and Cultures,* 8th Edition. Boston, New York: Pearson.

Dill, Claudia (2017). "What are the Top Risks to Doing Business in Latin America?" *World Economic Forum.* www.weforum.org/agenda/2017/03/risks-business-latin-america, accessed March, 2018.

Fay, Mariane, Luis Alberto Andres, Charles Fox, Ulf Narloch, Stephane Straub, & Michael Slawson (2016). *Spending Better to Achieve More.* Washington D.C. U.S.: The World Bank.

Fleischmann, Alan (2017) "Latin American the Next Frontier for Long-Termism." www.forbes.com/sites/alanfleischmann/2017/11/02/latin-america-the-next-frontier-for-long-termism/#4d3ac1574244, accessed March, 2018.

Frayer, Janis Mackey (2017). "China Ventures into America's Backyard: Latin America." www.nbcnews.com/news/world/china-ventures-america-s-backyard-latin-america-n740001, accessed March, 2018.

Gendreau, Brian C. & Timothy E. McLendon (2017). "2017 Latin American Business Environment Report." University of Florida: Center for Latin American Studies.

Gonzalez, Elizabeth, (2015). "Weekly Chat: Latin America's Informal Economy." www.as-coa.org/articles/weekly-chart-latin-americas-informal-economy, accessed April, 2018.

Hunkar, David (2014). "The Top 100 Latin American Multinational Companies 2014." *topforeignstorks.com*. http://topforeignstocks.com/2014/11/04-the-top-100-latin-american-multinational-companies-2014, accessed January, 2018.

Kapowicz, Izabela, Troy Matheson, & Svetlana Vtyurina (2016). "Investing in Infrastructure in Latin America and the Caribbean." Washington D.C. U.S.: International Monetary Fund.

Kelly, Nataly (2015). "How Marketing is Evolving in Latin America." *Harvard Business Review, Digital Review.* https://hbr.org/2015/06/how-marketing-is-evolving-in-latin-america, accessed January, 2018.

Latin Trade Infrastructure Index (2017). http://latintrade.com/latin-trade-infrastructure-index-2017, accessed August, 2017.

Lederman, Daniel, Julian Messina, Samuel Pienknagura, & Jamele Rigolini (2014). *"Latin American Entrepreneurs Many Firms but Little Innovation." International Bank for Reconstruction and Development.* Washington D.C. U.S.: The World Bank.

Lozada, Lucal Iberico (2013). "In Sweatshop, The Brazilian Dream Goes Away." *World News Reuters.* www.reuters.com/article/us-brazil-immigrants/in-sweatshops-the-brazilian-dream-goes-awry-idUSBRE98004L20130901, accessed April, 2018.

Lustig, Nathan (2017). "New Era for Start Up Investigation in Latin America." https://techcrunch.com/2017/05/19/a-new-era-for-startup-investing-in-latin-america, accessed January, 2018.

Martinez, Alonso, Ivan de Souza, & Francis Liu (2003). "Multinationals vs. Multilatinas: Latin America's Great Race." *Strategy + Business.* www.uky.edu/~wallyf/multilatinas, accessed April, 2018.

Mendoza, Naki B. (2015). "Minding the Gap: Evaluating SME financing in Latin America." www.devex.com/news/minding-the-gap-evaluating-sme-financing-in-latin-america-86957, accessed January, 2018.

Microfinance (2009). www.iadb.org/en/microfinance, accessed January, 2018.

Modern Beer Plant (2018). Gallo Beer Plant in Guatemala, Central America. Author's photo.

Momentum (2017) "Momentum to Do Business in Latin America and Caribbean." www.expo-f.com/m_article/3-Press-Release-2.html, accessed January, 2018.

Mueller, Marco (2017). "Digital Transformation in Latin America: Firms need to Invest More to Level the Playing Field." www.digitalistmag.com/digital-economy/2017/05/25/digital-transformation-in-latin-american-firms-need-to-invest-more-to-level-playing-field-05115403, accessed April, 2018.

Obiols, Maria (2017). "World's GDP Growth by Region 2017, Global Finance." www.gfmag.com/global-data/economic-data/economic-dataworlds-gdp-growth-by-region, accessed March, 2018.

Orantes, Luis (2015). "Building a winning supply chain in Latin America." www. linkedin.com/pulse/building-winning-supply-chain-latin-america-luis-orantes, accessed January, 2018.

Oxford Economics (2017). "SME Strategies for Success, A Global Study that Reveals the Key Drivers of Success for SME's in 2017 and Beyond." www.businessoffashion.com/ articles/global-currents/latin-americas-160-billion-fashion-opportunity, accessed April, 2018.

Reaching the Last Mile: SME Finance in Latin America (2015). *Center for Inclusive Growth.* https://mastercardcenter.org/insights/reaching-last-mile-sme-finance-latin-america, accessed January, 2018.

Srinivasan, Mandyam, M., Theodore P. Stank, Phillippe-Pierre Dornier, & Kenneth Petersen (2014). *Global Supply Chains: Evaluating Regions on an EPIC Framework – Economy, Politics, Infrastructure, and Competence.* New York: McGraw-Hill.

The Economist (2018). "Infrastructure in Latin America." March 10, 2018, pp.35–36.

The World Bank (2016). "Global Logistic Performance Rankings." https://lpi.world bank.org/international/global/2016, accessed March, 2018.

The World Bank Flagship Report (2016). "Doing Business 2016 – Measuring Regulatory Quality and Efficiency." 13th Edition. *World Bank Group, World Bank.* Washington D.C. www.doingbusiness.org/~/media/WBG/DoingBusiness/Documents/ Annual-Reports/English/DB16-Full-Report.pdf, accessed March, 2018.

Transparency International (2017). "Corruption on the Rise in Latin America and the Caribbean." www.transparency.org/news/feature/corruption_on_the_rise_in_latin_ america_and_the_caribbean, accessed April, 2018.

Vanek, Joann, Martha Alter, Francoise Carre, Jane Heintz & Raf Hussmaans (2014). "Statistics on Informal Economy: Definitions, Regional Estimates and Challenges, Informal Employment Women in Informal Employment Globalizing and Organizing, Working Paper No. 2." www.wiego.org/sites/default/files/publications/files/Vanek-Statistics-WIEGO-WP2.pdf, accessed April, 2018.

Waterpower (2014). www.waterpowermagazine.com/contractors/construction-general/ mwh-americas-inc/mwh-americas-inc3.html, accessed February, 2018.

Wisner, Joel D., Keah-Choon Tan, & G. Keong Leong (2009). *Principles of Supply Chain Management: A Balanced Approach.* Boston, MA, U.S.: Southwestern Cengage Learning.

World Bank Doing Business (2016) "2016 Fact Sheet: Latin America and the Caribbean." www.doingbusiness.org/media/~/media/WBG/DoingBusiness/Documents/Fact-Sheets/DB16/FactSheet_DoingBusiness2016_LAC_Eng.pdf, accessed January, 2018, http://info.aliceapp.com/hubfs/Amex-Small-Business-Strategies.pdf?t=1497027864089, accessed January, 2018.

World Bank Group Flagship Report (2016). "Doing Business 2016 – Measuring Regulatory Quality and Efficiency Regional Profile 2016, Latin America, 13th Edition." http://documents.worldbank.org/curated/en/588691467991948478/pdf/103368-WP-PUBLIC-ADD-SERIES-DB2016-DB16-Latin-America.pdf, accessed January, 2018.

Zerin, Phoenix (2014). "3 Key elements negotiating in Latin America." *Nomad Capitalists.* http://nomadcapitalist.com/2014/05/09/three-key-elements-negotiating-latin-america, accessed January, 2018.

Ziegler, Tania, E.J. Reedy, Annie Le, Bryan Zhang, Randall S. Kroszner, & Kieran Garvey (2017). "The 2017 Americas Alternative Finance Industry Report, Hitting, CME Group Foundation Stride." www.jbs.cam.ac.uk/fileadmin/user_upload/ research/centres/alternative-finance/downloads/2017-05-americas-alternative-finance-industry-report.pdf, accessed January, 2018.

9

THE MARKETING PROCESS

Introduction

This chapter describes and discusses the major marketing topics that relate to assessing consumer behavior and developing marketing plans to meet the needs of the customers in Latin America. Using the marketing mix concept as a major framework, the authors will investigate and report on the traditional and non-traditional marketing approaches that companies use to satisfy their customers. A general overview indicates that a blanket approach to marketing does not work in Latin America. Monitoring product life cycle is an important function of any Latin American marketer. The retail sector in Latin America is fragmented into three major markets: the formal market that is comprised of the legally established businesses, the informal market that is an important aspect of many Latin Americans' daily lives, and e-commerce. Understanding how the marketing mix fits these three major markets is an important discussion in this chapter. The emergence of the middle class and their consumer inclinations is also an important dimension that will be discussed. Finally, the issue of social media and online marketing will be part of the overall discussion as it relates to Latin Americans' consumer behavior.

International Marketing in Latin America

International marketing can be defined as "the performance of business activities designed to plan, price, promote and direct the flow of a company's goods and services to consumers or users in more than one nation for a profit" (Cateora, 2009, p.9). As such, selecting a marketing strategy wisely requires an accurate understanding of consumer behavior and market segments. Those living in Latin

America benefit from a dynamic consumer economy. Because this region of the world has young populations and generally large households, the promise of future economic growth is great. However, the fabric of the culture and the buying patterns of its members are in constant change. As a consumer group, the family or household resembles any other group with problems to solve and decisions to make (Lindquist & Sirgy, 2003). The globalization of markets in Latin America over the last two decades has forced marketers to analyze consumer behavior from a variety of different dimensions. Because there is a demand for consumer products in virtually all countries of the world, planning a global or an international marketing strategy requires a firm to consider how local customers and their attitudes will affect consumer behavior. In different cultures, however, products are used differently and under various conditions to meet differing buyer needs. Thus, international marketers must analyze these factors and decide the merits of standardizing or adapting their products for foreign markets. On one end of the continuum, a firm's entire marketing strategy might be standardized and used intact in foreign markets; at the other extreme, all strategic elements can be adapted to meet the foreign market's needs. In many cases, products must be made to meet different conditions for foreign markets. Products are often the most costly to adapt, but sometimes adjustments must be made because the product is used to meet different buyer needs or because specific attributes of a product have no value or meaning in foreign markets. When a firm has limited resources or limited goals for foreign sales, it may choose to standardize its products even if demand for them will be limited. Conversely, a firm may be forced to adapt.

Regional Differences – Regional Marketing versus Individual Country Marketing

Regional marketing relates to a variety of marketing functions that are directed at achieving marketing goals in a geographic region of a country or a much larger area that may include several countries. Regional marketing involves the application of basic marketing techniques and tactics used to successfully promote and market products and services. Marketers may segment geographic regions because one is richer or poorer than another. The products they sell may appeal to one of the two segments. An example of this would be marketing to an urban versus a rural population. Segmenting the market further by demographics is a popular technique in international marketing. There are clear differences in needs among the people of the north, south, east, and west of Latin America. Clothing and equipment in the mountainous areas is different than the clothing and equipment needs in the lowlands. These characteristics motivate marketers to create products and services that meet the needs of these segmented or targeted markets. Some examples of the regional differences are presented below:

1   Peru now has Tambor + a convenience store business model that is posing a real threat to the traditional barrio grocer. Tambo + is attractive because it offers a broad range of products and it is very affordable for the Peruvian people. It operates 24/7, which is one step ahead of the traditional barrio small grocery store.

2   Ecuador – remains tradition but modern with its traditional neighborhood stores. Modern channels that have emerged similar to small super markets. While this architecture and business model is attractive, Ecuador's tax and import policies are presenting major challenge to this modern approach.

3   Costa Rica has a trend towards locally made products – yet high end. There is government training to promote this approach to business. Remaining local seems to challenge the reliance on multinationals like Wal-Mart.

4   Uruguay – The government supports the traditional channels. The traditional channel remains strong.

5   Bolivia – entrepreneurial competitiveness among retailers. A movement called *800 tiendas de barrio* has benefitted from local government sponsored programs called *Mi Caserits* (Euromonitor International, 2016).

Market Research

Entering an international market requires the marketer to understand a host of market dynamics. The need for accurate marketing research is essential in order to make appropriate decisions about the types of customers, target markets, product acceptability, promotion strategies, and competitive intelligence. Failure to complete marketing research in all designated countries can lead to poor decisions and a serious misallocation of resources. Additionally, marketers can miss great opportunities that could enhance their profitability.

Market research is not a one-time activity. It requires the marketer to continuously investigate the changing markets. Market research is broader than just focusing on the customer. It encompasses the investigation of company and government policy and regulatory changes that may be occurring in regions of the country or. The investment and trading activities of a country or region can provide important information that can affect marketing decision-making.

The Latin American marketplace is complex, and therefore the importance of market research cannot be over emphasized. Statistics about the size and composition of the market are crucial to developing marketing strategies to meet the needs of the customers. The following tables provide a perspective on the size and capabilities of the market in Latin America.

The preceding table provides valuable information regarding the demographics of the region. To marketers, this information is crucial for forecasting sales. There are two interesting statistics in this table: a.) the median age in most countries is relatively young, and b.) many of the countries have very large urban areas. This gives the marketer in Latin America information about various

TABLE 9.1 Population Statistics 2018

Country	Population	Median Age	Urban Population	% of Population that is Urban
Argentina	44,688,864	31.0	39,791,287	89.0
Bolivia	11,215,674	24.3	8,053,683	71.8
Brazil	210,867,954	31.7	179,930,745	85.3
Chile	18,197,209	34.1	16,530,223	90.8
Colombia	49,464,683	30.5	39,603,748	80.1
Costa Rica	4,953,199	31.8	4,106,600	82.9
Ecuador	16,863,425	26.9	19,923,259	118.1
El Salvador	6,411,558	26.1	4,455,699	69.5
Guatemala	17,245,346	21.3	9,246,101	53.6
Honduras	9,417,167	23.4	5,031,591	53.4
Mexico	130,759,974	27.9	103,527,244	79.2
Nicaragua	6,248,757	25.6	3,889,910	62.3
Peru	32,551,815	27.8	25,706,179	79.0
Uruguay	3,469,551	35.0	3,313,395	95.5
Venezuela	32,381,221	27.7	29,051,213	89.7

Source: Worldmeter.Info (2018).

products that would serve these two market segments. Young people have various inclinations towards various products and services. Likewise, urban dwellers have much different needs and desires when compared to those people living in the rural sectors of the country. Marketers can build their marketing strategies and plans from this vital information.

Where are the Markets in Latin America?

Latin America is home to active and lucrative markets. Many of the markets are the traditional retail markets that are popular all over the world, e.g., storefront retailers and malls. These outlets have been the way people have exchanged goods for decades. Many consumers in Latin America are not focused on expensive, image-oriented goods to use as necessities in their daily lives. They buy them because of the image they portray. Latin Americans like to present the image of being successful. This inclination should tell marketers that knowing the consumer in their respective country and the specific locality is critically important to successful selling in Latin America (Li, 2011). Additionally, it is important to hire employees who know the product brand, needs, and desires of the local consumer. Electronic communication of ideas is an effective way to convey the message to rich customers. Within this context, it is imperative that the public image of the product is honestly presented. The companies that promote and sell products through luxury branding must prove themselves and their company to the consumer. Some people are saying that the market that exists in Latin America has many of the same attributes of China. There is evidence of rapid capital inflows, very strong domestic demand, and low inflation. These are conditions that motivate marketers to think seriously about the region, the countries, and the opportunities.

One of the major factors affecting market growth is the internet. In the 21st century, we see a major new approach to marketing becoming a dominant force in Latin America. The internet, or e-commerce, has become the all encompassing, 24/7 marketing and shopping environment. The internet has become the hub for connecting with business partners in Latin America. Using websites, e-mail, and other computer interaction mechanisms are vital to the success of most businesses in Latin America. Even itinerant vendors have cell phones, which allow them to do purchasing and selling electronically.

A digital class is growing and increasing all across Latin America. This new digital middle class is transforming the way consumers are acting and responding in the market. This class is alert, current, and has money. They are also knowledgeable about products and services because they can instantly receive advertising and promotions. They are interested in the discovery and exploration process. As such, they are able to find and investigate products and services more rapidly. The Latin American internet population is 375.1 million internet users as of 2018 (Statista, 2018). This online capability provides them with communication, social connections, information, and commerce.

Table 9.2 summarizes the extent of internet connection and potential use in respective countries.

While there are many visitors to Latin American e-commerce sites who make purchases online, many e-commerce retailers continually encounter barriers in drawing consumers to the new way of shopping. One of the major fears that deter online shopping is security. Another barrier is the selection of products. Consumers do not have the ability to physically examine the product

TABLE 9.2 The Extent of Internet Connection and Potential use in Respective Countries

Country	Millions of People
Brazil	139.1
Mexico	76.0
Argentina	34.8
Colombia	28.5
Peru	20.0
Venezuela	19.6
Chile	14.1
Ecuador	13.5
Bolivia	5.3

Source: Statista (2018).

that is offered. Additionally, some customers have problems with payment options. When some people only want to do business on a cash basis, and the online purchase requires credit cards, it creates a problem. The internet market is still in its embryonic stage and growing. It has enormous potential once retailers can work out the obstacles that are obstructing consumer involvement in this shopping environment. The consumer can always be linked with new products or advertisements about the onset of new products and services. The internet is a prime outlet for marketers to present their goods and services. The large number of people that are connected to the internet and use it as indicated by the foregoing table demonstrates that the e-commerce opportunities are substantial. This is a large market for marketers to exploit.

Since the internet is the gateway to the world, this tool can be a company's (big or small) gateway to increased sales and reduced costs. Using Facebook for advertising and product and service identification is a powerful mechanism for conveying company messages to the public. Blogging is another means of getting business exposure to local, national, and international business audiences. Lack of knowledge about these modern information devices among some Latin American business people and entrepreneurs has created some reluctance to use them. This is a disadvantage for business development, marketing, and business growth. Businesses must understand that the constantly changing media mechanisms mean that they may not always be selling products and services directly to the customer per se, but rather they are selling the value and information about the product and service. When good, genuine value and information is part of the message, then the company will get attention. Once they have the attention the customer wants to discuss more details of the product and this can lead to negotiations to purchase the product or service. Latin American business people are learning about these new customer-connecting devices and are finding out that they are valuable selling instruments that they cannot hesitate to adopt.

Table 9.3 summarizes selected Latin American countries' consumer potential based on disposable income and e-commerce potential.

TABLE 9.3 Latin America Countries Consumer Potential Based on Disposable Income and E-Commerce Potential

Country	Population	Per Capita GDP in US$	Household Disposable Income	E-Commerce in US$ Billions
Argentina	43.4	27,400	12,200	5.0
Brazil	206.6	15,800	11,665	19.8
Chile	17.5	23,800	15,500	2.3
Colombia	46.7	14,000	n/a	5.7
Mexico	121.7	18,500	13,370	6.0

Source: Latin American Consumer Overview (2015).

Table 9.3-consumer potential for e-commerce based on population and household disposable income. Customer buying and shopping habits are in constant flux. The marketing concept is still alive, but it is being presented to the market in different ways. The existence of social media, blogs, texting, e-mails, and all the other aspects of e-commerce have created a different landscape for marketers. The marketers of today need to focus on the dynamic buying behavior of customers. The information in Table 9.3 can assist the marketer in projecting trends and shopping potential in e-commerce area of retail.

Table 9.4 summarizes the potential for retail e-commerce in Latin America.

The information in Table 9.4 reinforces the preceding table with a glimpse of what the projected retail e-commerce potential. This is just another perspective on the large opportunity that exists in e-commerce among Latin American consumers.

The majority of Latin American businesses are market-oriented. This means that they focus on the customer to obtain information about his/her needs and desires. The buyers of industrial and consumer goods in Latin America are very much demanding and informed customers. One of the major rules among marketers is not to ignore or fail to recognize a customer's cultural origins.

The traditional old-fashioned marketing approach (production mentality – we make it, you buy it) to customer needs has given way to modern ideas advanced by the globalization process which requires major changes in market orientation and analysis (Becker, 2011). While industrial products need less cultural adaptation – e.g., bottling machines, conveyers, or earth moving equipment – consumer goods are very culturally bound and connected. This is especially true in the local geographic areas around each respective country (Becker, 2011).

As most consumer marketers in Latin America will testify, women are important to succeeding with the new digital class. This gender group is the principal purchaser and almost always the main decision maker for product

TABLE 9.4 Retail e-commerce in Latin America 2014–2019 (US$ billions)

Amount	Year
33.35	2014
40.98	2015
49.83	2016
59.81	2017★
68.94	2018★
79.74	2019★

Source: Statista (2018).

Note
★ Estimates.

selection and purchase. Attracting the female digital class is absolutely essential to penetrating this market.

Brazil is the 5th most populated country in the world and has the 12th largest economy. With this size, number of consumers, and buying power, marketers would be foolish not to aggressively pursue market and selling opportunities in Latin America.

Many people think that Latin America is composed of the traditional "open markets" where vendors spend long hours selling products from dawn to dusk for low salaries. While the traditional "open markets" do exist all across Latin America and provide for the livelihood for millions of vendors, there are other markets such as retail stores, malls, and warehouse vendors (SAMs) that are also competing for consumer attention.

Figure 9.1 illustrates the contrast of street vendors and the regular storefront vendors. Incredible competition that harmoniously function with each segment pursuing their customers and aggressively promoting their products to the public.

Here is a small example of how itinerant vendors present their goods to the public. Everything is out in the open and easy to see and inspect. This method of selling has been around for centuries.

FIGURE 9.1 Informal Market – They Exist across Latin America

The middle class – Reports indicate that the Latin American middle class is playing a critical role in market development, purchasing power, and consumer consumption. Based on various reports, the middle class is a heterogeneous group, but it has a different connotation in Latin America than in North America or Europe. When official government bodies refer to the "middle class," they are referring to a section of the population that has extricated itself from poverty yet does not have all of the characteristics of a well-to-do citizenry. The middle class we refer to in Latin America remains susceptible to economic problems and crises. Generally, this class does not hold a college degree, does not have stable employment, and remains a significant distance from being comfortable in their socioeconomic status. They still face threats because of their lack of achievement in education and economic status. The greatest increase in the middle class has taken place in Brazil. The criteria for classifying people in this country, as middle class was whether their income and earnings were four times that of what constituted the poverty line. Based on recent statistics, 61 million Brazilians can be classified as middle class (Money. cnn, 2018). In total, the Latin American middle class increased by 56 million since 1999. This has had a major effect on purchasing and consumer consumption. While there has been an increase in the middle class in Brazil, statistics show a decline in middle class in Argentina. This is equally evident in Colombia primarily due to the drug warfare that has been going on for so long in that country. Latin America has only six countries that have a large middle class. Table 9.5 Latin American Countries and the size of their middle Class:

Knowing the size of the middle class in respective countries provides marketers with a perspective on the consumer base for presenting product offerings. Since the middle class has a purchasing power and product inclination profile, marketers can begin to think about appropriate products and services that this group of consumers want and need. To achieve an improved quality of life, middle class members need to spend money on goods and services that will provide a higher quality of life. Marketers need to know these profiles to serve the customer more fully.

TABLE 9.5 Latin American Countries and the Size of their Middle Class

Country	% of Population in Middle Class
Argentina	4.0
Brazil	8.1
Chile	22.3
Colombia	15.3
Mexico	17.1

The Marketing Process

In the contemporary business environment, business people have no other choice but to market their goods and services internationally. The borderless world gives businesses freedom to move from one market to another with few constraints. Just look at the European Union – 27 countries can cross borders without encountering any bureaucratic strains of visas and immigration controls.

While such freedom seems great for market entry, it opens the marketing manager's options to a variety of known and unknown variables. Some of these variables encompass socio-economic, resource, legal, financial, and labor constraints. Such complexities make the marketing manager's task much more difficult. These managers have to have not just two strategies ready for implementation, but also an arsenal of culturally appropriate market strategies ready for implementation all the time. The marketing mix, or the 4 ps (product, price, promotion and place), become extremely important but must be measured against the variables mentioned above.

There are many combinations and permutations of the marketing mix that can be developed to address the interaction of the variables. International marketing managers need to know whether they have to standardize their products and approaches in world markets or if it is necessary to customize the marketing mix based on country and local conditions, needs, and variables. Standardizing is much easier, but it fails in many cases to meet the needs of the local customer (Geringer, McNett, Minor & Ball, 2012). Since product strategy development is at the core of all marketing mix arrangements, the product must first satisfy the customer's needs. If the product does not meet the customer's need, then there is no need to look at or analyze the other three parts of the marketing mix. In the first instant, the product must be presentable and beneficial to the customer. In other words, it must satisfy their needs. Two of the major constraints in this area are the issues of culture and laws. In various foreign countries, products and services must be changed or altered to meet the particular laws or culture. The need for customization necessitates a modification in the marketing mix strategy and thwarts the efforts to maintain a standardized approach to global marketing This action creates a modification in the marketing mix strategy and the efforts to maintain a standardized approach to global marketing (Geringer et al., 2012). Besides the legal and cultural constraints, there are also economic and physical forces that determine a different path for marketing products in foreign countries. Marketing in developing countries illustrates this dilemma. Many consumers in these countries do not have the income level that allows them to purchase products or services offered at standardized prices. Equally, the climate and the geography of the country run counter to standardization process. Such issues as dirt, sand, heat and power output many times are so substantial that it is not possible to sell products or services in countries without these elements in existence (Geringer et al., 2012).

Marketing Strategies

Marketing strategy singles out the firm's target market, its related marketing mix, and the methods which it intends to use in order to maintain a competitive edge (Grewal & Levy, 2017). Marketing strategy is created based on marketing research and focused on the right marketing mix in order to achieve maximum profit and sustain the business. Marketing strategies are part of the marketing plan, which is composed of a series of activities in the marketing mix that focus on addressing consumer and business needs. Providing the customer with value is a critical part of implementing marketing strategies. It is critically important to determine the target market and focus marketing strategies based on consumer information. One aspect of marketing strategy in Latin America relates to focusing on the local market. It is an effective method of market entry in various countries around the region. One of the popular marketing approaches is content marketing strategy. This method depends on the audience. Content marketing involves the creation and sharing of online material such as videos, blogs, and social media. It does not promote brands but initiates interest in products or services being offered (Arista, 2017).

Another approach is inbound marketing. This is a technique for attracting customers using company-created internet content. It is a routine where the customer comes to the company rather than the marketer going after the customer. Finally, another marketing strategy is to use the search engine optimization (SEO) method. By this method, the marketer is getting traffic from the

FIGURE 9.2   Typical Retail Outlet in Guatemala

free, organic editorials, or natural search results. With this information the marketer can follow leads and prospects that hopefully lead to a closed sale. Clearly this technology is an enabler of change (Arista, 2017).

Marketers focus on giving consumers the most value possible for their products and services. To achieve this goal, the marketer must have an excellent product, an efficient business and operations model that responds to consumers' needs and desires, and a distribution or logistics mechanism that brings the right products to the right customer at the right time in the right condition, quality, and price. Latin American consumers are very product quality and price sensitive. Efforts must be directed towards making these elements of the marketing process excellent. The marketing strategies are implemented using the marketing mix.

The Marketing Mix – Global Marketing

Product

At the core of the marketing mix is the product. People buy products to satisfy their needs and/or desires. When a product does not meet these criteria, repeat business will not occur. One of the major requirements when marketing a product is to sell the entire product, including the physical product itself, brand name, warranties, and other aspects that customers assume will accompany the product. While consumer products require more adaptation than industrial products, marketing managers must be alert to sensitivities to product types when marketing to different cultural locations (Geringer, 2012). Understanding what Latin America is and how it is composed is very important. Looking at data that shows the most popular demands for your product is important. This is an important and time-consuming activity because information about the country, locale, and region are in many cases difficult to obtain.

Promotion and Advertising

The next part of the marketing mix is promotion. This feature allows the marketers to communicate their message about a product to the public. It is the one factor that not only tries to convince the customer or user of its utility and value but also must appeal to the other members of the distribution channel, such as the retailers, wholesalers, jobbers etc., Personal selling, advertising, and public relations are the main vehicles whereby the marketer attempts to link the product name, type, and message to the customers' needs and desires. Personal selling and advertising are the two most prevalent methods of marketing a product in Latin America (Geringer, 2012).

Modern technologies (e.g., cellphones, TVs, internet, and social media) are so pervasive and used so frequently to advertise, marketers can now extend their

TABLE 9.6 Latin American Global Consumer Spending and Global Advertising (US$ millions)

Latin America Consumer Spending		Latin American Advertising Spending	
Year	Amount	Year	Amount
2009	38,035	2009	14,510
2010	45,099	2010	17,124
2011	55,381	2011	19,056
2012	66,305	2012	70,845
2013	75,010	2013	22,918
2014	83,436	2014	26,053
2015	91,690	2015	28,866

Source: McKinsey&Co (2015).

message, products, and services to a significantly larger customer market base. These new technological methods of contacting the customer have cut across both income and cultural domains. As such, the customer is more informed and more knowledgeable about the products and services that are being offered (Becker, 2012).

The advertising or promotion component of the marketing mix presents all the indications that Latin America is a very promising arena to do business. Countries such as Brazil, Mexico, and Argentina are among the major areas for opportunity.

The preceding table provides another perspective on the size and potential of the market in five of the major countries in Latin America. Marketers can use this information to establish their marketing strategies. Since household disposable income is a very important variable in predicting consumption patterns, marketers can use this information to plan their strategies in their target markets.

Mobile marketing is growing at a very fast pace, but it is not something to be taken for granted or understood as a linear entity. Some countries are different and have different areas of penetration due to varying economic power, culture, and infrastructure. Latin America loves apps. Mobile advertising is a business function of commerce in Latin America. There has been an explosion of mobile phones in Santiago, Sao Paolo, Medellin, and other places (Wright, 2017). Mobile internet advertising in Latin America is increasing rapidly; the projected value of this advertising is US$7.92 billion by 2019. Digital ad spending in Latin America has already reached new levels. While TV is still a forceful vehicle for ads, it represents only 40% of all advertisements. Additionally; TV is not where the audience is. 9 out of 10 people with internet connection in Latin America own a smartphone and spend 37 hours per week on internet compared to only 7 hours on TV. The implications are significant (Wright, 2017).

From another perspective, high context culture marketing generally relies on symbolic and emotional substance as a mechanism to appeal to the customer. Essentially this type of promotion focuses on two levels of consumer:

1   The low-structured context – which needs humor and picture presentation.
2   The high-structured context – which needs expert subscribers (Becker, 2012).

Marketers have to listen to the market. For example, the people who live in the mountains and on the coast generally are more informal and want more informal products and services to satisfy their needs. The people who live in the mountains are more conservative, and thus they need a different approach that has more formal structure to it to satisfy their needs. Knowing these two types of markets exist helps the marketer arrange and rearrange their marketing mix strategies to satisfy the customers. When a marketer has agreed on the specific target market, he or she needs to find the best medium to communicate that his or her product or service is now available to the public. One of the most popular mechanisms for spreading the message is through radio, newspapers, magazines, and community forums. Many areas in Latin America still have outdoor selling events that provide wide exposure to the products and services being offered.

Pricing

Price has always been an important part of the marketing mix in Latin America. The onset of more comprehensive and instantaneous information as well as access to ways to compare and assess the value of a product has caused price sensitivity among Latin American consumers to become a challenge among marketers. These phenomena should motivate marketers to concentrate more on product and service value rather than price. When the relationship between price and value can produce a perception of benefit, the consumer will pay attention and be more inclined to buy the product or service. This approach can increase product and service sales and, as a result, increase the profit margins. When marketers know the income levels and behaviors of a Latin American consumer, they can better gauge and position their pricing strategy. This will ultimately increase sales and/or profit margin (Becker, 2012).

The sale of products and services is not complete until the customer pays the price of the product. Making sure that the price is right to make a profit or achieve a reasonable profit margin is a very important part of the marketing process. Too high or too low a price can disrupt the business deal. The issue of price sensitivity needs to be recognized in cross-cultural negotiations. While fixed prices are part of many deals in many Latin American countries, there are also a great many deals that are concluded using the bargaining method to achieve price agreements. In many of the central markets, bargaining is the rule rather than the exception.

Place, Channels, and Distribution

The place aspect of the marketing mix relates to distributing products or services to the customer. This effort requires the marketer to deliver the goods at the right place, at the right time, and in the right condition (Sharma, 2015). Depending on the geographic location, the distribution will have different forms. In urban areas, the distribution will be much like that of most North American or other Western developed countries: manufacturer to distributer to retailer. In Latin America, with many towns and villages, the traditional approach to getting goods and services to the customer is through the *tienda*, local storefront shopkeeper or the local community central market.

Modernization of the distribution process has expanded the channel options available to the local customer. Now they can go the mass merchandising outlets like Jumbos in Chile, Wal-Mart in Guatemala, or SAMs in Mexico. These mega department stores carry all the products available in the *tienda* and much, much more. While the neighborhood central market, *tiendas*, and shopkeepers are important for convenience, their role in the community has been significantly diminished because of the powerful mass-merchandising entities. This modernization effect has given the consumer a broader, more comprehensive line of offerings that expands the market significantly. It has also created a large supply chain requirement that the marketers must address (Becker, 2012).

Latin America represents an example of the importance of considering geography in marketing. Economic and social systems are explained in part based on the geographic characteristics of the area. South America has many natural barriers that inhibit both national and regional growth, trade, and communication. It has vast landmass with population concentrations on the periphery and an isolated, almost uninhabited interior. One example within Colombia demonstrates the arduousness of travel. To get from Bogota to Medellin takes 30 minutes by plane. To get there by land, it takes 10–12 hours. This certainly is a major task by land (Cateora, Gilly, & Graham, 2016).

What Products, Branding, and Packaging are Appropriate or Needed?

Structural and societal changes in Latin America are creating incredible opportunities. Consumers in Latin America are looking for the best products even when the price is high. They look for value in the consumer goods that they buy. The common premium goods across the consumer groups of Millennial, baby boomers, Generation X, and age 65+ include dairy products, hair care, oral care, baby care, and tea and coffee. Millennials consider deodorants and cosmetics to be premium products. Generation X says rice and grains are premium products (Kadar, 2018).

The products presented in Table 9.7 are a representation of the types of products that are trending among the consumer population. We could classify them into technologies and consumables, e.g., food and events/entertainment.

Some of the top brands among Latin American countries have had an impact on consumer spending and behavior. The subsequent table summarizes the 15 most popular brands in Latin America.

Since most Latin Americans are brand conscious, it is important to know what brands are most popular among the consumer population. Some of the brands that are listed in Table 9.7 show that brands do not go away. Corona, Televisa, and CEMEX have been around for a very long time. They indicate quality and longevity, or people really like the product. This is good for marketers to know in order to build their marketing strategies and planning around the notion that branding is very important. Product quality and the name of the product go hand in hand. This idea is illustrated with a photo of a typical retail store in Guatemala.

The preceding photo is a picture of a typical retail store that could be seen anywhere in Latin America. The brands, products, and consumables are all presented in a very organized fashion. It is similar to the way retailers in U.S., Europe, and Asia present their products.

TABLE 9.7 Popular Products According to Latin America Countries

Country	Product A	Product B	Product C	Product D
Argentina	Plane Tickets	Hotel Reservation	Mobile Phones	TVs
Bolivia	Electronics	Games Apps	Service Payments	Streaming
Brazil	Books	Appliances	Fashion Accessories	Health Care Products
Chile	Clothing	Technology	Plane Tickets	Tickets to Events
Colombia	Fashion Products	Electronics	Food	Beauty
Mexico	Clothes and Accessories	Digital Downloads	Furniture and Appliances	Games and Entertainment
Peru	Accessories and Apps	Technology Products	Clothes and Shoes	

Source: AMI Perspective, Marketing Insights for Success in Latin America (2016).

TABLE 9.8 Summarizes the Most Popular Brands in LA

Brand	Product
SKL	Beer
Corona	Beer
Telcel	Communication provider
Bradesco	Bank
Falabella	Retail
Televisa	Communication provider
ITAU	Bank
Brahma	Beer
Aguila	Beer
Modelo	Beer
Telmex	Communication provider
Brancolombia	Bank
Sodimac	Retail
Bodega Aurrera	Retail
Cemex	Industry

Source: Millward Brown & WWP Brand Z (2015).

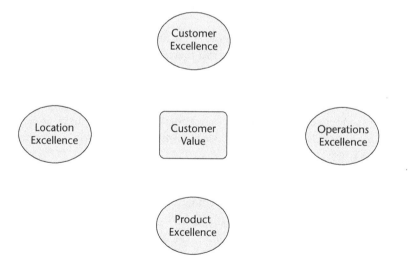

FIGURE 9.3   Customer Value and How it Relates to the other Components of Marketing Strategy

Other Marketing Information Needed to do Business in LA

Informal markets are part of the fabric of Latin America. Every city, town, and village has some type of informal market. It would be naïve to think about marketing in the region without thinking about the informal market, itinerant vendors, or role of informality. This form of marketing has been in place for centuries, and as one travels throughout Latin America, one sees its pervasiveness and its impact on individuals and local economies. Generally, each city in Latin America has a central open market. Here vendors have situated themselves in positions of heavy traffic so that they can implement their daily ritual of selling, buying, negotiating, and exchanging money for goods and goods for goods. This approach to marketing has been passed down through the centuries and is very similar across Latin America. In a central market, a consumer can sell or buy a vast array of goods from groceries to baby toys. As an observer, one begins to ask a variety of questions about this way of marketing. Is it effective? How much do the vendors make in profit when there is so much competition? When margins are so thin, isn't there a huge opportunity cost? Is it possible for an outside supplier to conduct business regularly and make it profitable? Many of these questions can provide important information and possibly opportunities for one who is concerned about selling goods in that country.

People who have traveled to various Latin American countries will note that the informal markets have several dimensions:

1   All countries have a central market where basic groceries and household consumables are sold;
2   Most countries have a central market for the typical goods (*Tipicos*) of that country. For example, in Guatemala there are two central markets: one for consumables and the other for the typical goods. This is also evident in the countries of Peru, Ecuador and Bolivia;
3   Itinerant vendors set up shops on the streets. Many are directly in front of a freestanding retail shop. Others are sporadically set on street corners, in plazas, on roadsides, and at any location where traffic or access to customers are available;
4   Vendors are on the street walking around and changing their location constantly using all their personal selling skills to make a sale. One could label this as "in-your-face-marketing." The vendor is persistent, creative, and generally friendly even if he or she doesn't make a sale;
5   Generally, these vendors are family oriented; the mother and father are both involved in the business, and they bring their children to the place of business on a street corner;
6   Many of the sidewalk vendors are very young – some as young as eight years old. They are taught at a very young age how to sell and market their goods and basically survive economically. The vendors jump on just about any opportunity to make a sale. The spontaneous vendors work with each potential buyer, presenting his or her product as cheap yet important. They go so far as using step ladders to climb to the windows of stopped buses to make a sale (again, in-your-face-marketing) or boarding a bus to sell goods, getting off, and finding another bus to do the same thing. Some ventures

generate lots of sales; others are not so lucky. In a majority of cases the reason for such perseverance of the informal vendors relate to a need for survival. Yet, a more underlying reason is due to numerous institutional requirements necessary to start a business.

Conclusions

As one walks the streets of Latin American cities, towns, and villages, one can see selling and buying on just about every corner. It seems to be a way of life and a true implementation of capitalism. In this chapter, we have described the marketing environment. Within this landscape there are both opportunities and weaknesses. These factors can be summarized as the following:

1   Growing population – As one reviews the population table, it is evident that the number of people in Latin America is growing with young citizens becoming a larger part of the population. This tells marketers that products and services need to focus on this segment.
2   Focus on the middle class – Marketers need to realize that the middle class, while not growing as fast as it has in the past, is still a vibrant part of the population and has the capacity to buy products and services. In many cases the per capita income has a solid purchasing power. This is good news for marketers.
3   Digital/internet market – This part of the economy is growing each year. People in Latin America have more access to the internet, and as a result, they have found that buying through this channel is easy, convenient, and in many cases less expensive. This is a wide-open environment that seems to be giving more and more opportunities each year.
4   Informal market – Let's not forget this formidable segment of the market. All cities, towns, and villages across Latin America have informal markets. They are on every corner and always seem to have the attention of a large segment of the population. Selling to them is as important as selling to other market segments in Latin America.

Building a marketing strategy that addresses all of the above areas is a major task, but it has great potential. The answer to marketing strategy development in Latin America is the development of a marketing mix that focuses on the product quality with a realistic price and a delivery system that is convenient to the customer. Marketing messages are quite pervasive and effective in Latin America. It is getting the product, price, and place elements of the marketing mix right that is so crucially important. This is a continuous improvement process. The potential in resources and opportunity are there; it just takes effective entrepreneurship and management to attain the ultimate marketing success. Latin America is ready. Now it is the marketers' turn.

CASE

CEMEX

International Monetary Fund, IMF, ranks Mexican economy at number 16 in the world based on the nominal terms. It also ranks the country at number 11 worldwide based on the purchasing power parity. The strength and the confidence of the economic activity in the country continue to be restored by the sensible responses of the fiscal policy, resilience to the shocks, gradual improvements in the management of the external environment, and sensible monetary response. Mexico has had strong recovery with external trade. This has been contributing vigorously to the growth of the country's GDP through the increased net exports. The Mexican exports have also been revived because of the increasing external competitiveness, derived from currency depreciation. This has been occurring for the last three years because of the United State's continued strengthening industrial production. Mexico's private consumption is also expanding at a steady pace despite the fact that the increase in inflation in the country is dampening purchasing power of the consumers by limiting the growth of the real labor income. This is the second year when the total investment of the country remains flat. This has been linked with the country's public investment, which has been falling for the two years hence dragging the total investment to the same position. At the beginning of the year 2017, the country experienced an increase in the consumer price inflation to 6.7%. This was caused by the hiking of the prices of the domestic fuel together with the accumulated currency depreciation's pass-through. In response to the increase in the consumer price inflation, the central bank of Mexico hiked its rate of monetary policy by 125 basis points (The World Bank, 2017b).

Because of NAFTA, Mexico becomes the third largest trading partner with the United States. The fact is that ending NAFTA would have huge influence on Mexico more than the United States. Many factories moved their manufacturing facilities to Mexico because of the cheaper labor. Thousands of Mexicans are able to get a job because these factories need huge amount of labors for their production. If NAFTA were ended, the employment problem might be one of the major issues Mexican government has to face. Other than this, Mexico benefits a lot from NAFTA because they were able to trade with the United States and Canada with less constrains and barriers (Chen, Chen, & He, 2017). This has strengthened the economy and provided many business opportunities for local companies. One of the companies that has a long history of success in Mexico and around the world is CEMEX.

CEMEX of Mexico is a global leader operating a large materials company in 50 countries around the world. The company is focused on providing the best solutions in cement, ready-mix and aggregates. Its mission is to provide cement and aggregates and concrete that will satisfy the highest global standards while having the least possible environmental impact. The company was founded in 1906 with the CEMENTOS plant in Hidalgo, Mexico. The production of materials was halted in 1912 because of the Mexican Revolution. This political action cutoff energy, communication and access to labor for a lengthy period of time. It had a negative impact on the company's operations. Cement could not be delivered which cause profits to significantly decline. CEMENTOS muddled through until 1921 when the Revolution had become history and stability had returned. In 1921 the company began full operation again and began to grow the business. CEMEX which the company eventually was named, embark on and expansion process by merging with Pollaras, Monterrey to for CEMENTOS Mexicanos, S.A. This became a very productive venture and established the foundation for more expansion. In the early 1940s Cementos Mexicanos became CEMEX, Monterrey. With the change in name came a gigantic increase in production capacity. CEMEX continued to grow through the merger and acquisition process. Production again expands rapidly. In 1976 CEMEX is listed on the Mexican stock exchange. This is a major advancement in business development. CEMEX continued to grow through the 1980s and the 1990s. In 1996, CEMEX became the third largest company in the materials supply industry with more M&As in Colombia, Costa Rica, U.S.A. and Thailand, among other around the world. CEMEX'S composed of three major values: (1) safety, (2) focuses on the customer and (3) pursue excellence.

From an operations percentage point of view, the following table provides a summary of how their product line sales composition is constructed:

	Product	Sales Percent
a	Cement	45%
b	Ready – mix	39%
c	Aggregates	16%

With regard to sales by region the break out is as follow:

	Country	Percent Sales
a	Mexico	22%
b	U.S.A.	28%
c	South &Central America	13%
d	Europe	25%
e	Asia, Middle East & Africa	12%

Annual sales in U.S. dollars was $13.40 billion.

By 2006 CEMEX had 50,000 employees and celebrated its 100th anniversary. As the first decade of the 21st century rolled forward, CEMEX continue its success. In 2010 it overcame the complex financial issues of this era by adapting its operations to the new market dynamics. In 2012 CEMEX lists it South and Central American operations on the Colombian Stock Exchange. Also, in 2016 CEMEX is listed on the Philippines Stock Exchange. These were significant achievements in the CEMEX international business exposure. It opened major opportunities for growth in international business dealings.

CEMEX and its Marketing. Marketing supports the CEMEX's strategy. Differentiating products from their competitors is a major task for CEMEX marketing professionals. Value added offerings that meet the needs of the market are the main focus of the marketing strategy. CEMEX professionals collaborate with other areas of the company to meet customer needs. This is completed through a process that focuses on customer loyalty and support where customer service become and important ingredient. The use of customer service is a vehicle to promote sustainability of the customer base. CEMEX uses continuous research methods to understand customer needs. Researchers are constantly reviewing, investigating and understanding customer needs. In addition, learning about construction trends is an important part of the research process. Within this context, the company promotes its reputation and products through an emphasis on sustainability and innovation. Working with the CEMEX R&D department, new products and services are developed to meet customer needs and industry trends. With this superior products development and innovation, CEMEX attempts to maintain its leadership position in the industry. Sales force training and development is a critical part of the efforts to keep current with the customers' evolving needs. All of these activities and enhancements can only be achieved when there is good communication and teamwork skills are available among all of the company's marketing employees. These professionals need to understand the basic marketing principles associated with CEMEX and the industry. Additionally, they must be knowledgeable of the branding issues and product development and marketing capabilities issues in order to implement a successful marketing program at CEMEX.

Source: www.cemex.com (2018)

References

Adekane, Joshua (2011). "Marketing Latin America Revealed." www.eliteproduct sourcing.com/wholesale/marketing-latin-america-revealed, accessed December, 2017.

Ami Perspectiva (2016). "Market Insights for Success in Latam." https://amiperspectiva. americasmi.com/tag/ami-perspectiva/, accessed March, 2018.

Arista, Carlos Garcia (2017). "Content Marketing: 3 Global Strategies for Latin America, Digital Marketing." https://isragarcia.com/content-marketing-3-global-strategies-for-latin-america, accessed April, 2018.

Becker, Thomas, (2011). *Doing Business in The New Latin America: Keys to Profit in America's Next-Door Markets*, Second Edition. Denver, Colorado and California: Praeger, and Denver-California.

Cateora, Phillip (2009). *International Marketing*. New York: McGraw Hill Higher Education.

Cateora, Philip R., John Graham & Mary C. Gilly (2016). *International Marketing*, 17th edition. New York: McGraw-Hill.

Chen, Sixiuzhu, Zeyu Chen, & Xixian He (2017) *Mexico International Business Mexico Overview*. St. Louis University: Undergraduate International Business Class, U.S.

Geringer, Michael, Jeanne M. McNett, Michael S. Minor, & Donald A. Ball (2012). *International Business*, 1st Edition. New York: McGraw-Hill.

Grewal, Dhruv & Michael Levy (2017). *Marketing*, 6th Edition. New York: McGraw-Hill.

Kadar, Isabel (2018). "Latin America Seeks Value in Consumer Goods, Global Edge." https://globaledge.msu.edu/blog/post/55570/latin-america-seeks-value-in-consumer-go, accessed February, 2018.

Lindquist J.D. and Sirgy, M.J. (2003). *Shopper, Buyer, and Consumer Behavior: Theory, Marketing Applications and Public Policy Implications*, 2nd Edition. Cincinnati, Ohio: Atomic Dog Pub.

Li, Hao (2011). "Marketing to Latin America: It's All About Image." www.ibtimes.com/articles/123445/20110316/marketing-to-latin-america-brand-image.htm, accessed July, 2018.

Latin American Consumer Overview (2015). www.fungglobalretailtech.com/research/latam-consumer-overview/, accessed January, 2018.

Middle Class Percentages (2018). http://money.cnn.com/infographic/economy/what-is-middle-class-anyway/index.html, accessed March, 2018.

McKinsey&Co (2015). (2015)." "Global Media Report, Global Industry Overview: Latin American Global Consumer Spending and Global Advertising." McKinsey&Co.: WikofskyGruen Associates, www.mckinsey.com/~/media/McKinsey/dotcom/client_service/Media%20and%20Entertainment/PDFs/McKinsey%20Global%20Report%202015_UK_October_2015.ashx, accessed March, 2015.

Millward Brown & WWP Brand Z (2015). "Top Most Valuable Latin American Brands." www.millwardbrown.com/brandz/top-latin-american-brands/2015, accessed January, 2018.

Money.cnn (2018). http://money.cnn.com/infographic/economy/what-is-middle-class-anyway/index.html, accessed March, 2018.

Sharma, Aditya (2015). "International Marketing Mix." www.linkedin.com/pulse/international-marketing-mix-aditya-sharma, accessed March, 2018.

Statista (2018). www.statista.com/statistics/186919/number-of-internet-users-in-latin-american-countries/2018, accessed March, 2018.

Worldmeter Info (2018). www.worldometers.info/population/, accessed March, 2018.

Wright, Blanca (2017). "Why Latin America's Mobile Advertising Market is Growing." *IDG Connect*. www.idgconnect.com/abstract/23665/why-latin-america-mobile-advertising-market-growingbile advertising market is growing", accessed April, 2018.

10

ENTREPRENEURSHIP AND INNOVATION

Introduction

Economic and social development depends on a constant flow of new ideas that will create wealth and prosperity for the citizens of Latin America. Economic growth has been relatively good over the last few years, and its sustainability is dependent on the entrepreneurship and innovation of people with business development ideas. Entrepreneurship is a key to the future for every country in Latin America. The need to build business and innovate in established businesses is an imperative task that must be continuously addressed. Latin America is rich in natural and human resources, which provides the opportunity for substantial business development and economic growth. Chile, Brazil, Argentina, and Colombia have demonstrated sustained development and transformation based on entrepreneurship and innovation. The necessity of making entrepreneurship and innovation part of the fabric of Latin American business life is apparent.

What is entrepreneurship? In basic terms, entrepreneurship is the capacity and willingness to develop, organize, and manage a business venture along with any risk it may present for the purpose of making a profit (Business Dictionary, 2018). It combines the factors of production, land, labor, and capital to produce revenues that ultimately get translated into profits. Entrepreneurs are people who convert ideas into moneymaking businesses. By and large this activity demands specialized talents such as risk taking, persuasiveness, and perseverance. The ability to create new products and search for new markets is a fundamental practice that entrepreneurs must pursue each day. Not only are entrepreneurs' great idea developers and converters but they also have to manage people and efficient production processes and allocate the necessary resources that their business demands (Lederman, Messina, Pienknagura & Rigolini, 2014). In addition to talents and abilities, entrepreneurs also need a business environment that has positive economic conditions, which encourages investment in innovation and development. When these conditions exist, entrepreneurs are more inclined to take risks and initiate more productivity that becomes the catalyst for economic development. This activity creates a multiplier effect spurring on other businesses to develop as buyers or suppliers of the new enterprises. Replication of this activity promotes serial entrepreneurship and economic development (Lederman et al., 2014). The bottom line is that entrepreneurship drives economic development.

Innovation and entrepreneurship require a market economy. These activities provide the economic growth and development, which gives society a better standard of living that can translate into a better quality of life. Entrepreneurs take risks by pursuing new ideas that can be converted into business ventures. They are interested in change and progress. Entrepreneurs provide the catalyzing energy for innovation by presenting new ideas that many times need new production processes and methods of operation. This activity attracts other people with similar and collaborative desires. One business venture creates several other business connections, which multiplies the value chain and helps other people to benefit from the new economic activity. The market economy is conducive to entrepreneurship and innovation because it offers incentives to pursue these activities. A major benefit is the creation of wealth for the entrepreneur and all the stakeholders associated with the business venture (Hill, 2011).

One of the major and fundamental elements that is required for innovation and entrepreneurship to be viable or feasible is the existence of a business environment in which strong property rights are established. The absence of strong property rights creates a risk of expropriation by the government of profits, structures, and other assets of the business. Property rights that are not properly enforced reduce the incentive for innovation and entrepreneurial activity (Hill, 2011). The existence of strong property rights depends on the political system in each country. Historically, Latin America has not enjoyed consistent or fair property rights. Several countries have especially struggled with weak property rights, including Peru, Venezuela, and other countries where dictators have reigned for lengthy periods of time. If a country has a market economy and strong property rights enforcement, then entrepreneurship and innovation activities can function and provide potential economic benefit for society (Hill, 2011).

Business Development

Entrepreneurship is the process of creating a new business. It can involve both the establishment of a start-up business in addition to the creation of new types of an existing business such as technology, merchandise or agricultural. These ventures benefit from the knowledge and funding of risk-taking entrepreneurs. It can also include a firm's entry into new or existing markets (both domestic and foreign). They launch new products to the market, and organizational improvements that allow firms to perfect the quality or price of their products or realize more efficient methods of production (Lederman et al., 2014). Imaginative entrepreneurs are, generally, outpacing the most dynamic and productive firms. These firms innovate, expand production, and generate jobs at a relatively rapid pace. They generate employment opportunities and better employment (Lederman et al., 2014). Entrepreneurs are main players in the conversion of low-income societies regarded as low productivity and often subsistence self-employment into vibrant economies exemplified by innovation and a growing number of well-paid workers (Lederman et al., 2014). If a supporting environment exists, entrepreneurs take risks and invest in innovation, which encourages productivity. The entry and existence of the firm produces innovations that foster economic development (Lederman et al., 2014).

Unfortunately, Latin America suffers from too little rather than too much competition, particularly in the markets for inputs and non-tradable services. Without a perceived necessity to innovate, the private sector may not give birth to invention. Underneath the absence of innovation in Latin America appears to be its human capital gap. This for the most part relates to the quality of education. The region has a large shortage of a specific type of human capital such as engineers and scientists. These are professionals that are the people who are likely to produce innovative entrepreneurs. Innovation gaps exist among small and large firms in the same way. Actually, even the regions big name entrepreneurs, exporters and multilatinas, have fallen behind in important dimensions of innovation (Lederman et al., 2014).

Enterprises and businesses make up our social order. In our capitalistic market-oriented system, buying and selling goods and services are the essence of how society operates. Entrepreneurship is fundamental to the market system. Without its existence, the market system would not function. Entrepreneurs are the central players in changing low-income societies to productive, active environments that promote sustainable businesses and good paying jobs for those who want to work (Lederman et al., 2014).

Why Entrepreneurship and Innovation are Important Variables

The concept of entrepreneurship is relatively new in Latin America, notwithstanding the fact that for centuries Latin Americans have been creating and operating business of all forms and types. From the rural agricultural districts to the pueblos to the large cities, business development has been intense and massive. Just look at the streets of Latin American towns and cities. Just about every corner has an itinerant vendor or a formal business of some type that sells, buys, or trades a variety of products and services. Brazil, Colombia, and Chile have been the leaders in elevating entrepreneurship to a more sophisticated level with the introduction of large business enterprises and multinational companies.

We have known for a very long period of time that these countries have taken the initiative to build business and have embedded into the DNA of their culture the value of market driven solutions to complex social problems. Latin Americans are isomorphic. That is, they like to imitate each other. So, if Joe creates a business selling tacos across the street then Luis will see that Joe is making money and thus he, Luis, will build his own taco stand and attract his own customers. This is the multiplier effect in action, and it is the primary way businesses emerge in Latin American countries. Many more lucrative and more sophisticated businesses emerge because the entrepreneur has more resources, connections, and probably experience, but in essence the end result is the same, only on a different scale.

Start-up investment is increasing in Latin American as there is more capital available than there was in the past. While the investment resources are available, the majority of the investments are being made in Mexico and Brazil. Beyond Brazil and Mexico, start-up funds available from venture capitalists or angel investors are scarce and difficult to find. Generally, the investments are US$50,000 to US $100,000. Countries other than the two just mentioned rarely find start-up investments of US$3 million to US$5 million. Even though start-ups have the major problem of funding, they have been finding ways to succeed without the million-dollar investments (Lustig, 2017).

The fundamental element that allows businesses to sustain themselves is innovation. It is through new ideas and creative destruction that businesses remain competitive with product differentiation or pursuing a specific niche that focuses the business on a very special product or service area.

While entrepreneurship in Latin America is rapidly expanding, innovation is not growing at the same pace. Generally, entrepreneurship precedes innovation; however, once a business is established, innovation must become a regular ingredient in the business planning and business model of the organization. One factor that has limited innovation in Latin America is the lack of a good education system in many of the countries. Countries struggle to produce skilled entrepreneurs who can develop ideas, convert them into innovations, and take them to market. Human initiative and innovation are the keys to survival and sustainability of any business operation (Oliveria, 2017). Sometimes the absence of competition makes firms complacent. Then the world moves forward without them, and they are not able to catch up. Firms in Latin America are 20% less likely to innovate than companies in Europe and Asia (Oliveria, 2017).

Behind all of this is a bright spot with innovations relating to online shopping. This approach to consumer shopping is rapidly spreading all over the region. Latin America is one step behind China in online growth rate in e-commerce. It is expected to grow by 20% in the near future. Also, there is real hope among the youth in Latin America as they have developed motivation and initiative to pursue entrepreneurship as a career. Chile has been a leader in entrepreneurship and understands the importance of this concept. It has created the program Start-Up Chile an initiative for development of both Chilean and foreign start-up companies with funding and technical assistance. This is an innovative push in the right direction (Oliveria, 2017).

Entrepreneurship in Latin America

The CAF is a multilateral development bank currently owned by 19 countries in Latin America, the Caribbean, and Europe as well as 14 private banks from the Andean region. In their report on entrepreneurship in the region, they indicate that entrepreneurs can be one of two types: one group who is high productivity oriented and high growth enterprises and a larger group of subsistence entrepreneurs. The regular profile of the entrepreneur of the region consists of a low level of education and income. It is an unstable worker who goes from one venture to another. This profile is much different than the more dynamic entrepreneur like Elon Musk or Steve Jobs. Essentially, entrepreneurship in Latin America is not a lifestyle choice, it is a survival approach because of the dearth of other good employment opportunities (Entrepreneurship, 2014).

Colombia is an international leader in entrepreneurship in Latin America. It has a high potential for innovation, job creation, and growth. Yet in Colombia, inequality is high with a Gini coefficient of 0.54. The Gini coefficient measures the level of poverty ranging from 0 to 1.0. Any coefficient near 0 is low poverty. Those who are above 0.50 would be considered to have high levels of poverty. It has low food production and many issues related to the country's historical conflicts. While to many these conditions would be discouraging, to Gabriel and Felipe Maya, brothers and founders of a small eco-cosmetics company. Their company has achieved national and international recognition with a constant attitude towards continuous improvement and lifelong learning. The partners have built a successful company that is benefiting its employees, their community, and the economy of Colombia. It has also now begun selling their products internationally, entering global markets, and using the export method as a market entry strategy (Partners, 2017).

Chile and Colombia are Latin American countries that lead the world in entrepreneurship. The Chilean method focuses on the issue of changing cultural norms towards entrepreneurship while Colombia has concentrated on creating a strong institutional framework for growing the number of ventures in business development. The way of creating entrepreneurs in an economy takes many forms. Mimicking, often seen in Chile or the Silicon Valley approach used in Colombia are possible.

Governments need to focus their attention on:

1 Number of entrepreneurs
2 Their ability to innovate
3 Sustaining growth ambitions

Dealing with and incentivizing these three components is the most advantageous way to make entrepreneurship happen. Context is a critical feature in entrepreneurship. Chile and Colombia are the only countries that have escaped the deceptions from naysayers and government obstructionists by creating environments for entrepreneurship and innovation to thrive. Both these countries have high levels of new business creation. Chile has some high impact entrepreneurs who innovate and thus create jobs for the rest of society.

In Chile, the government has made various structural changes, which promote business development. One example that illustrates the incentives is a national online website that allows entrepreneurs to begin a new business in one day with no cost at all (Espinosa, 2015).

Should these Two Concepts be Separated?

At the onset of a new business, entrepreneurship and innovation are separable. However, shortly after the start-up begins operation, the sustainability of the business depends on innovation. In a highly competitive global environment, innovation is absolutely critical. Innovative ideas are what distinguish one business from another. Innovation will help the start-up grow. Innovation is not just creating a new product or service, but it also can be an improvement of a process or a product or a service that already exists. Because innovation is not something that causes immediate results, entrepreneurs need to invest time and effort to make the innovation a successful pursuit.

Innovation is an instrument used to solve problems. It becomes a prime mover of entrepreneurship. To be successful a concentration on imagination, initiative, and strategic business practices is a must.

Entrepreneurship can and will be a necessary and important player in developing nascent business start-ups in emerging markets. It can be the driving force that encourages prospective business people into taking a chance with starting a new business. It provides hope for the youth and women in Latin America. It provides a vehicle for innovative solutions that is desperately needed among communities in emerging markets. The pursuit of entrepreneurship will also promote a higher quality of life among the citizens of these developing and emerging economies.

Advances in technology is pushing innovation. With the internet and low-cost online education, people can acquire the knowledge and wherewithal to begin start-ups. The introduction of continuous innovation to work and workplace procedures and tasks is altering the ways entrepreneurs begin start-ups and sustain them in the long-run (Rajendran, 2017).

Innovation is an important part of business development, growth, and sustainability. Without it, few businesses are able to compete successfully. The creative destruction concept is alive and well in the developed world, but unfortunately in many of the developing countries it has not been a constant. This is the case in Latin America. The following table summarizes the world-wide rankings of some of the Latin American countries.

Table 10.1 shows the worldwide rankings of countries throughout the region.

Again, Chile is leading the region with Costa Rica and Mexico not far behind. Clearly there is a need for many of the countries in the region to become more ambitious in the pursuit of more innovations. The table shows that Latin American countries are not very innovatively driven. Additionally, it would behoove the national governments to create environments that incentivize companies to initiate and follow through on innovations and innovative projects. Everyone benefits from innovation. The economic growth of the region depends on the continuous innovation of companies located in these countries.

Promoting innovation in today's dynamic world requires leaders of countries and companies to be open to collaboration. There is a need for companies to go after collaborators that can give them contact with new ideas. Sharing ideas can be mutually beneficial. OECD data about innovative companies from 30 economies reveals that Latin American firms are the least collaborative. Brazilian executives are more inclined to focus on in-house business development than their peers worldwide who are engaged in strategic alliances and joint ventures. Collaboration in Latin America appears to be very tenuous (Ovanessoff & Framil, 2016). The issue of collaboration and partnering among others relates to the Latin American leaders' mindset or the way they think about innovation. There appears to be a very profound, embedded, preconceived notion regarding the strategic options in front of business leaders. Collaboration in innovation does not seem to be popular in this region of the world. In reality, the issue boils down to trust; this is at the core of any collaborative relationship. There is an important test confronting Latin American business leaders: Collaborate in

TABLE 10.1 Global Innovation Index

Rank	Country	Rank	Country
42	Chile	88	Paraguay
51	Costa Rica	89	Dominican Republic
57	Mexico	99	El Salvador
62	Panama	101	Guatemala
67	Colombia	104	Bolivia
68	Uruguay	113	Honduras
70	Brazil	119	Ecuador
71	Peru	130	Nicaragua
72	Argentina	132	Venezuela

Source: Myers (2016).

innovation or not. There is a choice, and that choice has consequences and managerial implications. A recent comparison of inter-personal trust among 59 countries was completed worldwide. In the Latin American region, the major economies ranked low with Brazil, Ecuador, and Colombia at 54, 55 and 57 respectively (Ovanessoff & Framil, 2016).

Innovation requires a trusting relationship between collaborators. Building trust is not an issue of funding; it is an issue of time and effort. A focus on priorities, interests, and capability development are crucial and at the core of collaboration.

Global businesses are changing rapidly. The urgency of seeking out valuable partners is front and center. Changing the mindset to focus on access to new skills, technologies, and capabilities is critical to overcoming the challenges in Latin American economies (Ovanessoff & Framil, 2016).

Some parts of Latin America have proven that innovation can be accomplished. Brazil has the fifth highest business start-ups in the world. In Chile, Start-Up Chile has been recognized as one of the best incubators programs. These countries are important examples to the rest of Latin America and a testament to what can be achieved.

Latin American businesses and government leaders need to remove the barriers to communication between collaborative groups. The potential is there. The policy makers and business leaders just need to act.

The future of innovation exists in collaboration. Latin America needs to update itself and move forward quickly with partners and collaborators. It is the only way to achieve a successful approach to innovation. (Ovanessoff & Framil, 2016).

Regional Innovation Hubs

Competitive advantages through innovations are a basic tool of emerging economies. With the productive transformation process occurring that associates technology gap reduction with important goals and objectives for enhancing this vital area, Latin American countries are allocating resources strategically using public and private participants and conduits.

Technology capacities in many Latin American countries indicate serious deficiencies in regional infrastructures. Public technology institutes are weak in this area. Some manifest deterioration of the technology and innovation efforts that exist in their institutions. In many cases there is no clear direction or evidence that modernization or acquisition policies exist.

Having said the above, there are five Latin American countries that have established and are continuing to manage and upgrade their technology and policies related to innovation. Identification and brief summary of their approach to technology and innovation is presented (Barroeta, Gomez Prieto, Paton & Palazuelos, 2017).

The discussion below outlines the status and progress of the five Latin American countries mentioned above:

1   Chile – the National Council for Innovation manages the innovation system of Chile for Competitiveness. This agency provides guidelines for development of National Innovation Strategy and execution of innovation policy. The implementation of the policy resides in the Chilean Economic Development Agency. This agency has four strategic units: corporate innovation, entrepreneurship, technology transfer, and innovation environments. Chile has made great gains in pursuing and implementing regional innovation strategies.

2   Brazil – Invests a lot of money in R&D. Specifically it allocates 1% of its GDP to R&D. It has an extensive network of institutions that do the design, promotion, and execution of science and technology policy. Brazil has various institutes that implement policies related to science technology and innovation. The research and innovation fund furnishes capital for projects in energy, gas, health, aerospace, and many more endeavors.
    Colombia – Science and technology is directed from the national level. There is the Administrative Department of Science, Technology and Innovation that exists as an agency of the Colombian government. This entity coordinates both public and private organizational involvement with technology and innovation. Private institutes are of great importance regionally to promote and drive the policies that come from the national level.

3   Mexico – has both national and state or regional levels. The General Council for Science, Research and Technology Development is the primary agency for the technology and innovation efforts in Mexico. State governments are responsible for promoting and coordinating technology and innovation activities in their regions.

4   Peru – Science and technology is primarily a public responsibility and resides at the national level. A Council of Technology and Innovation develops policy and coordinates activities. Regional governments are responsible for pushing and implementing technology and innovation policies in their respective regions.

5   Argentina – The national government is responsible for the design, management and coordination of research and innovation policies (Barroeta et al., 2017).

Entrepreneurship Interest, Intent and Pursuit

The subject of entrepreneurship remains a topic of interest. The relationship between perception and intentions remains at the core of understanding why people become entrepreneurs. Finding the contributing factors to an individual's intentions to pursue a successful career path will contribute valuable business entrepreneurship (Zellweger, Sieger & Halter, 2011). Learning what initially drives people to be open to the thought of starting their own business has been of great interest to entrepreneurship research and education (Carey, Flanagan, & Palmer, 2010). Many motives for innovation and entrepreneurship have been studied. Lack of courage, skill and fear of failure have a negative effect on entrepreneurial attitudes (Szerb & Inreh, 2007). Other studies have shown that being in an entrepreneurial family is a motivating factor. The subsequent three tables clearly outline the ideas that a cross section of Latin Americans thinks about entrepreneurship from several different perspectives. These data indicate that there is a lot of thinking about and in some cases a lot of doing of entrepreneurship. Specifically, Table 10.1 shows that there is a substantial recognition of the opportunities associated with entrepreneurship and a good showing of persons having entrepreneurial intentions. They would like to become an entrepreneur and believe that they have the capabilities to be an entrepreneur. This is consistent with some of the other literature that has indicated that there is a growing cohort of entrepreneurs throughout Latin America. On the negative side, there is a considerable number that have a fear of failure. Overall the trends presented in these data is very encouraging and only shows that there is great potential for entrepreneurship in Latin America even in countries that have had turbulent political and economic times, e.g., Guatemala, Colombia, and Peru.

Table 10.2 provides a view of reality. This table shows that while there may be positive intentions, the real percentage of the population that engages in entrepreneurship is relatively small. It is interesting that El Salvador and Peru are the most active in entrepreneurship. Clearly, being an employee is by far the most popular occupational choice among most Latin Americans.

Tables 10.3 and 10.4 provide an interesting perspective on the relationship between social class and entrepreneurship. Social mobility is an important social structure component in Latin America. Preferably, individuals want to move

TABLE 10.2 Entrepreneurial Attitude and Perceptions (Percentage)

Country	Perceived Opportunity	Perceived Capabilities	Fear of Failure	Entrepreneurial Intentions
Argentina	40.9	61.7	24.9	31.0
Brazil	50.9	52.6	38.7	27.2
Chile	68.4	59.6	28.0	46.5
Colombia	67.7	57.8	31.8	54.5
Ecuador	57.3	74.3	34.8	39.9
Guatemala	58.8	66.4	33.3	39.0
Mexico	53.6	58.5	31.6	16.9
Peru	61.0	62.2	25.7	33.9
Uruguay	47.9	61.1	26.9	25.3

Source: Adapted from Rubach, Bradley & Kluck (2015).

TABLE 10.3 Occupational Groupings (Percentage of Working Population)

Country	Entrepreneur	Self-employed	Employee
Argentina	6.3	20.6	73.1
Bolivia	5.3	38.5	56.2
Brazil	6.3	22.1	70.8
Colombia	3.5	44.4	52.2
Ecuador	7.1	45.8	47.1
El Salvador	9.6	33.9	59.2
Mexico	8.3	31.7	60.0
Peru	9.9	44.4	45.7
Uruguay	5.3	–	–

Source: Adapted from Castellani & Lora (2014).

TABLE 10.4 Entrepreneurs and Social Origin (Percentage of Social Class)

Country	Lower Class	Middle Class	Upper Class
Colombia	1.8	5.3	21.4
Mexico	5.7	7.6	16.9
Uruguay	1.5	5.8	15.3

Source: Adapted from Castellani & Lora (2014).

from a lower class to an upper class. One of the major benefits of entrepreneurship is its capability to move people from a lower class to a higher class. We mentioned in Chapter 4 that the middle class has grown by about 30% over the last two decades. Entrepreneurship contributes to some of this growth.

Table 10.5 summarizes how entrepreneurs are divided by social origin among four major Latin American countries. One of the important strategies for entering the entrepreneurial and innovation arena is through networking and partnership building. The next section will discuss some of the approaches that are used to achieve this goal.

TABLE 10.5 Entrepreneurs: By Social Origin

Country	Lower Class	Middle Class	Upper Class
Argentina	23.3	63.9	12.8
Brazil	19.8	61.3	18.9
Colombia	34.4	46.3	19.3
Ecuador	42.3	50.6	7.0
El Salvador	51.6	44.2	4.2
Peru	62.0	33.2	4.8

Source: Castellani & Lora (2014).

Finding a Partner

There are several ways to create a partnership for doing entrepreneurship and innovation. Some of these popular methods are listed below:

1   Work with universities – Most research universities are eager to partner with entrepreneurs. They want to become partners with businesses because the potential for a win/win relationship exists. The university has the experts while the entrepreneur has the idea(s), location, and organization for the experts to work in. Pursuing this relationship is a no-brainer. There are many universities across Latin America that have the expertise and desire to establish these strategic relationships (How to Foster Innovation, 2018).

2   Strategic partnerships where two or more entities cooperate in various aspects of a business venture – These relationships may be difficult to negotiate, but they are very powerful if they can be harmoniously operated in business ventures. Most entrepreneurs are not experts in all fields. As such, there are aspects of a business venture where the entrepreneur needs experts to assist in achieving certain goals. One example is research on certain complex aspects of a product or service. Outsourcing this the activity yet keeping control of it can be a tremendous help to the growth and development of an entrepreneur's business venture.

3   Personal relationships – Business is about networking. Personal contacts and interactions can produce a variety of outcomes. Purposely finding people and organizations that can help with the development of innovation ideas and implementing them is a critical activity. Building networks of experts will in the long run provide the resources and capabilities for achieving the entrepreneurial and innovation goals that are needed to be successful.

Entrepreneurship and innovation are two activities that are not managed in a vacuum. Both require connection with experts who can help advance the mission and vision of the enterprise. Acquiring the correct talent or capabilities in order to pursue and generate innovation is crucial. Having the know-how is without question at the core of the innovative process.

Intellectual Property Issues

Intellectual property (IP) is an important part of business and, in the contemporary world, everyday life. With the digital society becoming the norm, more ideas, or intellectual products, are becoming a way of life. Protecting intellectual property is of immense importance when we think about copyrights, trademarks, patents, and the like. As we conduct more and more cross-border business and transactions, the need for this protection becomes more urgent. The Latin American region historically has a reputation of having one of the lowest standards of intellectual property protection in the world. Latin

American companies have been declared guilty of copyright infringements for copying U.S. brand names. Recently, however, there has been great progress in remedying these errors and improving and elevating the standards of protection for intellectual property. Three major economies in Latin America have taken important steps in applying the generally accepted intellectual property standards. The three countries and their improvements are:

1 Argentina – has made major improvements in IP protections. Presently Argentina and its National Directorate of Copyright and the National Institute of Industrial Property have been implementing TRIPS standards. These are agreements on trade-related to aspects of intellectual property. Using this mechanism, they can address some of the egregious violations associated with IP.
2 Brazil – generally has implemented some strong protections but limited in scope. Brazil has also put into place a strong law against software piracy. Even with this law, pirating continues to occur in Brazil.
3 Mexico – has distinct agencies that provide protection in the IP area. One advantage of Mexico's IP laws is that they only recognize IP that has industrial use. Works of authorship and copyrights are protected. All of this may change if NAFTA is renegotiated. While this small sample of Latin American countries consisting of only three countries are doing good things to protect IP rights, it does show that there is recognition of the problems that can be resolved with laws and standards. Latin American countries are moving in the right direction (Seling, 2017).

Short-Term and Long-Term Benefits

Chile and Colombia are the only countries in Latin America to "break out of the trap" and become all-around entrepreneurs. For the size of their economies they have high level, high impact start-ups, which frequently innovate, and increase the number of jobs. Chile implanted a serious of private and public initiatives called start-up Chile to build the biggest start-up community in the world. In the short term these countries need continue their efforts to promote entrepreneurship in the short run because those ventures that are successful in the short run generally have great potential for long run success (Espinosa, 2015).

What Role should Government Play in the Fostering of Entrepreneurship and Innovation?

Without question, government and government policies are important for fostering entrepreneurship and innovation. Government can become the initiator and the funder for important projects that catalyze the imagination of individuals for innovative ideas and ideas that have already been presented. Throughout

Latin America, because economic development is so important to economic growth and jobs, governments have been continuously active in pursuing initiatives that can ignite the economic engines and get business started and people working. Chile has been a major player in this effort. The government of Chile has been instrumental in developing policy that has become the foundation for more involved projects that get entrepreneurs started and innovations.

Government Incentives and Initiating New Projects

Latin American countries are presently developing and implementing policies to encourage productive development and innovation. Establishing incentives and new forms of financing is a critical piece of the strategies for development of start-ups. Different countries have embraced different support models. Specifically, countries are engaging in ambitious activities that focus on making entrepreneurship and innovation a primary business development area.

1   Argentina has major research projects that have given rise to spin-offs that are translating into new business ventures. It has been successful in getting performance-based standards applied to its incubator;
2   Brazil because of its size has the most active business sector with innovations occurring. Along with Chile, Brazil has created incentives to promote start-ups.
3   Chile has been focusing on the international stage attempting to attract talent to help grow its start-up in the international arena (OECD Dev, 2013).
4   Colombia and Peru – developing new finance and training methods to help champion new enterprises. Both of these countries have constructed new devices suitable for supporting new start-ups. Additionally, they have been investing seed capital and training regimens for the newly created enterprises (OECD Dev, 2013).

Government efforts to encourage new innovation firms are a sign that the region is making progress. Public policies can go a long way in producing incentives that create new firms and encourage expansion.

While many things across Latin America are the same, many economic and business methods are different. Support mechanisms for new enterprises vary from country to country; however. two major themes emerge when studying the policies and strategies for entrepreneurship and innovation. These themes are:

1   There is an increased involvement of regional and local governments. They want the business development to occur and continue to provide economic development and opportunities;
2   There is increased participation of large companies in financing and training entrepreneurs in start-ups. This is a new approach and strategy for the expansion of innovation in Latin American countries (OECD Dev, 2013).

Innovation has been growing more slowly in Latin America than in OECD countries. However, there is an increasing recognition in Latin America of the importance of innovation. Start-ups in Latin America confront significant impediments such as the access to finances. Latin American financial markets are less mature, and regional banks are less prone to lend money to new start-ups that have a risk factor associated with them. That is why incentives and the government supports are so critically important (OECD Dev, 2013).

Conclusions

Latin America is a region of entrepreneurs. This is evidenced by the large number of business owners per capita relative to countries with similar incomes per capita. (Lederman, 2014). Pursuing entrepreneurship seems to be a career path that many Latin Americans can achieve. Many small and medium size enterprises were born and have grown into stable productive businesses. They have contributed significantly to the economic development of the Latin American societies across the continent. Desire and action do not seem to be major issues among Latin American people. Lots of entrepreneurs exist. One feature of Latin American entrepreneurship is that new firms do not grow as much as firms in other regions. They tend to remain small. They may not be the most sophisticated entrepreneurs, but they are successfully operating their businesses and, in some cases, helping create other entrepreneurs among their peers and citizens of their communities. A variety of reasons exist for firms remaining small; one of them is the lack of innovation. Latin America is weak in the pursuit of innovation. Supporting innovation and productive development is a key tool in development strategies of open global economies.

In order to grow – or even survive – firms need to continuously innovate. Despite substantial reform, business regulations may still hamper innovative behavior. Many formal firms in the region are engaged in some form of innovation, but the intensity of innovation tends to be low or poorly suited to raise productivity. The region has many entrepreneurs but little innovation. If entrepreneurship is the cause of productivity growth, then there are opportunities for using policy mechanisms to speed up the development process by improving the incentives and supportive institutions that facilitate innovation by entrepreneurs (Lederman et al., 2014).

Innovation will begin to occur when company managers and executives realize that there needs to be a new way of solving problems. Historical approaches do not work in a new, technologically/digitally driven global environment. This will require managers to develop an innovation strategy, take risks and execute their innovation strategy effectively (Kinicki, 2018).

CASE

ARAUCO Forestry Co.

When thinking of top destinations for foreign investment in Latin America, Chile is often overlooked among larger countries such as Brazil, Argentina, or Mexico. However, ranked the most competitive country in the region in recent years, Chile has gradually made a name for itself in the global economy as well (Economic Forum, 2017).

Given the pro-business environment, political and economic stability, and the low corruption level, Chile is a prime destination for foreign investors. Based on the 2016–2017 Global Competitiveness Report, Chile has a GDP of US$240.2 billion and a GDP per capita of US$13,340.90. Chile is ranked 33rd in the 2016–2017 Global Competitiveness Report and is ranked the highest out of all countries in Latin America. Also, in the report, Chile is ranked very high among all countries for higher education and training (#28) and financial market development (#23), but lower for health and primary education (#71) and innovation (#63) (Economic Forum, 2017). By and large however, Chile beats the other nations in Latin America in all categories other than health and Primary Education. Within the last 10 years, and even as far back as the last 20 years, Chile's economy, measured by GDP, has increased at a rapid rate. According to the World Bank, Chile's GDP was measured at US$69.737 billion in 2002, US$172.389 billion in 2009, and US$247.028 billion in 2016 (Economic Forum, 2017). The unemployment rate is currently at 6.3% and the inflation rate is at 4.3%. (The World Bank, 2016). The country is a strong investment for foreign investors not only for the obvious reason of being the most competitive country of the region, but also in that it is a very low risk country, is a relatively free market, and finally that it has a very globally integrated economy. Among other countries in the region, Chile stands out among the rest because of its political, economic, and social stability. For example, since 2000, Chile has seen very sustainable GDP growth; Chile stands out among its Latin American competitors in that it is very politically stable. Finally, Chile's free market can also be explained through the low corporate tax rates, which are extremely attractive for foreign investors. For example, from 1997–2016, the corporate tax rate in Chile averaged 17.58% whereas the Latin American average floats around 32%. This lower tax rate draws businesses and consumers into the country and could explain the positive GDP growth outlined previously (Pomerleau, 2015). A Chile stand out among its Latin American competitors in that it is very politically stable the Chilean business environment is the relatively free market. For example, Chile ranks tenth out of 180 countries on the Economic Freedom scale which measures the transparency and consistency of regulation rights, how secure and stable property rights are, and how fair the judicial system (The Heritage Foundation, 2017).

Along with that, efforts to increase innovation in the country can be seen with the program Start-Up Chile. According to Start-Up Chile's website, "Start-Up Chile is a public start-up accelerator created by the Chilean Government for high-potential entrepreneurs to bootstrap their start-ups and use Chile as a foundation," with goals to ensure that Chile remains a world hub for technological innovation and to be known as drivers of technological enterprises. The program aims to attract new tech start-ups and bring entrepreneurs from around the world to make Chile the innovation hub of South America. The organization chooses 100 start-ups each round from all around the world for the six-month program and each receives US$40,000 in equity free funding, a one-year, temporary visa and mentoring and coaching (Start-Up Chile, 2017). Within this context, ARUCO Forestry has become a formidable company in Chile. It is innovative, progressive and profitable. environmental and social standards commitment to the world. ARAUCO has taken full advantage of the value of its forest products by continued research and implementing global best practices regarding sustainability and safeguarding the biodiversity and forests of the future. ARAUCO is one of the five major producers of forestry resources in the world. Presently, it has a workforce of 13,000 employees. It has 30 production plants in Chile, Argentina, Brazil, Uruguay, the U.S and Canada. It also has an existence in 80 countries around the world. ARAUCO uses renewable resources to develop products that are useful and healthy for people to increase the quality of their life. The company is adept at producing differentiated products through innovation with the intent of adding value to these products. ARAUCO's p-products are sold on five continents using the traditional sales and marketing methods such as sales offices, sales representatives etc., Sales offices have been established in 12 countries. It maintains a sophisticated supply chain management system for transportation, distribution and service for the products it sells. It provides this arrangement to 3,500 customers using 220 ports around the globe.

ARAUCO's vision is to improve people's lives through forest products yet still dealing with the challenges of sustaining the world. Within this context, ARAUCO values: safety, commitment, excellence and innovation, teamwork and good citizenship. ARAUCO's organizational management is composed of a senior management team reporting to the CEO. This group is involved in all the decision making with an emphasis on transparency and responsibility. The management team respects all the shareholders and the stakeholders that participate in the company operations directly or indirectly.

In 2016 ARAUCO was awarded first place in the "Most Innovative Companies Chile 2016." This award is granted to the nation's most innovative company in their respective industry.

References

Barroeta, Belen, Javier Gomez Prieto, Jonathan Paton, & Manuel Palazuelos (2017). "Innovation and Regional Specialization in Latin America, JRC Report." European Commission, European Union.

Business Dictionary (2018). "Entrepreneurship." www.businessdictionary.com/definition/entrepreneurship.html, accessed April, 2018.

Carey, Thomas, David J. Flanagan, & Timothy B. Palmer (2010). "An Examination of University Student Entrepreneurial Intentions by Type of Venture." *Journal of Developmental Entrepreneurship*, 15(4), pp. 503–517.

Castellani, Francesca, & Eduardo Lora (2014). "Is Entrepreneurship A Channel of Social Mobility in Latin America?" *Latin American Journal of Economics*, 51, pp.179–194.

Espinosa, Jose Ernesto Amoros (2015). "Why Chile and Colombia Lead the World for Entrepreneurship, World Bank Forum," www.weforum.org/agenda/2015/01/why-chile-and-colombia-lead-the-world-for-entrepreneurship/, accessed March, 2018.

Hill, Charles, W. L. (2011). *International Business: Competing in the Global Market Place.* New York: McGraw-Hill.

How to Foster Innovation (2018). "Through Strategic Partnerships." www.bdc.ca/en/articles-tools/start-buy-business/buy-business/pages/how-foster-innovation-through-strategic-partnerships.aspx, accessed April, 2018.

Kinicki, Angelo, & Brian K. Williams (2018). *Management: A Practical Introduction*, 8th edition. New York: McGraw-Hill.

Lederman, Daniel, Julian Messina, Samuel Pienknagura, & Jamele Rigolini (2014). "Latin American Entrepreneurs Many Firms but Little Innovation." International Bank for Reconstruction and Development, The World Bank.

Lustig, Nathan (2017). "4 Lessons U.S. Entrepreneurs Can Learn from Latin American Startup Culture." www.entrepreneur.com/article/297227#, accessed April, 2018.

Myers, Joe (2016). "These are the world's most innovative economies." *World Economic Forum.* www.weforum.org/agenda/2016/08/these-are-the-world-s-most-innovative-economies/, accessed January, 2018.

OECD Dev (2013). "Development Centre Studies – Start-up Latin America – Promoting Innovation in the Region." Paris, France: OECD.

Oliveria, Kevin (2017). "Entrepreneurship in Latin America." www. startuprounds.com/entrepreneurship-Latin-America/, accessed April, 2018.

Ovanessoff, Armen, & Leonardo Framil (2016). "What Can Latin American Leaders Do to Make the Region More Innovative?" *The Economic Forum.* www.weforum.org/agenda/2016/06/what-can-latin-america-s-leaders-do-to-make-the-region-more-innovative, accessed March, 2018.

Partners (2017) "Partners for Economic Growth and Entrepreneurship in Colombia." http://partners.net/sites/default/files/images/Success%20Story_F2F_Zen%20Naturals.pdf, accessed April, 2018.

Pomerleau, Kyle, & Alan Cole (2015). "International Tax Competitive Index." Washington D.C.: Tax Foundation.

Rajendran, Anand (2017). "Why Innovation is Increasingly Becoming Critical to Entrepreneurship." *Entrepreneur India.* www.entrepreneur.com/article/296912, accessed April, 2018.

Rubach, Michael, J, Don Bradley, III, & Nicole Kluck (2015). "Necessity Entrepreneurship: A Latin American Study." *International Journal of Entrepreneurship*, 19, pp.126–139.

Seling, Tyler (2017). "How Latin and South America Protects Intellectual Property." *International Law Review*. Michigan University, College of Law.

Start-Up Chile (2017). "About Us." www.startupchile.org/about-us, accessed April, 2018.

Szerb, Laszlo & Szaboles Inreh, (2007). "Fifth International Conference on Management Enterprise and Benchmarking," July 10, 2007. Budapest, Hungary.

The Heritage Foundation (2018). "Economic Freedom Index." www.heritage.org/index/, accessed April, 2018.

The World Bank Report (2016). www.worldbank.org/content/dam/Worldbank/Publications/WDR/WDR%202016/WDR2016_overview_presentation.pdf, accessed April, 2016.

Zellweger, Thomas, Sieger, Philipp, & Halter, Frank (2011). "Should I Stay or Should I Go? Career Choice Intentions of Students with Family Business Background." *Journal of Business Venturing, Elsevier*, 26(5), pp.521–536.

11
CONCLUSION

Latin America presents a complex, challenging, yet potentially rewarding business environment. Each chapter in this book provided analysis and insights into important factors that must be considered when seeking to do business in Latin America. An essential theme to note is that although the region shares similar historical, cultural, political, and economic roots, the individual countries differ widely from one another. By almost every metric, there are countries in Latin America that are on opposite ends of the scale whether it comes to strength of institutions, political freedom, or GDP growth, for example. It is not enough to study Latin America as a whole; to be successful in business, one must understand how each country presents its own unique challenges and opportunities. However, although there are exceptions to every rule, there are general themes that we have seen appear time and time again.

Economically, Latin America is growing quickly and shows room for even more growth. As an overall trend, GDP and GDP per capita are rising, and the quality of life is improving in most countries. This is due largely to the gradual turn to open markets and free trade. Governments seem to gradually be shaking the protectionist measures implemented with ISI policies. While it is true that Latin America was burned before by export dependency, turning to the other extreme only closed the region off from the rest of the world and stunted its growth as global economies boomed. Now, Latin America is once again opening its doors by participating in the global economy and forming more free trade agreements both within and outside its borders. Instead of relying heavily on export-led growth, countries have begun to diversify and shift from agricultural and industrial dependency to service sector-based economies. Developed countries still turn to Latin America for natural resources (especially in the way of oil, natural gas, and minerals), but the region is becoming more competitive in high-skilled service industries. High-skilled labor is a strong asset to the region, and it is bolstered by the quality of private institutions, particularly universities and business schools. A well-educated and well-trained workforce is an attractive attribute for any company looking to begin operations in Latin America. The continued improvement of private institutions contributes to improving competitiveness of the region.

On the other hand, public institutions are still an obstacle for efficient business practices and free market growth. Various indices have shown the poor rankings of countries in Latin America in terms of important factors to promote the ease of doing business such as enforcing contracts, protecting property rights, and trading across borders. While Latin America is generally becoming more receptive to open-market principles, it still has a tendency to turn towards protectionist measures when faced with foreign competition. Consumer demands are increasingly pressuring governments to enact free trade policies as the people of Latin America are seeing the benefit of a greater quantity and improved quality of goods from increased competition. However, institutional reforms are difficult to approve and slow to implement. Still, more politicians are making the effort to correct decades of unproductive policies and unchecked spending. Brazil and Argentina in particular are leading the way in committing to fiscal responsibility. Of course, the danger of state intervention still looms as populist, socialist leaders hold on to power and support in the region. The most striking example is Venezuela. As other countries progress towards higher GDP and better quality of life, economic and social conditions in Venezuela are spiraling downward with no apparent end in sight. Even amid crisis and suffering from the population, Nicholas Maduro and his populist regime still hold on to power. Venezuela is a stark reminder that the political turbulence of Latin America can shake a once prosperous nation and entirely change its business environment and outlook for the future.

Hand in hand with weak public institutions and political instability is corruption. Corruption has been a pervasive part of business and politics in Latin America for decades. Bribery appeared to be the law of the land, and investments were not protected or safe as money did not always end up where it was intended to go. Distrust of the government is widespread, but with the corrupt politicians holding the power, there were seemingly no repercussions. However, political leaders are no longer untouchable. Countries in Latin America are seeing a wave of national courts cracking down on corruption. The general population is demanding justice and insisting that no one is above the law, especially not the leaders who are chosen to represent the best interests of the people. Although it remains to be seen whether the political environment truly does become more transparent in the long-term, prosecuting on corruption gives investors more assurance that their investments will be protected. A shift towards more fair and democratic political processes is a win for business too.

Latin America seems to have turned a corner in terms of development and investment. It is an attractive opportunity for investors who can tolerate a certain level of risk, with some countries being much riskier to invest in than others. Yet, now could be a golden opportunity for investment in Latin America for those who can tolerate a region still coping with political uncertainty, shaky democratic processes, and underdeveloped infrastructure. Costs are relatively low due to weakening exchange rates and there is much less competition than there will be several years down the line if the region continues its current trajectory.

In summary, there is no one clear-cut formula to doing business in Latin America. The approaches, processes, and possibilities are as diverse as the countries that make up the region. It is impossible to provide a simple answer to the question of how to succeed in business in Latin America. It is equally impossible to provide an analysis that will stand the test of time in a dynamic and ever-changing environment. However, by exploring the challenges, opportunities, and new realities of the region, this book provides a strong foundation for anyone wishing to do business in Latin America.

INDEX

Page numbers in **bold** denote tables, those in *italics* denote figures.

"twenty-first-century socialism" program 95, 105, 124
"*800 tiendas de barrio*" movement (Bolivia) 193

advertising, in Latin America 202–4
Afro-descendant populations, across Latin America 52
agribusiness, in Latin America 119
AJE Group 187
Alibaba 129
Amazon.com 129
Apertura Petrolera program (Venezuela) 104
ARAUCO Forestry Co. 229–30
Argentina: credit rating 56–7; economic and fiscal reforms 54–5; exchange rate of peso against dollar 54, 55; Falklands War (1982) 55; financial crisis 119; floating rate accrual notes (FRAN) bonds 55–6; government incentives and initiating new projects 227; impact of ISI policies on borrowing in 55–7; innovation system of 222; intellectual property standards 226; labor unions 55; pro-market policies 55
arms proliferation 90
art and literature, appreciation of 61
Auteco, Colombia 15–16
authoritarian regime, notion of 92, 94, 99

balance of payments 45, 47
Ban, Ki-moon 33
banking crises 38
Barcena, Alicia 82
beefs: exports 24; foot-and-mouth disease 24; tariffs on 24
Bolivarian Revolution 105
Bolivar, Simon 105
Bolivia 5, 73, 77, 99, 113, 115, 121, 134, 175, 177, 180; "*800 tiendas de barrio*" movement 193; entrepreneurial competitiveness 193; GDP per capita 20; growth rate 19; indigenous population 58, 64; manners and customs 71; *Mi Caserits* program 193; natural gas reserves 19; political risks 94; poverty level in 65; safety and security risks 175; sweatshop conditions in 184
boom and bust cycles 11
brand management 188
brand names 202, 226
Brazilian economy: e-commerce industry 129; entrepreneurship and innovation 129; government incentives and initiating new projects 227; income inequality index 128; innovation system of 222; intellectual property standards 226; investment opportunities 128; major scandals 184; middle-class labor force 128; Operation Car Wash 88,

140; state enterprise share in **53**; technology and retail industries 129
Bretton Woods scheme 48
Brexit 23
bribery 184–5, 234
budget allocation, for education 70
bureaucracy, in Latin America 74, 187
business decisions 7
business development, process of 3, 7–8, 62, 166, 170, 172, 175, 196, 211, 214, 215–16, 218–20, 227
business environment, changes in 19, 69, 103, 163, 175–6, 188, 200, 215, 229, 233
business establishment, in Latin America 162–3; changing the business environment and 175–6; corporate social responsibility (CSR) in 183–5; corporate strategy for 163–4; distribution and focus of 173–4; factors affecting business strategies 170; financing alternatives 171–2; informal markets 168–70; investment, finance and start-up funding 170–1; microfinancing for 172–3; multinationals 164–8; negotiation patterns and partners 180–3; other supply chain management (SCM) Issues 175; physical infrastructure of 177–80; small and medium size enterprises (SMEs) 168; supply chain management issues 173–4
business in Latin America: categories of 163–4; economic progress 18; environment and trends of 18; establishing of *see* business establishment, in Latin America; foreign direct investment (FDI) 7; globalization, impact of 7; history of 7–8; major trends affecting 19–24; multinationalization of 165
business networks 153
business sophistication 134, 136, 153–4, **154**, 159
business start-ups: in emerging markets 219; in Latin America 228; Start-Up Chile program 218, 230
business strategies, factors affecting 170
business transactions 68–9, 72; cross-border 74; instrumental in making 59; international 16

CAF development bank 218

capital flows, to Latin America 8, 18, 49, **172**
Caribbean Transportation Infrastructure Projects **179**
CEMEX case study 163, 206, 210–12
Chavez, Hugo 95, 98, 104–6
child labor 146, 183
Chile: ARAUCO Forestry Co. 229–30; Chile for Competitiveness 222; Economic Freedom scale 229; Global Competitiveness Report 229; government incentives and initiating new projects 227; high-quality education 124; inflation rate 229; innovation system of 222; internet usage 117; market-oriented policies 76; market size differences 153; MASISA company 76–8; National Council for Innovation 222; quality of management schools in 146; Start-Up Chile program 218, 221, 226, 230; unemployment rate 229
collective bargaining 24, 126
Colombia: current business environment in 33–6; drug cartels in 34; government incentives and initiating new projects 227; homicide rates 34; internet usage 117; Marriott Hotels 35; Medellín city 34; peace accord in 177; pro-business climate 34
commercial protectionism, idea of 46
communication, in Latin America 69–70; for cross-cultural management 69; face-to-face 69; nonverbal language 69
communist terrorism 86
competitiveness, of Latin America 134–56; business sophistication (eleventh pillar) 153–4; classification by each stage of development **134**; defined 135; efficiency-driven 135; factor-driven 135; financial market development (eighth pillar) 149–50; Global Competitiveness Index (GCI) 134, 135–8; goods market efficiency (sixth pillar) 146–7; health and primary education (fourth pillar) 143–4; higher education and training (fifth pillar) 144–6; infrastructure (second pillar) 140–1; innovation (twelfth pillar) 154–6; institutions (first pillar) 138–40; labor market efficiency (seventh pillar) 148–9; macroeconomic environment (third pillar) 142–3; market size

competitiveness *continued*
(tenth pillar) 152–3; Operation Car
Wash (Brazil) 140; Panama, case study
of 158–9; regional comparison of 156;
technological readiness (ninth pillar)
150–2
Conditional Cash Transfer programs 29,
52
ConocoPhillips 104
consumer demands 234
consumer potential, based on disposable
income **196**
consumer price inflation 210
contracts, enforcement of 175
copyrights 225; infringement of 226
corporate ethics, quality of 96–7, 139
corporate social responsibility (CSR):
bribery 184–5; child labor 183; in
Latin American businesses 183–5;
making the choice 185; sweatshop
conditions 184
corporate strategy, for business
development 163–4
Correa, Rafael 92
corruption: bribery 234; Corruption
Perceptions Index 87, *88*; impact on
business and politics in Latin America
234; Operation Car Wash (Brazil) 88,
140; in public institutions 87; public's
perceptions of 87; and transparency
issues 87–8
Corruption Perceptions Index 87, *88*
Costa Rica 88–9, 94, 98–9, 115, 120, 124,
126, 135, 141, 183, 187, 220; business
environment in 175; business
sophistication 153; energy investment
178; healthcare system 144; innovation
in business 156; locally made products
193; mobile phone penetration 141;
wage determination 149
credit rating, of Argentine economy 56–7
credit risk, in Latin America 97
crime and violence, in Latin America
84–7; civil war violence 86; communist
terrorism 86; corruption and
transparency issues 87–8; corruption in
public institutions 87; criminal and
political violence 86; economic cost of
86; FARC rebel group 86; homicides
per 100,000 people **85**; political stability
and absence of violence **87**
cultural artifacts, in Latin America 73
cultural intelligence 74

cultural issues, affecting business: analysis
of 59; art and literature, appreciation of
61; bureaucracy 74; business and
cultural activities 67; communication
69–70; components of 59; contracts 73;
cultural artifacts 73; cultural
competency 63; cultural context and
content of 72; culture and business
leadership 74; education 70–1;
individual *vs.* collectivisms 62; *machismo*
(men) and *marianismo* (women) 60–2;
manners and customs 71–2; masculinity
vs. femininity 62; national values and
attitudes of 60–2; power distance 61;
regional subcultures 62–4; religion,
impact of 68–9; social structures 64–7;
uncertainty avoidance 62; work ethic
and appreciation of family life 61
currency depreciations 42, 210
customs union 30; administration costs 31;
advantage over free trade area 31; and
freedom of movement of people 31

debt-based transactions 171
debt crises 38, 48–9
debt restructuring 49
de Silva, Lula 88
developed economies 23, 45, 64
diligent entrepreneurship 168
distribution of products and services,
process of 205
Doing Business Index 132; rankings of
selected indicators from **133**; of Trading
Across Borders 133
Dominican Republic–Central America
Free Trade Agreement (DR-CAFTA)
32
Double Taxation Agreements 117
drug trafficking 12

e-commerce 129, 175, 195; consumer
potential for **196**, 197; in Latin America
197
economic and social development 3, 9,
214
economic climate, in Latin America
108–9; economic liberalization 109–20;
human development 120–6
economic competitiveness 50
Economic Decline indicator 89–90
economic dependency 39, 41; postcolonial
40
economic expansion, of Latin America 41

Economic Freedom scale 29, 229
economic globalization indicator 117
economic liberalization 49; composition
  of production 117–20; economic
  climate in Latin America 109–20;
  globalization 117; gross domestic
  product 111–13; inflation targeting and
  109–11; trade 113–16
economic nationalism, in Latin America
  40
economic slowdown 18
economic structure, of Latin America: in
  nineteenth century 38–45; during
  1870–World War I (1914–1918) 39–42;
  Catholic Church, influence of 39;
  diversification of 42–5; exploitation of
  natural resources 39; export boom and
  39–42; impact of export-led growth on
  42–5; influx of ideas from European
  immigrant market 39; retrograde
  institutions, influence of 38; tariff
  policies 44
economies of scale 84, 152
Economist Intelligence Unit's Democracy
  Index 92, **93**
economy ranking: according to ease of
  doing business **176**; on element for
  starting and doing business **176**
Ecuador 86, 92, 95, 115, 124, 144, 193;
  displacing of indigenous groups in 101;
  neighborhood stores in 193;
  performance of ISI policies 47;
  property rights in 100; super markets in
  193
education, in Latin America 70–1; budget
  allocation for 70; elementary 70; higher
  education 144–6, **145**; percentage of
  GDP per student 71; primary 143–4;
  quality of 52, 70, 144, 216; for skill
  development 70; tertiary education 144
electronic portal system 176
Elliott Capital Partners 56
El Salvador 56, 85–6, 88, 133–4, 138,
  144, 146, 175, 185; Catholicism in 69;
  coffee plantation in 101; education
  system in 146; entrepreneurial attitude
  and perceptions in 223
emerging economies 177, 219, 221
employment: in formal sector 126; in
  informal sector 125, **125**, 168, **169**;
  opportunities for 44; self-employment
  125–6
energy security 114

entrepreneurial competitiveness, among
  retailers 193
entrepreneurial ecosystem 170
Entrepreneurial Finance Lab (EFL) 171–2
entrepreneurship, in Latin America 214,
  218–19; attitude and perceptions of
  223; business development 215–16;
  concepts of 219–21; employment
  opportunities 216; government
  incentives and initiating new projects
  227–8; government's role in fostering
  of 226–7; innovation and 216–18;
  intellectual property issues 225–6;
  interest, intent and pursuit of 222–4;
  long-term benefits 226; occupational
  groupings **224**; partnership for doing
  225; regional innovation hubs 221–2;
  risk-taking entrepreneurs 215; short-
  term benefits 226; social origin of **224**
Environmental, Social and Corporate
  Governance (ESG) 170
equity-based transactions 171
European immigrant market 39
export boom 39–42
export-led growth, in Latin America 41;
  early model of 42
export processing zones 132
ExxonMobil Corp. 104

FARC 19, 33–4, 86
financial market, development of 46, 136,
  149–50, **150**, 156, 228–9
financing alternatives, in Latin America
  171–2
fiscal and monetary policies, in Latin
  America 46; Keynesian notions of 46
fixed-broadband internet 151
flawed democracy, notion of 92, **93**
floating rate accrual notes (FRAN) bonds
  55–6
foot-and-mouth disease 24
forced labor 42
Foreign Corrupt Practices Act, U.S. 95
foreign debt 48–9; holdings 47; obligations
  45–6
foreign direct investment (FDI) 7, 22–4,
  150, 165, 175; ECLAC's report on 23;
  liberalization of 51; market-seeking
  capital 23; net inflows of 22, **23**
foreign technology, sources of 150
Fragile States Index 89, **89**
Freedom House 90
Freedom in the World 90, **91**

freedom of movement of people 31
free market, growth of 12, 50, 53, 105, 229, 234
free trade 30, 46, 153; with advanced nations 95; agreements for 233; benefits of 40; disintegration of 45; Free Trade Zones 115; open markets and 233; purposes of 32
Fund for Peace 89

General Agreement on Tariffs and Trade (GATT) 48
geography of Latin America 3–5
Gini Coefficient, of Latin American Countries **66**, 122, 123, **123**, 125, 218
Global Competitive Index (GCI): Component Ranks **96**; components of 96, *136*; of Latin America 134, 135–8; overall **137**; pillar median ranks by region **157**
global competitiveness: doing business in Latin America 132–4; of Latin America 134–56
global consumer spending **203**
global fascism, struggle against 46–7
global financial crisis of 2008/2009 50, 82, 138
global financial system 45
global industrial power 25
Global Innovation Index **220**
Global Investment Advisors 54
globalization: impact of 7; KOF Index of 117, **118**; level of 117
global marketing 200, 202–9
global start-up network 171
Good Neighbor Policy 46
goods market efficiency 146–7
Great Depression (1929–1939) 41, 45, 47
gross domestic product (GDP) 19–21, 111–13; annual inflation growth rate *112*; growth per capita **48**; impact of religion on 68; labor productivity and 24; per capita by country **20**; per capita by region **43**; by sector *119, 120*
Guatemala 12, 69, 206; child labor in 183; coffee industry in 39; competitive and price-sensitive market 147; corruption and transparency issues in 87–8; crime in 84; criminal and political violence in 86; cultural artifacts in 73; forced labor in 42; indigenous populations in 58, 63–5; manners and customs in 71; multinational corporation in *167*; Old

Ruins in Petén *73*; political crisis in 94; primary education in 144; private education in 70; revenues from exports of agricultural and mining products 42; safety and security risks 175; supply chain management (SCM) issues in 175; workforce in the agriculture sector 121

health insurance schemes 29
health services: access to 143–4; basic requirements index 144; state-funded 29
hedge funds 56
higher education 144–6; and training **145**
high-skilled service industries 234
high-tech value chains 154
Hispanic heritage 61
Hofstede, Geert 61; cultural workplace relationship framework 61
homicides 34, 84, **85**, 103
household income, sources of 29, 82
Huanza Hydroelectric Project, Peru *180*
human capital 44, 168, 216
human development, in Latin America: in agriculture sector 121; impact on economic climate 120–6; inequality and 122–5; informal economy sector 125–6; percentage of individuals working by sector *121, 122*; poverty reduction, impact of 120
human initiative and innovation 217
hybrid regime, notion of 92
hyperinflation 106

immigration flows 39, 42
import substitution industrialization (ISI) 44, 45–8; for achieving developmentalist aims 46; commercial policies 47; components of 53; effects on Latin America 38; impact on borrowing in Argentina 55–7; spillover effects of 38
income distribution gap 82
income hierarchy, of world regions 42
income inequality 65, 66
income inequality index 128
indigenous communities, of Latin America 61
inflation targeting 109–11
informal business 163–4, *198*; characteristics of 169
informal economy sector 125–6

informal employment 26, 125–6, 168, **169**, 170
informal markets 64, 163, 168–70, 191, *198*, 207–9
infrastructure and industrialization projects 48
infrastructure bonds 177
infrastructure investment projections, in Latin America **179**
innovation, in Latin America 216, 219; collaboration in 220; competitive advantages through 221; emerging economies and 221; government's role in fostering of 226–7; partnership for doing 225; regional innovation hubs 221–2; technological innovations 41, 154–6, **155**
innovative entrepreneurship 167, 216
intellectual property (IP): in Argentina 226; in Brazil 226; in Mexico 226; protection of 225–6; protection rankings 101–2
Inter-American Development Bank (IDB) 86, 172, 177
internal domestic market, development of 46
International Labor Organization (ILO) 125
international marketing, in Latin America 191–2
International Monetary Fund (IMF) 38, 49, 210; structural adjustment policies 50
International Tribunal for the Law of the Sea 56
internet market 129, 196, 209
inter-personal relationship 72–3
investment grade 98
itinerant vendors 163–4, 195, 198, 207–8, 216

job markets, in Latin America 14; formal-sector 25
job security 62, 184
judicial system 11–12, 230

Keynesian economics 46, 109
Keynesianism, displacement of 50
Keynesian monetary policies 47
knowledge transfer 167
KOF Index of Globalization 117; change in **118**
Kraus, Brad 159

labor force: growth of 25; scarcity in 38
labor formalization 24
labor markets 25, 126; efficiency of **148**, 148–9; skills gaps in 145
labor mobility 38–9
labor productivity: calculation of 24; in Latin American countries **25**
labor protection systems 126
labor unions 55, 98
laissez-faire age 42
Latin American society: categorization of 40; corruption in 12; economic development of 228; masculinity *vs.* femininity dimension 62; opportunities of doing business 58; social classes in 65; social relationships in 67
Latin-derived languages 1
Latin Trade Infrastructure Index 180
leadership, in Latin America 139, 212; culture and business 74
leftist threat, in Latin America 94–5
legal rights index 149
lithium reserves 20
living standards, deterioration of 50
Logistic Performance Rankings (LPI) **174**
"lost decade" for Latin America 50
low-income societies 216

Macri, Mauricio 54–7, 100
macroeconomic environment, stability of 135, 142–3, 156, 158
Maduro, Nicholas 13, 86, 91, 98, 103, 106, 234
making the choice, in Latin America 185
malinchismo 40
map, of Latin America 4
"market-based" economies 51
marketing information, needed to do business 207–9
marketing mix 200; and marketing information needed to do business 207–9; place, channels, and distribution 205; pricing 204–5; product 202; products, branding, and packaging 205–7; promotion and advertising 202–4
marketing process, in Latin America: for active and lucrative markets 194–9; business environment for 200; individual country marketing and 192–3; for international marketing 191–2; marketing mix 202–9;

marketing process *continued*
marketing strategies 201–2; market
research 193–4; regional differences in
192–3
marketing strategies, in Latin America
201–2
market-oriented education and culture 2
market research 193–4
markets: globalization of 192; in Latin
America 194–9
market-seeking capital 23
market segmentation 192
market size, in Latin America **152**,
152–3
Marriott Hotels 33, 35
MASISA company, Chile 76–8; business
model of 77; business principles of 77;
founding of 76; high performance work
teams 77; main products 76; mission
and vision of 77; revenues generated
from sales 78; trust-based relationships
with customers 77
Mayan empire 73
MERCOSUR 7, 30–2
merger and acquisition (M&A) 165, 211
Mexico: CEMEX case study 210–12;
consumer price inflation 210;
currency depreciation 210; Economic
Decline indicator 90; economic
forecast for 90; economic ranking of
210; employment problem 210;
innovation system of 222; intellectual
property standards 226; stock exchange
211
Mi Caserits program (Bolivia) 193
microenterprises 126, 173
microfinance, among Latin American
businesses 172–3
middle class: growth of 28; in Latin
America 199; occupations of 40; size of
199; and social contract 28–30
money transfer 173
Monotax 126
Moreno, Lenín 92, 124
Multilateral Investment Fund (MIF) 172
Multinational Corporations (MNCs) 76,
166–7
multinational enterprises (MNEs) 163,
164–8; business development and
growth 166; cross-border activity of
167; economic environment of 166;
financing for 171; merger and
acquisition (M&A) deals 165; non-Latin

ownership of 164; Top Latin American
Multinationals **165**; total multilatinas'
revenue 167

national banks, creation of 46
National Council for Innovation, Chile
222
nationalization of industries 104
natural gas reserves 19
natural resources, exploitation of 39
negotiation patterns and partners, in Latin
America 180–3
Nicaragua 5, 19, 94–5, 101, 115, 138,
146, 175, 187; Catholicism in 69;
competitiveness of 135; corruption and
transparency issues in 87; education
system in 146
North American Free Trade Agreement
(NAFTA) 21, 30, 32, 90, 95, 210

Odebrecht Construction Co. 184–5
oil-importing countries 49
oil industry, development of 104
oil prices, rise in 49
old-age pension 29
on-the-job training 144
OPEC oil cartel 49
open markets 198, 208, 233, 234
Operation Car Wash (Brazil) 88, 140
Organization for Cooperation and
Development (OECD) 70
Organization of American States 94
organized crime 90, 92, 147
Oxfam 66

Panama 94, 98, 102, 115, 120, 132, 135,
140–1, 144–5, 149, 155–6, 183; City of
Knowledge 146; competitiveness of
158–9; customs union 31; education
system in 145; free trade agreement 31;
GDP growth in 19; Panama Canal 42,
140; political systems in 89; value of
goods imported 113
partnership, for doing entrepreneurship
and innovation 225
patents 225
personal relationships 72–3, 225
Peru: AJE Group 187; economic growth
186; GDP per capita 186; government
incentives and initiating new projects
227; Huanza Hydroelectric Project *180*;
inflation rate 186; innovation system of
222; Tambor + (convenience store

business model) 193; tourist industry 186; visa schemes 187
petrodollars 49
physical infrastructure, in Latin America 177–80
Platt Amendment 46
political climate, in Latin America: political risk 92–9; political systems and 89–91; poverty and inequality 81–4; regional political issues 84–8; rule of law and other obstacles 99–102
political risk, management of 97–9
political violence 86, 90
polychromic cultures 74
population rate of change 2
population statistics, of Latin America **194**
poverty and inequality: Gini Index **123**; impact on human development 120, 122–5; indigence rates of 82; political climate 81–4; political economic systems 82; rate of reduction 81; social structure and 64; structural reforms 26–8; urban poverty and destitution 82–4; urban/rural divide 82, **83**
poverty umbrella, concept of 82
pricing, issue of 204–5
production, in Latin America 117–20
product marketing, in Latin America 202
promotion of products and services 202–4
property protection ranks **101**
property registration 175
property rights 82, 215, 230, 234; intellectual property rights 102; legal security for 51; policy recommendations 50; protection of 99; ranking of 100, **101**; rule of law 100–1
protectionist policies, in Latin America 45
public education, state-funded 29
public safety and corruption 11–13; map of *13*
public-sector spending 49; on science and technology 24
public services 11, 28, 29, 128, 184
public technology institutes 221
public *vs.* private institutions, in Latin America 95–7
purchasing power parity (PPP) 26, 210

quality of goods 234
quality of life 7, 65, 77, 166, 177, 199, 215, 219, 233–4

regional innovation hubs 221–2

regional integration 14
regional marketing, in Latin America: functions of 192; goals of 192; *vs.* individual country marketing 192–3; techniques and tactics of 192
religion, in Latin America 68–9; distribution percentage **69**; influence on GDP 68; religious affiliation memberships 68
research & development (R&D) collaboration 167, 188, 212, 222
resource-planning systems 173
risk-taking entrepreneurs 215
Rousseff, Dilma 13, 88
Rule of Law indicator 99–102
rural campesinos 184

safety and security risks 175
Sapelli, Claudio 124
search engine optimization (SEO) 201
self-employment 125–6
service sector-based economies 233
sidewalk vendors 208
single-commodity exports **52**
slave labor 42
Small and Medium Size (SME) businesses 76, 163, 168, 228
Smoot-Hawley Tariff Act (1930), U.S. 45
social classes, in Latin America 65
social contract 28–30
social insurance 29, 126
"Social Panorama of Latin America 2012" report 81
social protection, of entrepreneurs and employees 126
social security payments 28
social security systems 28, 82
social structure, in Latin America 64–7; class structure 64–5; of family 67; Gini Coefficient of **66**; graphical depiction of *67*; income inequality 65; major social classes 65; poverty level 64; redistribution of wealth 66; social relationships and 64, 67
specific industries, that thrived or failed 52–3
staff training 144
stakeholders, in cross-border negotiations *183*
start-ups: boot camp 171; funding for business 170–1, 217; investment 217; Start-Up Chile program 218, 221, 226, 230

state enterprise share, in Brazilian economy **53**
state enterprises, privatization of 51
state-owned-enterprises (SOEs) 53
state ownership, rates of 53
storefront vendors 198
strategic partnerships 225
street vendors 125, 128, 164, 173, 198
structural reforms, in Latin America 24–30; middle class and the social contract 28–30; poverty and inequality 26–8; tax revenues and 28
Sub-Saharan Africa 84, 177
supply chain management (SCM) 162, 173–4, 205; businesses regarding 174; other issues 175; training and capability development 174
sustainable development 138, 170
sustainable energy and power 180
sweatshop conditions 184

talent acquisition and retention 149
tariffs on beef 24
tax revenues 28; from exports 119; Monotax 126; zero-tax zones 115
technological innovations 41, 154–6, **155**
technological readiness, in Latin America 150–2, **151**
technology transfer 151, 166, 222
telecommunication/communication systems 175
Temer, Michel 30, 88, 92
Thomson Financial 165
tiendas 193, 205
trade: in goods and services 113–16; liberalization 51; restrictions, practices of 45
trademarks 167, 225
trading blocs, in Latin America 19, 30–2
trading partners, of Latin American countries **116**
Trans-Pacific Partnership 19
Transpacific partnership (TPP) 32–3
Transparency International 87, 104, 184
transportation management system 175
trends, in Latin America 13–14

United Fruit Company 53
United Nations Children's Fund (UNICEF) 123

urban neediness, issues of 84
urban poverty 82–4, 102
Uruguay 10, 21, 45, 69, 86, 88–9, 96, 99, 102, 113, 139, 151, 177, 230; beef exports 24; channels of marketing 193; corporate ethics ranking 97; destination for exports 115; foreign direct investment in 22; GDP per capita 24; informal employment in 126; labor markets 126; Monotax 126; reduction in inequality 124; transition to formal economy 126
U.S. Dollar 55–6, 119

Vanek, Joann 170
Vasquez, Paul 15
Vegh, Carlos 112
Venezuela: Apertura Petrolera program 104; austerity program 105; Bolivarian Revolution 105; business environment of 103–4; economic reforms 105; foreign investors in 103; hyperinflation, issue of 106; IMF loans 105; nationalization of businesses 104; oil reserves in 103; political history of 104–6
venture capital 149, 170, 217
Viscidi, Lisa 114
Vive Digital plan, of investment and subsidization 117
vocational training 144
vulture fund 56

Wal-Mart 193, 205
Washington Consensus 38, 50–2; neoliberal reforms of 51
welfare state 29
Williamson, John 50
workforce competencies 170
work with universities 225
World Bank 28, 48, 177; Doing Business Project 132
World Competitiveness Report 6, 132
World Economic Forum 134–5
World Integrated Trade Solution database 114–15
World Trade Organization 132
World War II 39, 46–8
Worldwide Governance report 99

zero-tax zones 115, 116